I BET YA!

Which players have the highest career batting averages? What are some of the worst recent trades of active players? What players have the Mets given away to find a third baseman? Who was the only player ever killed during a major league game? What's Willie McCovey famous for?

This collection of baseball facts, stats, and opinion was put together to settle fights among fans—and to start them. Here are the best and worst players to ever become big league pros, the greatest and most grating, the most underrated, overrated, and overrated-underrated. From fielding feats to power hitting, opening day to post-season play, there's dream teams, moments of glory, fights on and off the field, champions, near-champions, losers, super-losers, and all the memorable runs, hits, and errors in baseball history. All? Well, You Wanna Bet?

Other Avon Books about Baseball

AARON TO ZIPFEL: BASEBALL PLAYERS OF
THE SIXTIES
by Rich Marazzi and Len Fiorito

AARON TO ZUVERINK: BASEBALL PLAYERS OF
THE FIFTIES
by Rich Marazzi and Len Fiorito

CHRYSANTHEMUM AND THE BAT: BASEBALL
SAMURAI STYLE
by Robert Whiting

DOLLAR SIGN ON THE MUSCLE: THE WORLD
OF BASEBALL SCOUTING
By Kevin Kerrane

TOUGH CALLS: THE ILLUSTRATED BOOK
OF OFFICIAL BASEBALL RULES
by Zach Rebackoff

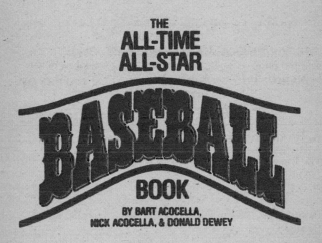

THE
ALL-TIME
ALL-STAR

BASEBALL

BOOK

BY BART ACOCELLA,
NICK ACOCELLA, & DONALD DEWEY

AVON
PUBLISHERS OF BARD, CAMELOT, DISCUS AND FLARE BOOKS

AVON BOOKS
A division of
The Hearst Corporation
1790 Broadway
New York, New York 10019

Copyright © 1985 by Nick Acocella, Bart Acocella, and
Donald Dewey
Baseball cards on cover © Topps Chewing Gum, Inc.;
cards from Renata, Galasso, Inc.
Published by arrangement with the authors
Library of Congress Catalog Card Number: 84-091235
ISBN: 0-380-89530-7

First Avon Printing, May 1985

AVON TRADEMARK REG. U.S. PAT. OFF. AND IN OTHER
COUNTRIES, MARCA REGISTRADA, HECHO EN U.S.A.

Printed in the U.S.A.

WFH 10 9 8 7 6 5 4 3 2 1

Dedicated to

FB—BEN ACOCELLA
SB—JOAN ACOCELLA
TB—ANTHONY CIMMINO
SS—CHRIS ACOCELLA
OF—PHEA CIMMINO
OF—DONNA LANDREY
OF—CHARLES DEWEY
C—TOM DEWEY
P—ADAM DEWEY

TABLE OF CONTENTS

INTRODUCTION

Major league baseball fans thrive on three things—statistics, conjecture and argument. A fan who doesn't know about Walt Dropo's 12 consecutive hits or Joe Adcock's 18 total bases in one game is someone who goes to the refreshment stand for a hot dog when the home team has the bases loaded in a tie game. A fan who doesn't wonder what might have happened to the Mets if they hadn't traded away Nolan Ryan and Amos Otis is someone without imagination. One who has no opinion about Roger Maris's 61 home runs in 1961 is someone better off playing computer games. Baseball is numbers, fantasy and creed. The baseball fan is someone who spends each season, Hot Stove League and spring training trying to marshal these three elements into an explanation of what actually takes place on the field. An uninformed few call it a pastime; the true fan knows that there is very little leisure involved.

The All-Time All-Star Baseball Book is a compendium of statistics, conjecture, and argument. Its format—the lineup—is not only baseball's most basic organizational unit, but also the scheme most commonly adopted by millions of fans when they muse about the best and the worst, the greatest and the most grating, the most underrated, overrated, and overrated underrated. Included, of course, are lineups which point up the achievements of the Ruths and the Robinsons, but also included are those which point out the uniqueness of the Bloodworths and the Southworths. On the following pages, the Kuenns become teammates of the Kluszewskis, the Dizzy Deans of the Dixie Walkers, the Sparky Andersons of the Gair Allies—and all for good reasons.

In general, there are three kinds of lineups to be found

1

in *The All-Time All-Star Baseball Book.* The first group consists of teams put together on the basis of cold numbers. Many players may have *seemed* great at this or that, but what do the statistical facts say? Included in this group are such lineups as the best hitters in the history of the game (none of whom are in the Hall of Fame), the worst hitters of all time (none of whom ever got a hit) and, perhaps the oddest collection of all, players who held down starting berths for one season, but otherwise never wore a major league uniform.

A second group of lineups concerns the identical, the co-incidental and simply the bizarre. Pitchers who have hurled for teams they didn't belong to? Catchers who were carried on rosters merely to instigate fights? An all-star team of players traded for Willie Montanez? Yes, indeed. And what about all those heralded rookies whose arrival in spring training hastened the retirements of the Gehringers and the Traynors? They're all here.

Last, but hardly least, are the lineups of the purest prejudice—those in which the authors reveal themselves for the fools they are. The only defense we have for the selections in this group is that of age: We never asked Cap Anson for an autograph; we never saw a Lou Gehrig or Chuck Klein home run from the bleachers. But it is also most of all in these lineups that *The All-Time All-Star Baseball Book* has its primary purpose—to start an argument.

> Bart Acocella
> Nick Acocella
> Donald Dewey

MOST INFLUENTIAL

Because boardroom and courtroom wrangles have been as crucial to the history of baseball as on-the-field heroics, a lineup of the game's most influential players is necessarily a mixed bag. For every player who made his impact with a bat or glove, another left a mark with the assistance of an agent or attorney. Some of those deserving of recognition were innovative in their skills and/or daring, others were caught up in situations over which they had little control. But whether because of what they did or what was done to them, all the members of the Most Influential Team hung up their spikes on a sport that was significantly different from the one they had known as rookies.

In one way or another, then, every other lineup in this book stems from a starting nine of:

> 1B—CHARLIE WAITT
> 2B—JACKIE ROBINSON
> 3B—JOE DUGAN
> SS—MAURY WILLS
> OF—BABE RUTH
> OF—CURT FLOOD
> OF—ROY THOMAS
> C—KING KELLY
> P—CARL MAYS

Waitt wore the first glove in 1875 and thereby steered baseball toward most of the defensive elements with which we associate it today. Take away Waitt's glove, in fact, and you would have to take away everything from a Walter Johnson and Nolan Ryan to a mean batting average of .250.

Robinson, of course, had the task of unraveling the 60 years of racism that had blanketed the sport from the 1880s until his arrival in Montreal in 1946 and in Brooklyn the following year.

Dugan's trade to the Yankees in August 1922 enabled New York to edge the St. Louis Browns for the pennant. When the Browns objected to such a late-season transaction (and the Cardinals filed a similar protest over another swap involving the Giants and Braves), Commissioner Kenesaw Mountain Landis imposed the June 15 trading deadline that has remained officially in effect to this day. Admittedly, owners have gotten around this restriction on numerous occasions through gentlemen's agreement waiver purchases, but when one considers the number of pennants decided by only a game or two over the last six decades, the consequences of the formal deadline must be seen as enormous.

Wills's virtual reinvention of the stolen base while with Los Angeles in the 1960s inspired a new emphasis on running that probably still hasn't reached its zenith. It should also be noted that, unlike his speedster contemporary Luis Aparicio, Wills played for a team that regarded the stolen base as an additional offensive weapon, not merely as a last resort for a punchless lineup, although he was a part of punchless lineups, too.

Ruth's home runs so impressed major league owners with their ability to draw crowds that the lively ball was introduced in 1921 in the interests of increasing numbers in both team home run columns and at the turnstiles. Ruth, of course, has also been without peer as a symbol of the game.

Flood refused to accept his 1970 trade from the Cardinals to the Phillies and took the reserve clause to court. Although he himself lost, his challenge proved to be the opening salvo in the player-management war that ultimately led to free agency.

It was Thomas's penchant for standing up at the plate and fouling off balls to his heart's content that prompted the National League in 1901 to introduce the rule that the first two fouls are to be regarded as strikes. (The American

League followed suit two years later.) Hitting .400 would never be as easy again.

Kelly's claims to importance are several. For one thing, he was the foremost exponent of the hook slide during his playing days for the Chicago and Boston franchises in the 1880s. For another, he was the first catcher to use finger signals with pitchers. Finally, and not least important, his antics as a "tenth man" off the bench (such as leaping up and announcing his presence in the lineup so he could catch a foul ball coming his way) led to very precise regulations about when and under what circumstances substitutes could be put on the field.

In 1919, Mays was traded to the Yankees by the Red Sox while under suspension by Boston. American League president Ban Johnson tried to block the deal, and the ensuing court case so undermined Johnson's authority as a member of a three-man ruling National Commission that the road was paved for the creation of a baseball commissioner and for the administrative structure of the sport as we know it today. A year later, Landis was installed in office.

Numerous other players merit special mention for the Most Influential Team. Filling out the roster are:

Infielders. Cap Anson refused, while manager of the Chicago White Stockings, to play an exhibition game against a minor league team that included black players, prompting the ban that excluded blacks until the arrival of Jackie Robinson. On a more positive note, Brooks Robinson's exploits afield in the 1960s and 1970s for Baltimore focused attention on defense generally and, most specifically, on the need to station something more than a boulder at third base.

Outfielders. Ned Hanlon, as player-manager for Pittsburgh in the 1890s, introduced the strategy of using righties against lefties and lefties against righties, mainly because of his own difficulties as a left-handed hitter against southpaw pitchers. Tommy McCarthy's habit in the 1890s of tapping fly balls back and forth between his bare and gloved hands while running toward the infield prompted the rule that says runners can advance as soon as a fly ball touches a fielder, not only when a clean catch or error is made. Dummy Hoy, a deaf mute in the nineteenth century, forced umpires to give hand, as well as verbal, signals for their calls.

Catchers. Moses Walker, a black who played with Toledo of the American Association in 1884, was Jackie Robinson's unsuccessful forerunner. It was Walker's defensive skills that embarrassed white players and made it easier for segregationist policies to be adopted. Fred Thayer, the author of "Casey at the Bat," also invented the first catcher's mask in 1875. Red Dooin's late-nineteenth-century machismo cost him general recognition as the first catcher to wear shinguards and a chest protector. In apparent dread of being criticized for less than manly behavior, the Philadelphia receiver slipped the gear *under* his uniform for more than two years and admitted to it only after Roger Bresnahan had begun wearing it openly.

Pitchers. Candy Cummings threw the first curve in competition in the early 1870s after several years of experiments. Charlie Sweeney is recorded as having thrown the first screwball in 1880. Tricky Nichols was the first to specialize in sinkers, in 1875. Ed Nolan was an 1876 overhand curve pioneer. Frank Corriden taught the spitter to Elmer Stricklett while both were laboring for a Newark team at the turn of the century; Stricklett in turn taught it to Ed Walsh, who popularized it with the 1904 White Sox. Al Spalding, also a promoter in the formation of the National League, was the first changeup artist in the 1870s.

Three pitchers who exerted a considerable influence on the game while away from the diamond were Andy Messersmith, Dave McNally and George Zoeterman. Messersmith and McNally were the first successful challengers to the reserve clause and opened the floodgates to free agency in 1975 when they secured their freedom from the Los Angeles Dodgers and Montreal Expos, respectively. Although Zoeterman never appeared in a major league game, it was his drafting from a Chicago high school in 1947 by the White Sox that prompted more stringent regulations with regard to plucking undergraduates out of the classroom. (It is not widely remembered today, but the White Sox were actually thrown out of the American League for two weeks in the autumn of 1947 when they refused to pay a fine over the Zoeterman affair. There is an argument to be made that Commissioner Happy Chandler's decisive action in the case was a conclusive reason why team owners elected much less resolute figures to the commissioner's chair in subsequent years.)

Another hurler who affected more than his own team's performance was Joe Page. While it is true that there had been other relief pitchers before Page (most conspicuously Johnny Murphy and Firpo Marberry), it was Casey Stengel's use of the left-hander exclusively in a bullpen role for the Yankees of the 1940s that truly launched the era of the fireman. Among Page's most immediate heirs were Jim Konstanty, Hoyt Wilhelm and Joe Black.

The rest of baseball's most influential franchise would have to include:

Manager. Harry Wright, who introduced what we now refer to as "professionalism" into the sport. Before 1869, the game had been theoretically amateur—meaning that the players were often paid under the table. In 1869, Wright, then manager and center fielder for the Cincinnati Red Stockings, ended the hypocrisy by openly paying members of his team.

Owner. Arthur Soden, who in 1879 introduced the reserve clause that was to prove to be the chief bone of contention between players and management throughout the history of baseball.

General Manager. Branch Rickey, who introduced the concept of a farm system, forced the racial integration of the game with the signing of Jackie Robinson and pioneered the use of batting helmets after seeing them used in the Negro leagues.

Umpire. Alexander Cartwright, who drew up the first written regulations of the game. Among other things, he is responsible for establishing nine players a side and 90 feet between the bases. The first game held under these rules took place at the Elysian Fields in Hoboken, NJ, on June 19, 1846, when the New York Nine beat Cartwright's Knickerbockers, 23-1. Cartwright umpired and fined one of the players for swearing.

Official. Harry Chadwick, who codified the rules of the game and who was baseball's first official scorer.

Entrepreneur. William Cammeyer, who built the first

enclosed stadium on Brooklyn's Union Grounds in 1862 and who had a big role in the construction of other parks.

Groundskeeper. The anonymous gentleman who, in 1884, misunderstood an instruction to increase the distance from the pitcher's mound to home plate from 50 feet to "six-six" feet and placed the rubber 60 feet and 6 inches from all future batters.

Inventor. George Cahill, who, as early as 1909, demonstrated the efficacy of a light tower that would make night baseball possible. Although another 30 years were to pass before the first night game, it is worth noting that it was the Cincinnati Reds who had the benefit of Cahill's demonstration and the same Reds who hosted the first night contest.

Business Manager. Luke Sewell, who, as manager of the Reds in the late 1940s, came up with the idea of having groundskeepers drag the infield after the fifth inning so fans could go to refreshment stands and contribute a little more to Cincinnati's coffers.

Chaplain. Brother Jasper of Manhattan College, who, while demanding that students sit rigidly while watching the school's athletic events, also realized that this might lead to physical problems. His compromise was the seventh-inning stretch.

Finally, let us not forget Oliver Wendell Holmes's Supreme Court Nine. In 1922, Holmes and his eight teammates decided unanimously for major league owners in a suit brought six years earlier by the Baltimore Terrapins of the disbanded Federal League. In its attempt to recover damages from the settlement reached between other Federal League owners and the National and American leagues, the Terrapins claimed that baseball was a monopoly in violation of antitrust laws and that the reserve clause in particular abrogated constitutional guarantees. Holmes wrote the decision holding that professional baseball was a sport in which no commodity was produced, no "chattel slavery" was involved and that, therefore, antitrust provisions were not applicable.

NATIONAL LEAGUE FRANCHISES

The all-time all-star team for every twentieth century franchise in the senior circuit. Separate teams for the Boston, Milwaukee and Atlanta versions of the Braves; the Brooklyn and Los Angeles Dodgers; and the New York and San Francisco Giants. Obviously, quality of play is the primary criterion here, but longevity and the ability to succeed personally when surrounded by a losing team certainly count for something.

BOSTON BRAVES

Want to know about the Boston Braves? Try this: Of the 20 most important offensive records established by Boston-Milwaukee-Atlanta players, only seven are held by members of the teams which played in Massachusetts, and four of these seven are the result of Tommy Holmes's 1945 season. When you consider that the Boston club existed for 53 years and the Milwaukee team (holder of most of the individual records) for only 13, it's easier to understand why the Red Sox were always Boston's first team.

BOSTON BRAVES

1B—FRED TENNEY
2B—BILL SWEENEY
3B—BOB ELLIOTT
SS—RABBIT MARANVILLE
OF—TOMMY HOLMES
OF—WALLY BERGER
OF—HUGH DUFFY
 C—KING KELLY
 P—VIC WILLIS

Honorable mention to Johnny Sain, Tommy McCarthy and Tommy Tucker.
Manager: George Stallings.

MILWAUKEE BRAVES

With the exception of Rico Carty, this is the team which won National League pennants in 1957 and 1958 and lost a season-ending playoff to Los Angeles in 1959.

1B—JOE ADCOCK
2B—RED SCHOENDIENST
3B—EDDIE MATHEWS
SS—JOHNNY LOGAN
OF—HANK AARON
OF—WES COVINGTON
OF—RICO CARTY
 C—DEL CRANDALL
 P—WARREN SPAHN

An honorable mention here to pitcher Lew Burdette.
Manager: Fred Haney.

ATLANTA BRAVES

Unless Rafael Ramirez proves to be the solution, the Georgia version of the Braves may soon become as infamous for their shortstops as the Mets have been for their third basemen.

1B—ORLANDO CEPEDA
2B—FELIX MILLAN
3B—BOB HORNER
SS—DENIS MENKE
OF—HANK AARON
OF—RICO CARTY
OF—DALE MURPHY
C—JOE TORRE
P—PHIL NIEKRO

Aside from Ramirez, the main pretender to this lineup would seem to be second baseman Glenn Hubbard.
Honorable mention to Felipe Alou.
Manager: Joe Torre.

BROOKLYN DODGERS

The Boys of Summer never really had a left fielder and had only Don Newcombe as a repeat 20-game winner. Otherwise, the nucleus of the teams that played in the 1949, 1952, 1953, 1955 and 1956 World Series remains the Ebbets Field Hall of Fame.

1B—GIL HODGES
2B—JACKIE ROBINSON
3B—BILLY COX
SS—PEEWEE REESE
OF—ZACK WHEAT
OF—DUKE SNIDER
OF—CARL FURILLO
C—ROY CAMPANELLA
P—DAZZY VANCE

Honorable mention to Babe Herman, Dolf Camilli, Dixie Walker, the ill-starred Pete Reiser and Burleigh Grimes.
Manager: Charlie Dressen.

LOS ANGELES DODGERS

It is an open question whether the nine-year longevity of the Garvey-Lopes-Russell-Cey infield was due to perfect chemistry, the need to give Garvey stretching exercise, or simple front-office fatigue with the comings and goings of the Jim Lefebvres, Ted Sizemores, Bobby Valentines and Bill Grabarkewitzes. Certainly, if no team has produced more Rookies of the Year than the Dodgers, few teams have produced as many sophomore or junior mediocrities, either. In any case, with one major reservation, we'll go with:

> 1B—STEVE GARVEY
> 2B—DAVEY LOPES
> 3B—RON CEY
> SS—MAURY WILLS
> OF—DUSTY BAKER
> OF—FRANK HOWARD
> OF—TOMMY DAVIS
> C—JOHN ROSEBORO
> P—SANDY KOUFAX

Our reservation concerns second base where, although he was a superior player in most categories to Lopes, Jim Gilliam simply did not play enough after the team's move from Brooklyn.

Honorable mentions, of course, to Don Drysdale and Don Sutton.

Manager: Walter Alston.

CHICAGO CUBS

Any starting nine that can't make room for Billy Williams must have something going for it.

1B—CAP ANSON
2B—BILLY HERMAN
3B—STAN HACK
SS—ERNIE BANKS
OF—RIGGS STEPHENSON
OF—HACK WILSON
OF—KIKI CUYLER
C—GABBY HARTNETT
P—MORDECAI BROWN

At .336 for 14 seasons, Stephenson holds the second highest career average for any player *not* in the Hall of Fame. (The highest mark is held by Joe Jackson, kept out of Cooperstown by the Black Sox scandal.)

Manager: Frank Chance.

CINCINNATI REDS

The greatest pitcher the Reds ever had was one they were in a great hurry to get rid of—Christy Mathewson. With that ill-fated transaction with the Giants at the turn of the century, Cincinnati unwittingly set itself on a course that would see the franchise consistently stress hitting over pitching, producing 20-game winners almost by accident. Even the team's most successful pitchers—Noodles Hahn, Paul Derringer, Bucky Walters—were very much within striking distance of .500 records when they completed their careers, and Hall of Famer Eppa Rixey probably wouldn't survive the first cut if Cooperstown ever had to reduce its roster. On the other hand, of course, there has also been more than one version of the Big Red Machine.

1B—TONY PEREZ
2B—JOE MORGAN
3B—PETE ROSE
SS—DAVE CONCEPCION
OF—FRANK ROBINSON
OF—EDD ROUSH
OF—GEORGE FOSTER
C—JOHNNY BENCH
P—EPPA RIXEY

The most obvious absentee here is Ernie Lombardi, but he just happens to be up against the catcher who holds most of the National League's offensive and defensive records. Ted Kluszewski? In the late innings of a close game we'll take Perez.

Manager: Sparky Anderson.

NEW YORK GIANTS

This is the only franchise that can boast a Hall of Famer at every position.

> 1B—BILL TERRY
> 2B—FRANKIE FRISCH
> 3B—FREDDY LINDSTROM
> SS—TRAVIS JACKSON
> OF—MEL OTT
> OF—WILLIE MAYS
> OF—ROSS YOUNGS
>   C—ROGER BRESNAHAN
>   P—CHRISTY MATHEWSON

Among the other Giant Hall of Famers not making the first team are Mickey Welch, Tim Keefe, John Montgomery Ward, Buck Ewing, George Kelly, Amos Rusie, Roger Connor, Johnny Mize, Carl Hubbell, Monte Irvin, Rube Marquard and Dave Bancroft.

Manager: John McGraw.

SAN FRANCISCO GIANTS

In their 25 years of existence, the West Coast Giants have become noted for their slugging and speedy outfielders and their sluggish and tweedy infielders. Only in the past year or two, in fact, has the team been unable to boast of a solid middle in the lineup. In addition to infielders capable of hitting their weight, the San Franciscans have also suffered from the lack of a dependable catcher—the Bob

Schmidts, Jack Hiatts, Dave Raders and Milt Mays coming and going like the winds in Candlestick Park.

1B—ORLANDO CEPEDA
2B—TITO FUENTES
3B—JIM DAVENPORT
SS—CHRIS SPEIER
OF—WILLIE McCOVEY
OF—WILLIE MAYS
OF—BOBBY BONDS
C—TOM HALLER
P—JUAN MARICHAL

If you prefer Cepeda in the outfield and McCovey at first, no problem: It would still be up to Mays to catch any fly balls hit to that side.
Manager: Alvin Dark.

PHILADELPHIA PHILLIES

Given the owners they had in the 1920s and 1930s, when Philadelphia players were considered only as good as the checks they could attract from other teams ready to buy them, it's a wonder the Phillies are still around at all. Despite those black years, the team below manages to span most of the twentieth century.

1B—FRED LUDERUS
2B—BILL HALLMAN
3B—MIKE SCHMIDT
SS—LARRY BOWA
OF—CHUCK KLEIN
OF—CY WILLIAMS
OF—RICHIE ASHBURN
C—ANDY SEMINICK
P—GROVER CLEVELAND ALEXANDER

Honorable mention to Sam Thompson, Robin Roberts and Elmer Flick.
Manager: Danny Ozark.

PITTSBURGH PIRATES

Despite the fact that they entered the 1985 season second only to the Giants in terms of lifetime winning percentage in the National League since 1900, the Pirates have had chronic weaknesses at the two most important positions—pitcher and catcher. Or, to put the problem in better perspective: The most reasonable alternatives to the battery choices below are two pitchers (Bob Friend and Vern Law) who each won 20 games only once and a catcher (Smokey Burgess) more noted for his pinch-hitting than nine-inning play.

1B—WILLIE STARGELL
2B—BILL MAZEROSKI
3B—PIE TRAYNOR
SS—HONUS WAGNER
OF—RALPH KINER
OF—PAUL WANER
OF—ROBERTO CLEMENTE
C—MANNY SANGUILLEN
P—RAY KREMER

When Stargell is inducted into the Hall of Fame, this lineup will include six Cooperstown residents. The others are Traynor, Wagner, Kiner, Waner and Clemente.

Manager: Danny Murtaugh.

ST. LOUIS CARDINALS

Very little needs to be said about this entry except that it includes five Hall of Famers, seven Most Valuable Player titles, and fifteen batting championships.

ST. LOUIS CARDINALS

1B—JOHNNY MIZE
2B—ROGERS HORNSBY
3B—KEN BOYER
SS—MARTY MARION
OF—STAN MUSIAL
OF—JOE MEDWICK
OF—LOU BROCK
  C—WALKER COOPER
  P—BOB GIBSON

Among the players left off this powerhouse lineup are Enos Slaughter, Frankie Frisch, Dizzy Dean and Mort Cooper. In fact, together with such Cardinal MVPs, offensive leaders and Cy Young winners as Chick Hafey, Orlando Cepeda, Joe Torre, Ted Simmons, Keith Hernandez, Terry Moore, Bruce Sutter and Bill White, there are the makings of a second team that could leave the rest of the league in the dust.

Manager: Billy Southworth.

HOUSTON ASTROS

Pitching has always been the name of the game in Houston, and the catcher has usually been named John Doe.

1B—BOB WATSON
2B—JOE MORGAN
3B—DOUG RADER
SS—ROGER METZGER
OF—CESAR CEDENO
OF—JIM WYNN
OF—JOSE CRUZ
  C—ALAN ASHBY
  P—J. R. RICHARD

Although Larry Dierker and Don Wilson turned in some impressive seasons, no pitcher in an Astros uniform ever came so close to dominating the league as Richard did for a few years. If Nolan Ryan turns in another good year or two, we might change our minds, but until then it's J.R.

Morgan, of course, enjoyed his greatest years with the Cincinnati Reds , but Houston is where he honed his skills and also where he returned in 1980 to lead the club into the playoffs.

Manager: Bill Virdon.

NEW YORK METS

The offensive story of the Mets is contained in the career of Ed Kranepool: Although barely a .260 hitter with indifferent power, he stayed on the team for 18 years. Of course, when you talk about the Mets, you have to talk mostly about pitching, and that essentially means talking about the glory days of Tom Seaver, Jerry Koosman, Jon Matlack and Tug McGraw. But the rest of the lineup? Well, pending longer tenure from Darryl Strawberry, we'll go with:

1B—KEITH HERNANDEZ
2B—FELIX MILLAN
3B—WAYNE GARRETT
SS—BUD HARRELSON
OF—CLEON JONES
OF—TOMMIE AGEE
OF—RUSTY STAUB
C—JERRY GROTE
P—TOM SEAVER

Ron Hunt, the first genuine player for the franchise, and Ken Boswell, a better hitter than fielder, are the infield reserves. New York being New York, Dave Kingman and Lee Mazzilli should also be mentioned for providing the kind of media hype that kept the turnstiles busy when there was very little to see on the field.

Manager: Gil Hodges.

MONTREAL EXPOS

Although the Expos haven't been a pennant contender until relatively recently, they usually have had at least one good hitter in the lineup since joining the National League in 1969. On the other hand, the team's pitching was until 1984 synonymous with the career of Steve Rogers.

```
1B—RUSTY STAUB
2B—RON HUNT
3B—LARRY PARRISH
SS—TIM FOLI
OF—ANDRE DAWSON
OF—TIM RAINES
OF  BOB BAILEY
 C—GARY CARTER
 P—STEVE ROGERS
```

And don't forget Jose Morales as the pinch-hitter. Manager: Dick Williams.

SAN DIEGO PADRES

San Diego is another team in which some of its "best" players are those who lasted longer at their positions than others.

```
1B—NATE COLBERT
2B—ALAN WIGGINS
3B—GRAIG NETTLES
SS—OZZIE SMITH
OF—CLARENCE GASTON
OF—DAVE WINFIELD
OF—GENE RICHARDS
 C—TERRY KENNEDY
 P—RANDY JONES
```

We'll wait another year before including Tony Gwynn.
Manager: Dick Williams.

ODDS AND ODDS

A lineup of National League franchise trivia:

1B—	JIM BOTTOMLEY	1922 Cardinals
2B—	LOU BIERBAUER	1891 Pirates
3B—	EDDIE MATHEWS	Career
SS—	EDDIE BRESSOUD	1962 Astros
OF—	GINO CIMOLI	1958 Dodgers
OF—	RUSTY STAUB	Career
OF—	OLLIE BROWN	1969 Padres
C—	HOBIE LANDRITH	1962 Mets
P—	TIM KEEFE	1885 Giants

Bottomley was the first regular developed through Branch Rickey's innovative farm system. Because of its allegedly unscrupulous behavior in signing Bierbauer, the Pittsburgh franchise was scornfully referred to as the Pirates. Mathews was the only Brave to play regularly for the Boston, Milwaukee and Atlanta versions of the team. Bressoud was the first player drafted by the expansion Houston team (then known as the Colt .45's). On April 18, 1958, at Seals Stadium in San Francisco, Cimoli became the first major league batter in California. Staub is both the oldest surviving Astro (he joined the team in its second year, 1963) and the only surviving member of the original 1969 Montreal Expos. Brown was the first player drafted by San Diego. Landrith was the first to be drafted by the Mets (though the first player *signed* to a New York contract was infielder Ted Lepcio). When the Giants purchased Keefe and infielder Dude Esterbrook from the American Association Mets, it was the last straw for Association owners convinced that the Giants were using their neighbors as a farm team. The Mets were drummed out of the American Association.

AMERICAN LEAGUE FRANCHISES

The all-time all-star team for every franchise in the junior circuit. Separate teams for the Philadelphia, Kansas City and Oakland versions of the Athletics; for both the Washington teams and their subsequent reincarnations in Minnesota and Texas; for the Seattle Pilots and the modern Milwaukee Brewers; and for the St. Louis Browns and the modern Baltimore Orioles. Also included are the best of two long-forgotten AL entries, the Milwaukee Brewers of 1901 and the Baltimore Orioles of 1901–02. Again, statistics are primary, but longevity matters.

BOSTON RED SOX

The Red Sox have traditionally had problems with pitching. Even their most famous pitcher had won a mere 88 games before being sold off to the Yankees in 1920 and forced to make his living with the odd home run here and there. We'll go with:

BOSTON RED SOX

1B—JIMMIE FOXX
2B—BOBBY DOERR
3B—JIMMY COLLINS
SS—JOE CRONIN
OF—TED WILLIAMS
OF—TRIS SPEAKER
OF—CARL YASTRZEMSKI
C—CARLTON FISK
P—JOE WOOD

Why Wood over Mel Parnell? Because Parnell's lifetime record was 123-75, while Wood, in his seven seasons in a Boston uniform, managed 125-56.

Manager: Bill Carrigan.

BALTIMORE ORIOLES I

The first American League version of the Orioles was a charter member of the junior circuit in 1901. The team's key figure was John McGraw, a star with the nineteenth-century National League team also known as the Baltimore Orioles who brought many of his former teammates with him to the new franchise. The AL Orioles had a first-year record of 68-65, but there wasn't room in that league (or any other) for two such forceful personalities as McGraw and AL founder and president Ban Johnson. After numerous clashes with umpires and Johnson, McGraw moved on to the National League Giants in July 1902, once again bringing star teammates along with him. The Orioles finished their second season in the cellar (50-88) and were moved to New York for the 1903 season. The franchise was eventually renamed the Yankees.

1B—DAN McGANN
2B—JIMMY WILLIAMS
3B—JOHN McGRAW
SS—BILL KEISTER
OF—MIKE DONLIN
OF—CY SEYMOUR
OF—KIP SELBACH
C—WILBERT ROBINSON
P—JOE McGINNITY

McGann was the best of nine first basemen. Williams batted .321 and .311 in the two seasons. McGraw was often hurt, but still outshone other third basemen. Keister hit .328 in 1901, Donlin .340 the same year. Seymour hit .302 and .278, Selbach .321 in 1902, Robinson in the .290s both seasons. McGinnity's records were 26-19 and 13-10.

NEW YORK YANKEES

The most astonishing thing about this team is that three of its members are *not* in the Hall of Fame. On the other hand, note the wealth of a club that has no room in its starting lineup for (among others) Yogi Berra, Lefty Gomez and Reggie Jackson.

1B—LOU GEHRIG
2B—TONY LAZZERI
3B—GRAIG NETTLES
SS—PHIL RIZZUTO
OF BABE RUTH
OF—JOE DiMAGGIO
OF—MICKEY MANTLE
C—BILL DICKEY
P—WHITEY FORD

The non-Hall of Famers, of course, are Lazzeri, Nettles and Rizzuto.

Manager: Casey Stengel.

PHILADELPHIA ATHLETICS

Somewhat like the Yankees, the old A's have become so fabled that it's something of a surprise to discover that they don't have every position covered by a Hall of Famer.

1B—JIMMIE FOXX
2B—EDDIE COLLINS
3B—FRANK BAKER
SS—JOE BOLEY
OF—AL SIMMONS
OF—MULE HAAS
OF—BING MILLER
C—MICKEY COCHRANE
P—LEFTY GROVE

The excluded are Boley, Haas and Miller.
Manager: Connie Mack.

KANSAS CITY ATHLETICS

The chief claim to fame of the Kansas City version of the Athletics (1955–1967) was the frequent accusation that it served as an unofficial farm club for the New York Yankees. As we show elsewhere in this book, the accusation was not without merit; as the lineup below indicates, some of the Yankees acquired for the Roger Marises and Art Ditmars were with merit.

1B—VIC POWER
2B—JERRY LUMPE
3B—ED CHARLES
SS—DICK HOWSER
OF—GUS ZERNIAL
OF—NORM SIEBERN
OF—BOB CERV
C—HAL SMITH
P—BUD DALEY

Power, Lumpe, Siebern and Cerv were obtained from the Yankees, while Howser and Daley subsequently ended up in the Bronx. Howser, of course, also served briefly as one of George Steinbrenner's managers.

It is also worth noting that Power ended up on Kansas City after the Yankee brass decided that his flashy kind of play would be "inappropriate" for the first black in pinstripes.

Manager: Lou Boudreau.

OAKLAND ATHLETICS

The only question mark here would seem to be at first base, where Oakland has been chronically unimpressive.

> 1B—MIKE EPSTEIN
> 2B—DICK GREEN
> 3B—SAL BANDO
> SS—BERT CAMPANERIS
> OF—REGGIE JACKSON
> OF—JOE RUDI
> OF—RICKEY HENDERSON
> C—GENE TENACE
> P—CATFISH HUNTER

Pinch-runner: Herb Washington.
Manager: Dick Williams.

CHICAGO WHITE SOX

In true White Sox fashion, this is a lineup that would have to scratch out every run.

CHICAGO WHITE SOX

1B—JIGGS DONOHUE
2B—EDDIE COLLINS
3B—BUCK WEAVER
SS—LUKE APPLING
OF—JOE JACKSON
OF—MINNIE MINOSO
OF—HAP FELSCH
C—RAY SCHALK
P—TED LYONS

The only player in this group to have hit more than 100 career homers was Minoso with 186. Next were Jackson at 54 and Collins at 47. When you consider that even many of these four-baggers were hit for other teams, you either begin wondering whether the White Sox have been on a 84-year plan stressing speed and pitching or whether their hitters have been facing the right walls when they go to bat at Comiskey Park.

Manager: Al Lopez.

CLEVELAND INDIANS

The Indians have been so dedicated to playing .500 or worse for so long that it's difficult to remember that they were once the Yankees' chief rivals. In fact, were it not for the Cleveland pennants in 1948 and 1954, the Yankees might have won an astounding 12 consecutive American League championships between 1947 and 1958.

1B—HAL TROSKY
2B—NAP LAJOIE
3B—AL ROSEN
SS—LOU BOUDREAU
OF—LARRY DOBY
OF—TRIS SPEAKER
OF—CHARLIE JAMIESON
C—STEVE O'NEILL
P—BOB FELLER

The Cleveland tale of recent years is in this: The most recently active player in this lineup is Doby, who retired in 1959!

Manager: Al Lopez.

DETROIT TIGERS

The strength of this lineup is reflected in the fact that the only non-Hall of Famers are a player with a lifetime batting average over .300 and a pitcher who turned in a record of 80-27 over a three-year span.

                1B—HANK GREENBERG
                2B—CHARLIE GEHRINGER
                3B—GEORGE KELL
                SS—HARVEY KUENN
                OF—TY COBB
                OF—HARRY HEILMANN
                OF—AL KALINE
                  C—MICKEY COCHRANE
                  P—HAL NEWHOUSER

Those not in Cooperstown are Kuenn (.303 lifetime) and Newhouser (who won 80 times between 1944 and 1946).

Manager: Hughie Jennings.

MILWAUKEE BREWERS I

Milwaukee fielded a team in the American League's first year, 1901. This earliest version of the Brewers finished dead last with a 48-89 record, 35½ games out of first. At the end of the season Ban Johnson, the guiding genius of the new league, decided that to be successful the Americans had to compete with the NL in St. Louis and moved the Milwaukee franchise to that city. The best of those who appeared in a Brewers uniform in 1901 were:

1B—JOHN ANDERSON
2B—BILLY GILBERT
3B—BILL FRIEL
SS—WID CONROY
OF—BILL HALLMAN
OF—IRV WALDRON
OF—HUGH DUFFY
C—BILLY MALONEY
P—BILL REIDY

Anderson, who batted .339, was the only legitimate hitter. Waldron was traded in the middle of the season. Maloney caught half the team's games, but managed a .293 average. Reidy was 15-18. And Duffy, alas, was the player-manager.

ST. LOUIS BROWNS

If you remember any of these players aside from the first baseman and the pitcher, you should run to the nearest quiz show.

1B—GEORGE SISLER
2B—MARTY McMANUS
3B—HARLOND CLIFT
SS—BOBBY WALLACE
OF—KEN WILLIAMS
OF—BABYDOLL JACOBSON
OF—JACK TOBIN
C—HANK SEVEREID
P—JACK KRAMER

The pinch-hitter, of course, is Eddie Gaedel (and if you don't know who he is, you better forget about the quiz show).
Manager: Luke Sewell.

BALTIMORE ORIOLES II

This won't please Boog Powell fans, but the fact is that most experts have been so busy predicting that Eddie Murray will be a great player, they have failed to notice that he has already become one.

1B—EDDIE MURRAY
2B—DAVE JOHNSON
3B—BROOKS ROBINSON
SS—MARK BELANGER
OF—FRANK ROBINSON
OF—PAUL BLAIR
OF—KEN SINGLETON
C—GUS TRIANDOS
P JIM PALMER

Triandos instead of Rick Dempsey? Well, one of the authors has the same doubt, but the other two insist that a little bit of Rick Dempsey goes a little way.

Manager: Earl Weaver.

WASHINGTON SENATORS I

These are the Senators who made Washington famous for being first in war, first in peace and last in the American League. In fact, however, they had their moments, especially in the '20s, and they never became quite as boring as the St. Louis Browns. Even the walking dead teams of the '50s had some oafish clout in Roy Sievers and Jim Lemon (the latter being the Dave Kingman of his time).

1B—MICKEY VERNON
2B—BUCKY HARRIS
3B—EDDIE YOST
SS—JOE CRONIN
OF—HEINIE MANUSH
OF—GOOSE GOSLIN
OF—SAM RICE
C—MUDDY RUEL
P—WALTER JOHNSON

The combined batting average of this team is .295—not bad for a legendary loser. And that's without taking into account Yost's thousands of walks!

Manager: Bucky Harris.

MINNESOTA TWINS

For some reason, the Twins have never had a dearth of good hitters and in this respect, at least, their farm system deserves comparison with those of the Dodgers and Cardinals. The problem, of course, is that most of these hitters were dispensed with as soon as they asked for salary raises and were replaced by players the Twins themselves would probably not have promoted to the majors.

1B—ROD CAREW
2B—CESAR TOVAR
3B—HARMON KILLEBREW
SS—ZOILO VERSALLES
OF—BOB ALLISON
OF—TONY OLIVA
OF—LYMAN BOSTOCK
C—EARL BATTEY
P—JIM KAAT

How well has the farm system produced hitters? Consider this: only Battey (the White Sox) and Tovar (the Reds) came from other teams.

Manager: Sam Mele.

CALIFORNIA ANGELS

The history of California's pitching is divided into three periods—Before Nolan Ryan, Nolan Ryan, and After Nolan Ryan.

CALIFORNIA ANGELS

1B—ROD CAREW
2B—BOBBY GRICH
3B—CARNEY LANSFORD
SS—JIM FREGOSI
OF—DON BAYLOR
OF—REGGIE JACKSON
OF—LEON WAGNER
C—BOB BOONE
P—NOLAN RYAN

Another good year from Brian Downing would squeeze him somewhere into the outfield.
Manager: Jim Fregosi.

WASHINGTON SENATORS II

These are the Senators who, existing as they did during the Laos and Vietnam war years between 1961 and 1971, made Washington famous for being last in war, last in peace and last in the American League.

1B—MIKE EPSTEIN
2B—BERNIE ALLEN
3B—KEN McMULLEN
SS—EDDIE BRINKMAN
OF—FRANK HOWARD
OF—DEL UNSER
OF—CHUCK HINTON
C—PAUL CASANOVA
P—DICK BOSMAN

Manager Gil Hodges liked Casanova.
Manager: Ted Williams.

TEXAS RANGERS

Deep in the heart of Texas there is a reason why this team has never produced the winners it should have, but the reason certainly hasn't been a lack of talent.

1B—MIKE HARGROVE
2B—DAVE NELSON
3B—BUDDY BELL
SS—TOBY HARRAH
OF—AL OLIVER
OF—JEFF BURROUGHS
OF—RICHIE ZISK
C—JIM SUNDBERG
P—FERGUSON JENKINS

Notice: Almost all of these players remained active into the 1984 season, but only Bell was still a Ranger. Enough said about the trading acumen of the front office.

Manager: Billy Martin.

SEATTLE PILOTS

The Pilots didn't know it at the time, but the only reason for their one-year existence in 1969 was to give some of their players the opportunity to be mentioned in this book.

1B—DON MINCHER
2B—JOHN DONALDSON
3B—TOMMY HARPER
SS—RAY OYLER
OF—WAYNE COMER
OF—TOMMY DAVIS
OF—STEVE HOVLEY
C—GERRY McNERTNEY
P—DIEGO SEGUI

As all trivia experts should know, pitcher Segui was the only player to be on both the Seattle Pilots and Seattle Mariners.

Manager: Joe Schultz.

MILWAUKEE BREWERS II

If this lineup seems familiar, it means you watched the 1982 World Series.

```
1B—CECIL COOPER
2B—JIM GANTNER
3B—PAUL MOLITOR
SS—ROBIN YOUNT
OF—BEN OGLIVIE
OF—GORMAN THOMAS
OF—LARRY HISLE
 C—TED SIMMONS
 P—ROLLIE FINGERS
```

If you want to cheat a little, you can move Cooper into the outfield in place of Hisle and put George Scott at first, but on balance we prefer it as is.

Manager: George Bamberger.

KANSAS CITY ROYALS

The pinball team that lost the American League playoffs regularly to the Yankees in the late '70s is still the best.

```
1B—JOHN MAYBERRY
2B—FRANK WHITE
3B—GEORGE BRETT
SS—FRED PATEK
OF—HAL McRAE
OF—AMOS OTIS
OF—WILLIE WILSON
 C—DARRELL PORTER
 P—DENNIS LEONARD
```

The guiding hand behind this team was, of course, batting instructor Charley Lau.

Manager: Whitey Herzog.

SEATTLE MARINERS

The only thing more difficult than coming up with an all-time all-star Mariners team is deciding whether or not Rick Sweet's good half-season in 1982 entitles him to be the starting catcher over such other half-season performers as Larry Cox, Jerry Narron and Jim Essian. We believe so.

1B—BRUCE BOCHTE
2B—JULIO CRUZ
3B—DANNY MEYER
SS—CRAIG REYNOLDS
OF—RICHIE ZISK
OF—RUPPERT JONES
OF—LEON ROBERTS
C—RICK SWEET
P—FLOYD BANNISTER

Definitely a team of the future—if for no other reason than it has no past.

Manager: Rene Lachemann.

TORONTO BLUE JAYS

When the Blue Jays entered the American League in 1977, it was clear that they were going to be Canada's second best baseball team for quite a while. It was only in 1982, however, that they began to show signs that they weren't also *Toronto*'s second best club.

1B—WILLIE UPSHAW
2B—DAMASO GARCIA
3B—ROY HOWELL
SS—ALFREDO GRIFFIN
OF—BOB BAILOR
OF—LLOYD MOSEBY
OF—JESSE BARFIELD
C—ERNIE WHITT
P—DAVE STIEB

An honorable mention to Rico Carty.
Manager: Bobby Cox.

ODDS AND ODDS

Some American League franchise trivia:

1B—DON MINCHER	Career	
2B—NAP LAJOIE	1905–09 Indians	
3B—JOHN McGRAW	1900 Cardinals	
SS—BOB BAILOR	1977 Blue Jays	
OF—ELMER VALO	Career	
OF—LOU SOCKALEXIS	Career	
OF—RUPPERT JONES	1977 Mariners	
C—PHIL ROOF	Career	
P—AL FITZMORRIS	Career	

Mincher spent his entire career with expansion or shifted franchises: both Washington teams, their successors in Minnesota and Texas, the Angels, Oakland Athletics and Seattle Pilots. During his player-manager days in Cleveland, Lajoie's team was commonly known as the Naps. It was McGraw's derisive reference to the Athletics as "those white elephants" that ultimately led Philadelphia to adopt the animal as its symbol. Bailor was the first player selected by the expansion Blue Jays. Valo moved with three franchises—with the Athletics from Philadelphia to Kansas City, with the Dodgers from Brooklyn to Los Angeles and with the Senators from Washington to Minnesota. Sockalexis, the first Native American in the majors, was the inspiration for renaming the Cleveland franchise the Indians. Jones was the first player drafted by Seattle. Roof was on the first-year squads of the Oakland Athletics, Milwaukee Brewers and Toronto Blue Jays. Fitzmorris was picked twice in expansion drafts—by the Royals in 1969 and the Blue Jays in 1977. (Bobby Shantz was the only other player selected in two expansion drafts—by the Astros and Senators.)

DECADES

All-star teams for every ten years from the 1880s to the 1980s. No distinction between leagues here. And one or two good years at the end or the beginning of a decade is insufficient to qualify.

THE 1880s

The 1880s was a time of turbulence in professional baseball. The National League matured. The American Association was born. The Union Association was born and died the same year. And great players abounded.

> 1B—CAP ANSON
> 2B—HARDY RICHARDSON
> 3B—EZRA SUTTON
> SS—JOHN MONTGOMERY WARD
> OF—TIP O'NEILL
> OF—PETE BROWNING
> OF—KING KELLY
> C—BUCK EWING
> P—TIM KEEFE

Dan Brouthers, one of the greatest hitters of all time (.349 lifetime) can't make this team because of Anson. And a galaxy of pitchers with extraordinary credentials—John Clarkson, Pud Galvin, Charlie Radbourne and Mickey Welch—come out as also-rans. But five Hall of Famers—Anson, Ward, Kelly, Ewing and Keefe—combined with O'Neill (who recorded baseball's highest season batting average, .492, in 1887) and Browning (who has the fourth highest lifetime average, .355, but is mysteriously absent from the Hall of Fame) make a stellar combination.

THE 1890s

With the failure of the Players' League in 1890 after only one year and the demise of the American Association a year later, the National League expanded to twelve teams for the remainder of the decade. Baltimore baseball—stealing bases, playing hit and run, and scrapping—became the standard of play from 1894 on. The Orioles won three pennants and placed four players on this team. But the Cleveland Spiders put two players on the team of the decade and won no pennants, while Boston won five pennants with only a single entry here.

1B—CAP ANSON
2B—CUPID CHILDS
3B—JOHN McGRAW
SS—HUGHIE JENNINGS
OF—JESSE BURKETT
OF—ED DELAHANTY
OF—WILLIE KEELER
C—WILBERT ROBINSON
P—KID NICHOLS

The four Orioles: McGraw, Jennings, Keeler and Robinson. The two Spiders: Childs and Burkett. Boston has many runners-up: Billy Hamilton, the stolen base champion; Bobby Lowe, who hit four home runs in one game; and Hugh Duffy, whose .438 in 1894 was the highest NL batting average ever. But it also has Nichols, who won 30 or more games in seven seasons. Honorable mention also to third baseman Denny Lyons, pitcher Cy Young, shortstop Ed McKean and outfielder George Van Haltren.

THE 1900s

The birth of the American League in 1901 ended the monopoly of the National League, which cut back to eight teams again with the onset of the twentieth century.

> 1B—JAKE BECKLEY
> 2B—NAP LAJOIE
> 3B—JIMMY COLLINS
> SS—HONUS WAGNER
> OF—TY COBB
> OF—GINGER BEAUMONT
> OF—SAM CRAWFORD
> C—JOHNNY KLING
> P—CHRISTY MATHEWSON

Of the four American Leaguers here, three (Lajoie, Collins and Crawford) were recruits from the National League and only one (Cobb) was an original product. The least familiar names in the lineup are Beckley, who hit over .300 every year from 1900 to 1904; Beaumont, who had a batting championship and six .300 seasons in the decade; and Kling, who was the starting catcher for the powerhouse Cubs from 1902 to 1910.

Of the superstars, Cobb didn't arrive until 1905, but still managed three batting titles for the decade; Wagner never batted below .329; and Mathewson won 30 or more games in four seasons, three of them consecutive.

THE 1910s

The fact that eight of the nine players of this decade were American Leaguers demonstrates that the new league had become a fixture.

THE 1910s
1B—GEORGE SISLER
2B—EDDIE COLLINS
3B—FRANK BAKER
SS—HONUS WAGNER
OF—TY COBB
OF—TRIS SPEAKER
OF—JOE JACKSON
C—RAY SCHALK
P—WALTER JOHNSON

This could be the best decade of them all. Sisler didn't come to the Browns until 1915, but immediately established himself as the best first baseman around. Collins and Baker were half of Connie Mack's $100,000 infield until Mack broke up the Athletics and sent Collins to the White Sox and Baker to the Yankees. Wagner was a fading star, but still the premier shortstop until 1916. Speaker batted over .300 nine times and took the only AL batting championship Cobb didn't win. Jackson batted over .300 every year from 1910 to 1919, reaching a high of .408 in 1911. Schalk was the backstop for the sterling White Sox pitching staff that dominated the league in the latter part of the decade.

Cobb? All he did was bat .387 over the ten years.

And Johnson? Well, he won 264 games with Washington Senators teams that ranged from mediocre to terrible.

THE 1920s

The Golden Age of Baseball—and a dramatically different kind of baseball as a result of the booming bat of a young pitcher-turned-slugging-outfielder named Babe Ruth.

1B—LOU GEHRIG
2B—ROGERS HORNSBY
3B—PIE TRAYNOR
SS—JOE SEWELL
OF—TY COBB
OF—TRIS SPEAKER
OF—BABE RUTH
C—MICKEY COCHRANE
P—DAZZY VANCE

Gehrig was the boy wonder of the second half of the decade. Traynor came to the Pirates in 1920 and within a few years was the finest third baseman of his time, or perhaps any other. Sewell was a remarkably underrated hitter who almost never struck out. Cobb and Speaker were aging stars, but still dangerous. Cochrane was a rookie in 1925, but an immediate star.

Vance had a few bumpy years, but won 20 or more three times with teams that finished sixth just about every year.

Ruth hit 467 home runs in these ten years.

Hornsby batted an astonishing .402 over five seasons (1921–25).

THE 1930s

Standout players abounded in the 1930s, a hitters' decade. After much debate we'll take:

1B—LOU GEHRIG
2B—CHARLIE GEHRINGER
3B—PIE TRAYNOR
SS—JOE CRONIN
OF—PAUL WANER
OF—MEL OTT
OF—JOE MEDWICK
C—BILL DICKEY
P—LEFTY GROVE

Gehrig (.329 and 119 RBIs or better for eight consecutive seasons) over Bill Terry (.401 in 1930) and Jimmie Foxx (two batting titles and four league-leading home run totals).

Ott (five home run titles), Medwick (414 RBIs in three years and a triple crown in 1937) and Waner (over .300 eight times) rather than Al Simmons (two batting titles) and Chuck Klein (three home run titles and a batting title).

THE 1940s

The war years interrupted most of these players' careers so their lifetime statistics are not up to the stats of other eras. Nevertheless, no one need be embarrassed by these selections.

1B—JOHNNY MIZE
2B—BOBBY DOERR
3B—STAN HACK
SS—LUKE APPLING
OF—TED WILLIAMS
OF—JOE DiMAGGIO
OF—STAN MUSIAL
C—ERNIE LOMBARDI
P—BOB FELLER

Mize was the most feared power hitter of his day. Doerr was a steady hitter whose average rose as high as .325. Hack faded as the '40s wore on, but was still a dangerous hitter. This was Appling's last hurrah, but it was loud enough for him to hit over .300 in seven full seasons and to lead the league once. The outfield needs no defense whatsoever. Lombardi won a batting crown in 1942 and hit over .300 in three other seasons. And Feller was striking out everyone in sight.

THE 1950s

The Yankees and the Dodgers dominated the 1950s, but the decade's most successful players were far more widely distributed. A glance at the lineup below shows that even such period stars as Brooklyn's Duke Snider and Roy Campanella, New York's Whitey Ford, Pittsburgh's Ralph Kiner, Milwaukee's Henry Aaron, Detroit's Al Kaline, and Philadelphia's Robin Roberts—Hall of Famers all—had some royal competition at their various positions.

1B—STAN MUSIAL
2B—JACKIE ROBINSON
3B—EDDIE MATHEWS
SS—ERNIE BANKS
OF—TED WILLIAMS
OF—MICKEY MANTLE
OF—WILLIE MAYS
C—YOGI BERRA
P—WARREN SPAHN

Among other things, this lineup produced eight batting championships, seven league home run leaders and eight Most Valuable Player awards. As for Spahn, his record between 1950 and 1959 was 202 wins and 131 losses.

THE 1960s

A decade of turbulence for the nation and of expansion for the national pastime. In 1961 came new franchises in the American League—Los Angeles (later California) and Washington (later Texas). And in 1962 the Mets and Houston joined the National. Then, in 1969, each league added two more teams: Seattle (which moved to Milwaukee after one season) and Kansas City in the AL, Montreal and San Diego in the NL. Expansion offered us a larger pool of players from which to choose, but not one of our selections ever starred for an expansion team.

1B—HARMON KILLEBREW
2B—BILL MAZEROSKI
3B—BROOKS ROBINSON
SS—LUIS APARICIO
OF—FRANK ROBINSON
OF—WILLIE MAYS
OF—HANK AARON
C—ELSTON HOWARD
P—SANDY KOUFAX

A superb fielding infield—except for Killebrew, who played first, third and the outfield equally badly, but who had to be here somewhere because of his bat.

The outfield needs no comment. Lou Brock can't crack this lineup. Neither can Roger Maris nor Mickey Mantle.

Howard won an MVP in 1963 and was a superlative successor to Yogi Berra.

And between 1962 and 1966 Koufax led the league in ERA five times, struck out 300 or more three times, pitched four no-hitters, and won 118 while losing only 34 for a .776 percentage.

THE 1970s

In the first full decade of divisional play, the dominant teams were the Orioles (six division titles and three pennants), Athletics (five titles and three pennants) and Yankees (three pennants) in the American League, and the Reds (six division titles and four pennants), Pirates (six division wins and two pennants) and Dodgers (three pennants and no finish below third) in the National.

1B—ROD CAREW
2B—JOE MORGAN
3B—MIKE SCHMIDT
SS—DAVE CONCEPCION
OF—WILLIE STARGELL
OF—REGGIE JACKSON
OF—PETE ROSE
C—JOHNNY BENCH
P—TOM SEAVER

The chief pretender here is George Foster, who batted .287 and hit 201 home runs for the decade. Stargell, however, rode his best years into a .286 batting average and 296 homers. In addition to his personal marks, Jackson played in seven Championship Series and four World Series for the decade.

Seaver gets the nod over Jim Palmer and Steve Carlton for having won 178 games despite being saddled with mediocre teams for most of the period.

THE 1980s

Even with only half the decade gone, we'll not shy away from a quick glance into our crystal ball.

1B—EDDIE MURRAY
2B—RYNE SANDBERG
3B—WADE BOGGS
SS—CAL RIPKEN
OF—DARRYL STRAWBERRY
OF—HAL BAINES
OF—DALE MURPHY
C—LANCE PARRISH
P—DAVE STIEB

The bet here, of course, is that Baltimore will not eventually find the shortstop it has been seeking for the past few years and put Ripken back at his natural position.

WHERE OR WHEN

Not so much what happened as *where* it happened (what city or ballpark) or *when* (what date or day).

HISTORIC FIRSTS

A relatively easy way of getting into the record book is to be around for the first major league game. For example:

1B—WES FISLER	1876	Philadelphia
2B—ROSS BARNES	1876	Cubs
3B—NED WILLIAMSON	1884	Cubs
SS—GEORGE WRIGHT	1876	Braves
OF—JIM O'ROURKE	1876	Braves
OF—OLLIE PICKERING	1901	Indians
OF—BABE HERMAN	1935	Reds
C—TIM McGINLEY	1876	Braves
P—LOU KNIGHT	1876	Philadelphia

In the very first National League game on April 22, 1876, between Philadelphia and Boston, Fisler became the first player to get three hits, Wright was the first batter, O'Rourke the first to get a hit (a two-out single in the first inning), McGinley the first both to strike out and score a run and Knight the first to deliver a pitch. Ten days later, Barnes became the first player to hit a home run. Eight years passed before Williamson went into the books as the first player to hit three homers in a single contest. Pickering was the first American Leaguer to stand up at home plate in the April 24, 1901 inaugural between Cleveland

45

and Chicago. As for Herman, he hit the first homer in a major league night game.

BALLPARK BAPTISMS (NL)

Civic leaders love to celebrate the opening of ballparks. These players had an extra reason for celebrating:

1B—VIC SAIER	April 20, 1916	Cubs
2B—OTTO KNABE	April 9, 1913	Phillies
3B—DICK ALLEN	April 12, 1965	Phillies
SS—ED SPIEZIO	April 8, 1969	Padres
OF—WALLY POST	April 10, 1962	Reds
OF—WILLIE STARGELL	April 17, 1964	Pirates
OF—RICO CARTY	June 30, 1970	Braves
C—JOE TORRE	April 12, 1966	Braves
P—SAM JONES	April 12, 1960	Giants

Saier's 11th-inning hit was Chicago's margin of difference over Cincinnati in the Wrigley Field opener. Knabe's double and an error in the outfield provided the only run for Johnny Seaton's opening day shutout at Ebbets Field in Brooklyn. Allen hit the first indoors home run at the Astrodome, and it gave Philadelphia a win over Houston. The unlikely Spiezio christened Jack Murphy Stadium with San Diego's first hit and first home run, enough to give the Padres a 2-1 win. Post dampened the Dodger Stadium opener by hitting a decisive three-run homer. Stargell went 4-for-5 with a homer to ruin the Mets' opener at Shea Stadium. Carty's homer and four runs batted in made the Reds wish they had opened Riverfront Stadium the next day. Despite Torre's long-ball hitting, Atlanta went down to defeat in its first home opener; Torre's two solo blasts came up against a two-run shot from the same Stargell who had left Shea Stadium fans dejected two years before. Jones won a masterful 3-1 game over the Cardinals in the first game ever played in Candlestick Park.

BALLPARK BAPTISMS (AL)

Those who have distinguished themselves in inaugural games in American League ballparks include:

1B—DOUG AULT	April 7, 1977	Blue Jays
2B—STEVE YERKES	April 20, 1912	Red Sox
3B—LENNY RANDLE	April 21, 1972	Rangers
SS—VERN STEPHENS	April 15, 1954	Orioles
OF—BABE RUTH	April 18, 1923	Yankees
OF—GEORGE STONE	July 1, 1910	Browns
OF—TY COBB	April 20, 1912	Tigers
C—MICKEY COCHRANE	July 31, 1932	Athletics
P—ANDY MESSERSMITH	April 7, 1970	Angels

Ault christened Toronto's Exhibition Stadium with two homers and a single in the first AL game in Canada. Yerkes had five hits to help Boston win the Fenway Park opener. Randle's three hits keyed a Texas victory in the first Arlington Stadium game. Stephens hit a big homer to help Baltimore open Memorial Stadium on a winning note. Ruth hit the first of his many Yankee Stadium homers in the first Bronx game. Stone helped to dampen the spirits of Chicago fans by getting a single, double and triple to boost St. Louis to a victory in the Comiskey Park opener. Cobb worked two double steals with Sam Crawford, including a steal of home, in the very first inning of play at Tiger Stadium. Cochrane batted in the lone run in the eighth inning in Lefty Grove's 1-0 masterpiece over Cleveland in the first Municipal Stadium contest. Messersmith four-hitted the Brewers in California's grim 12-0 win in Milwaukee's first AL County Stadium game.

Honorable mentions to John Mayberry who homered and drove in four runs in Kansas City's 12-1 victory over Texas in the 1973 inaugural at Royals Stadium and to Joe Rudi of the Angels who had three hits and four RBIs in the 1977 indoor opener at the Seattle Kingdome.

BOTH LEAGUES

Frank Robinson was the first black manager in both the National and American leagues, but that is only one of his accomplishments in both circuits. His teammates are:

1B—BOB WATSON	Astros and Red Sox
2B—NAP LAJOIE	Phillies, Athletics and Indians
3B—DICK ALLEN	Phillies and White Sox
SS—BILL ALMON	Padres and White Sox
OF—FRANK ROBINSON	Reds and Orioles
OF—SAM CRAWFORD	Reds and Tigers
OF—RON LeFLORE	Tigers and Expos
C—GUS TRIANDOS	Orioles and Phillies
P—JIM BUNNING	Tigers and Phillies

Watson is the only player to have hit for the cycle in both leagues. Lajoie had seasons for all three clubs when he led his league in runs batted in. Allen led both leagues in slugging percentage and was also one of three players (along with Frank Robinson and Dick Stuart) to have 35-homer seasons in the two circuits. On a negative note, Almon has led both leagues in errors (tie with Alfredo Griffin in the AL). Robinson did just about everything—homers, slugging percentage, being named MVP, etc. In the pre-Ruth era Crawford led both leagues in home runs. LeFlore is the only player to have led both leagues in stolen bases. Triandos was the first to catch no-hitters in the two leagues (Hoyt Wilhelm in the AL, Jim Bunning in the NL); Jeff Torborg subsequently did it with Sandy Koufax in the NL and Nolan Ryan in the AL. Bunning, the pitching equivalent of Robinson, won more than 100 games, pitched no-hitters, struck out at least 1000 batters, and was the starting pitcher in All-Star games for both the National and American leagues.

FOUR DECADES

Only 17 players have appeared in a box score in four different decades. Two of them appeared in a fifth decade. It's all a matter of combining longevity and good timing—or having an active public relations department.

1B—DAN BROUTHERS	1879–1896, 1904
2B—KID GLEASON	1888–1908, 1912
3B—JOHN RYAN	1889–1891, 1894–1896, 1898–1899, 1901–03, 1912–13
SS—EDDIE COLLINS	1906–1930
OF—MINNIE MINOSO	1949–1964, 1976, 1980
OF—TED WILLIAMS	1939–1960
OF—JIM O'ROURKE	1876–1893, 1904
C—DEACON McGUIRE	1884–1888, 1890–1908, 1910, 1912
P—EARLY WYNN	1939–1963

Only Wynn and Williams were legitimate players in their fourth decades. Collins, who was, of course, a second baseman and played only 40 games (in two of the decades) at short, never played the field at all in 1929 and 1930. The rest of these players appeared in a fourth decade as stunts. And O'Rourke did not play the outfield in 1904.

The others who appeared in four decades are Nick Altrock, Jack O'Connor, Jack Quinn, Bobo Newsom, Mickey Vernon, Willie McCovey, Tim McCarver and Jim Kaat—but only Quinn, Newsom, Vernon and Kaat did it for more than the glory of joining this exclusive club.

FOUR MAJOR LEAGUES

It has been categorically impossible for any player who was a rookie after 1891 to appear in a box score in four major leagues. These are the best of the handful who did just that.

1B—JOE QUINN	UA, NL, PL, AL
2B—FRED DUNLAP	NL, UA, PL, AA
3B—JOHN IRWIN	NL, UA, AA, PL
SS—BILL HALLMAN	NL, PL, AA, AL
OF—DUMMY HOY	NL, PL, AA, AL
OF—HUGH DUFFY	NL, PL, AA, AL
OF—EMMETT SEERY	UA, AL, PL, AA
C—DUKE FARRELL	NL, PL, AA, AL
P—GUS WEYHING	AA, PL, NL, AL

We cheated a bit here. Quinn played first base only in the Union Association and the National League and was primarily a second baseman. And Hallman never played shortstop in the American Association.

The most recent four-majors player was Lave Cross, perhaps the best third baseman of his day (1887–1907). But Cross played third only in the American Association, the National League and the American League; in the Players League he appeared only as a catcher.

The manager is Tom Loftus, the only man ever to manage in four leagues—with Milwaukee (UA); Cleveland (AA); Cleveland, the Reds and the Cubs (NL); and the Senators (AL).

WHICH LEAGUE IS THIS ANYWAY?

Back in the nineteenth century players exhibited a loyalty to certain cities rather than certain teams. These players stuck with their favorite cities through thick, thin and three leagues.

1B—DAN BROUTHERS	Boston	NL, PL, AA
2B—BILL HALLMAN	Philadelphia	NL, PL, AA
3B—JOE MULVEY	Philadelphia	NL, PL, AA
SS—WILLIE KUEHNE	Pittsburgh	AA, NL, PL
OF—LAVE CROSS	Philadelphia	AA, PL, NL
OF—PATSY DONOVAN	Washington	AA, NL, AL
OF—JIMMY McALEER	Cleveland	NL, PL, AL
C—KING KELLY	Boston	NL, PL, AA
P—PUD GALVIN	Pittsburgh	AA, NL, AL

Cross actually played with four Philadelphia teams, since he also appeared with the American League Athletics, although only at first base and third base.

Kuehne never played short for the Players League Pittsburgh franchise, but he comes closest among shortstops.

Both John McGraw and Wilbert Robinson played for Baltimore Orioles franchises in the American Association, the National League and the American League. But Kelly was a better catcher than Robinson; and McGraw never played third base with the AA Orioles.

UNFAMILIAR SETTINGS

Major league baseball has been played in several unlikely cities. Syracuse, NY; Worcester, MA; and even Altoona, PA, have all fielded major league teams at one time or another. But the following played major league ball in cities that did not have major league teams.

1B—ROGER CONNOR	Albany
2B—HOBE FERRISS	Canton and Columbus
3B—EDDIE MATHEWS	Jersey City
SS—JOHN MONTGOMERY WARD	Staten Island
OF—WALLY MOON	Jersey City
OF—WILLIE KEELER	Newark
OF—SAM CRAWFORD	Toledo
C—ROGER BRESNAHAN	Dayton
P—GEORGE MULLIN	Grand Rapids

The secret is that major league teams played away from their home grounds for a variety of reasons—to escape Sunday blue laws, to increase attendance at the end of a season, or to escape an untenable position.

Connor hit the first major league grand-slam while playing for Troy at a home game across the river in Albany. Ferriss hit homers for the Red Sox in both Canton and Columbus when the Indians and Tigers played a few home games there in the first decade of this century. Mathews is the only one to hit two homers while the Dodgers sojourned in Jersey City for a few games in 1956 and 1957. Moon hit the first homer in Jersey City's Roosevelt Stadium. Keeler and the New York Highlanders played a few games in Newark in the first decade of this century. Ditto Crawford and the Tigers in Toledo. In his brief sojourn in the American League, Bresnahan spoiled the Indians' Dayton home game by hitting the only major league home run hit in that city. And Mullin won the only major league game played in Grand Rapids, when the Tigers played a game there.

The classic story here is that of Ward and the 1889 Giants. In July of that year New York City decided to run a road through the old Polo Grounds and evicted the Giants, who ended up finishing their season on Staten Island where Ward, their captain, led them to a pennant and an early World Series victory against the American Association Brooklyn team. This means that there has been a World Series played in each of New York City's five boroughs.

LOUD OUTS

All these players did was strike out, ground out, or fly out. Their timing, however, was something else.

1B—RICH REESE	Sept. 27, 1973	Twins
2B—MARV BREEDING	Sept. 12, 1962	Orioles
3B—BRAD MILLS	April 27, 1983	Expos
SS—LEO DUROCHER	June 15, 1938	Dodgers
OF—CESAR GERONIMO	June 17, 1974	Reds
OF—TOMMY HUTTON	Sept. 3, 1976	Phillies
OF—AL FERRARA	April 22, 1970	Padres
C—JOHN STEPHENSON	June 21, 1964	Mets
P—AL DOWNING	April 8, 1974	Dodgers

Reese struck out on the last pitch of the season, thereby becoming Nolan Ryan's record-breaking 383rd strikeout victim of the year. Breeding contributed three crucial strikeouts to Washington pitcher Tom Cheney's mark of most strikeouts in an extra-inning game (21). Mills was the strikeout victim who enabled Ryan to pass Walter

Johnson's record of 3508 career whiffs. Durocher's fly was the last out in Johnny Vander Meer's second straight no-hitter. Geronimo was Bob Gibson's 3000th strikeout victim; seven years later he performed the same service for Steve Carlton. Hutton, usually Tom Seaver's chief nemesis, was at the plate when the Mets right-hander notched his 200th strikeout for the ninth consecutive year. The same Seaver blew away Ferrara as his record-making 10th straight strikeout victim. Stephenson fanned as the 27th out recorded by Jim Bunning in the first National League perfect game since 1880. Downing served up the pitch that Hank Aaron clouted into the Atlanta bullpen to break Babe Ruth's career mark of 714 homers.

LOUD CLOUTS

On the other hand, these players chose unusual moments to get a hit or deal some other blow to pitchers.

1B—BILL WHITE	Sept. 30, 1956	Giants
2B—LOU KLIMCHOCK	August 4, 1963	Braves
3B—BUCKY WALTERS	May 6, 1934	Red Sox
SS—LARRY BROWN	July 31, 1963	Indians
OF—JO JO MOORE	August 13, 1939	Giants
OF—ROGER MARIS	Sept. 26, 1961	Yankees
OF—SAM THOMPSON	August 17, 1894	Phillies
C—MIKE GRADY	August 17, 1894	Phillies
P—MIKE TORREZ	June 25, 1977	Yankees

White's two homers off Robin Roberts pushed the Philadelphia great into the record book for yielding 46 round-trippers in a season. When Roger Craig of the Mets tried to pick off Klimchock, he threw the ball away into his record-tying 18th consecutive loss. Walters tagged Firpo Marberry for an unprecedented fourth consecutive triple. Brown went Walters one better by clouting the fourth consecutive homer off Paul Foytack. Moore put Bill Kerksieck into the record books by hitting the sixth homer off the Phillies hurler in a game. Before he hit his 61st homer off Tracy Stallard, Maris tied Babe Ruth's seasonal mark by walloping No. 60 off Jack Fisher; the year before, the same

Fisher had given up the blast that marked Ted Williams's goodbye to baseball. Thompson and Grady together reached Louisville's Jack Wadsworth for 11 hits and insured the pitcher's grim mark of allowing the most hits (36) in a single game. Torrez put an end to Boston's incredible streak of 33 home runs over 10 consecutive games.

STAYING HOT

The first eight players were nightmares for pitchers over a span of several games, while the pitcher evened the score for fellow hurlers.

1B—FRANK HOWARD	1968 Senators
2B—TONY LAZZERI	1936 Yankees
3B—GEORGE BRETT	1976 Royals
SS—JOE CRONIN	1933 Senators
OF—RALPH KINER	1947 Pirates
OF—RIP REPULSKI	1954 Cardinals
OF—JIM NORTHRUP	1968 Tigers
C—JOHNNY BLANCHARD	1961 Yankees
P—JIM BARR	1972 Giants

Howard walloped 10 homers in six games. In back-to-back games Lazzeri amassed 15 runs batted in. Brett had six consecutive three-hit games. Cronin established the record for the most hits (13) in three consecutive American League games. Kiner connected for eight home runs in a four-game span. Repulski had ten consecutive games in which he had at least two hits. Northrup hit three grand-slams in one week. Blanchard had four consecutive homers spread out over a three-game stretch. Barr retired 41 straight hitters over two games.

Honorable mentions to Lee Lacy of the 1978 Dodgers and Del Unser of the 1979 Phillies, both of whom had three consecutive homers as pinch-hitters.

THE BEST YEAR OF THEIR LIVES

In 1945, these players were the cream of the crop. Two years later, with the last veteran home from World War II, they weren't even on a major league roster.

1B—NICK ETTEN	Yankees
2B—DUTCH MEYER	Indians
3B—CHUCK WORKMAN	Braves
SS—GLENN CRAWFORD	Cardinals and Phillies
OF—BUSTER ADAMS	Phillies and Cardinals
OF—JIMMY WASDELL	Phillies
OF—BOBBY ESTALELLA	Athletics
C—FRANK MANCUSO	Browns
P—ROGER WOLFF	Senators

Etten hit .285, had 18 home runs, and drove in 111 runs. Meyer batted a neat .292. Workman bolstered his .274 average with 25 homers and 87 runs batted in. Crawford, who also played some outfield, came in at .292 and struck out only 15 times in more than 300 at bats. Adams hit .287 with 22 homers, 109 runs batted in and 104 runs scored. Wasdell batted an even .300 with 60 runs batted in. Estalella finished one point below the magic circle at .299, but also walked 74 times. Mancuso contributed a solid .268 for a catcher. Wolff, a knuckleballer, won 20 and lost 10.

ALWAYS ON SUNDAY

In his 15-year career between 1950 and 1964, Charley Maxwell gained a reputation for hitting Sunday homers and, in fact, 40 of his 148 circuits were recorded on the seventh day. But Maxwell wasn't the only one who liked some moments and places better than others.

1B—LOU GEHRIG
2B—PETE ROSE
3B—KEN REITZ
SS—EDDIE JOOST
OF—CHARLIE MAXWELL
OF—WILLIE MAYS
OF—STAN MUSIAL
C—RUDY YORK
P—WALTER JOHNSON

Gehrig hit 14 homers against Cleveland in 1936 to set the major league record for damage against one team. In 1969 and 1970 Rose and Bobby Tolan led off three games by hitting back-to-back homers—the only twosome to have done it more than once. Rare was the April when Reitz, a lifetime .261 hitter, wasn't leading the National League in batting and rare was the June when he wasn't on the bench for not hitting. Joost set the AL mark for leading off the most games (six) with a homer in 1948, a year in which he otherwise reached the seats only ten times. Mays holds the record for the most home runs in extra innings (22). Musial was so scrupulous about not favoring home or away games that he ended his career with 1815 hits on the road and 1815 in St. Louis. York's 18 homers in August 1937 are the record for a single month. Johnson won nine Opening Day games.

YANKEES, NO HOME

Not all players who wore Yankees uniforms have the right to be called Bronx Bombers. And we don't mean just because they lacked offensive skills.

1B—BOB OLIVER
2B—FERNANDO GONZALEZ
3B—BILL SUDAKIS
SS—EDDIE BRINKMAN
OF—ALEX JOHNSON
OF—BOBBY BONDS
OF—WALT WILLIAMS
C—ED HERRMANN
P—CECIL UPSHAW

The faithful will, of course, recognize this as a lineup of players who never appeared in pinstripes in Yankee Stadium, having toiled for George Steinbrenner in 1974 and/or 1975, when the team played in Shea Stadium. There is also a manager—Bill Virdon.

BALLPARK ODDS AND ODDS

For these players the where was as important as the what.

1B—HUGH BRADLEY	1912 Red Sox
2B—JOHNNY EVERS	1909 Cubs
3B—CARNEY LANSFORD	1981 Red Sox
SS—LEE TANNEHILL	1910 White Sox
OF—FRANK ROBINSON	Career
OF—WILLIE STARGELL	1970 Pirates
OF—MEL OTT	Career
C—FRANK SNYDER	1926 Giants
P—ED WALSH	1910 White Sox

Bradley hit the first home run over Fenway Park's Green Monster; it was his only homer of the year. Evers set the tone for 4700 games at Forbes Field by getting a single as the first batter in the Pittsburgh park; in its 62-year existence Forbes Field never hosted a no-hitter. The Green Monster may be comfortable for right-handed hitters, but Lansford is the only Boston righty ever to win a batting championship (and during the split season at that!). Tannehill set a tone of sorts by hitting the first homer in Comiskey Park—a grand-slammer that *rolled* down the foul line and out through a fence; it was one of only seven homers hit by the power-poor White Sox that year. Robinson and Rusty Staub share the mark for homering in the most ballparks—thirty-two. Thanks to the midseason transfer from Forbes Field to Three Rivers Stadium, Stargell holds the National League record for homering in the most parks (13) in one season. Although he retired in 1947 with the most career homers (511) by a National Leaguer, Ott never hit one in nine years of playing in Philadelphia's Shibe Park. Snyder hit the first homer over the distant left field wall of Braves Field—ten years after the opening of the park! Walsh was an important consultant in the design of Comiskey Park and, oddly enough, suggested that the fences be set back far into the Plains. Despite the fact that he got his way, he lost the home opener, 2-0.

WHAT'S IN A NAME?

Just some fun. The criteria have nothing to do with ability. And lots of liberties with positions.

THE NAME OF THE GAME

Since there has never been a major leaguer named Willie NoHit or Al Grandslam, we'll go with:

1B—VIC POWER
2B—NEAL BALL
3B—STAN JOK
SS—GENE ALLEY
OF—LEE WALLS
OF—JOHN STRIKE
OF—CHARLIE SPIKES
C—MATT BATTS
P—EARLY WYNN

The reserves will, of course, be led by Johnny Bench.

THE SPORTING LIFE

Nor is there a Freddy Football or a Larry Lacrosse. So we'll go with:

1B—GENE TENACE
2B—BILLY CHAMPION
3B—RON HUNT
SS—MILT BOLLING
OF—CLINT HURDLE
OF—CHARLIE CADY
OF—GENE DERBY
C—JIMMY ARCHER
P—HARRY BILLIARD

Herb Score and Dave Downs round out the pitching staff.

GAMBLING MEN

Gambling may not be in the best interests of baseball, but . . .

1B—FRANK CHANCE
2B—CHARLIE PICK
3B—CHARLIE DEAL
SS—HERB WELCH
OF—OSCAR GAMBLE
OF—TINSLEY GINN
OF—HARLIN POOL
C—DAN POTTS
P—HUCK BETTS

. . . we're pleased to put this club on the diamond.

MONEY PLAYERS

These days financial information plays almost as large a role on the sports pages as hits, runs and errors. So this team was probably inevitable.

MONEY PLAYERS

1B—NORM CASH
2B—JOHN HAPPENNY
3B—DON MONEY
SS—ERNIE BANKS
OF—ELMER PENCE
OF—ART RUBLE
OF—BOBBY BONDS
C—DICK RAND
P—JOHN STERLING

Herman Franks is the manager. And honorable mention to infielder Jim Shilling, pitchers Chet Nichols, Wes Stock and Gary Fortune—and all the Bucs of Pittsburgh.

EATING

An absolutely delicious ensemble.

1B—JACKIE MAYO
2B—COOT VEAL
3B—GENE LEEK
SS—JOE BEAN
OF—DARRYL STRAWBERRY
OF—TONY CURRY
OF—GEORGE GERKEN
C—HENRY SAGE
P—EDDIE BACON

Bob Lemon is the manager.

And a well-balanced pitching staff for him to work with: Herb Hash as the main dish; Hap Collard and Harry Colliflower for vegetables; and Frank Pears, Earl Huckleberry and Mark Lemongello for dessert.

And what about Johnny Grubb?

LIBATIONS

We'll raise our glasses to:

LIBATIONS

1B—J.W. PORTER
2B—JACK COFFEY
3B—RUBEN AMARO
SS—BOBBY WINE
OF—GENE RYE
OF—ED HOCK
OF—CHARLIE MEAD
C—NORM SHERRY
P—CLARENCE BEERS

No free advertising, so omit pitcher Weedo Martini, first baseman-catcher Johnny Walker and outfielder Jack Daniels.

For different reasons leave out first baseman Johnny Lush and pitchers Chief Bender, John Boozer, Dan Tipple and Ed High.

Honorable mention to second baseman Mickey Finn and all the Houston Colt .45s.

GRAINS

It wouldn't be easy to grind these guys down.

1B—LEON DURHAM
2B—PEACHES GRAHAM
3B—HARRY RICE
SS—DICK GROAT
OF—GENE RYE
OF—ZACK WHEAT
OF—WILLIE MAYS
C—JOHNNY OATES
P—LEFTY MILLS

Gene Rye, the *nom de bal* of one Eugene Mercantelli, played in 17 games for the 1931 Red Sox and collected exactly 7 singles and 1 RBI in 39 at bats. However, he once hit 3 home runs, good for 8 RBIs, in one inning while playing for Waco in the Texas League.

FISH

They may not be great, but they don't stink.

> 1B—LEFTY HERRING
> 2B—CHICO SALMON
> 3B—ED WHITING
> SS—BOBBY STURGEON
> OF—LIP PIKE
> OF—KEVIN BASS
> OF—GEORGE HADDOCK
> C—BERT BLUE
> P—HARRY EELS

And the Trout family (Dizzy and Steve), Clarence Pickrel, Thornton Kipper and Preacher Roe round out the pitching staff.

BIRDS

See how you think these fly.

> 1B—GEORGE CROWE
> 2B—JAY PARTRIDGE
> 3B—SAMMY DRAKE
> SS—ALAN STORKE
> OF—BILL EAGLE
> OF—CANNONBALL CRANE
> OF—TOM PARROTT
> C—JOHNNY PEACOCK
> P—JOEY JAY

The bullpen would include Craig Swan and Ed Hawk.
Honorable mention to all the Blue Jays of Toronto, Cardinals of St. Louis and Orioles of Baltimore.

ANIMALS

Some ferocious, some tame, even a rodent and an insect.

1B—FENTON MOLE
2B—NELLIE FOX
3B—BERT HOGG
SS—BILL HART
OF—CHICKEN WOLF
OF—JOE RABBIT
OF—LYMAN LAMB
C—MIKE ROACH
P—JIM PANTHER

Panther barely beats out Lerton Pinto, Bob Moose, Al Doe, Joe Gibbon and Paul Jaeckel.

Honorable mention to the Tigers of Detroit and Cubs of Chicago.

COUNTRIES

The only thing more comprehensive than an all-star team is a United Nations team. For instance:

1B—FRANK BRAZILL
2B—BLAS MONACO
3B—TIM IRELAND
SS—RAFAEL SANTO DOMINGO
OF—BOB HOLLAND
OF—BUCK JORDAN
OF—MOE SOLOMON
C—HUGH POLAND
P—OSMAN FRANCE

The backup catcher would be Gus Brittain.

POINT OF ORIGIN

In some of those countries you might run into . . .

> 1B—GEORGE SCOTT
> 2B—LES GERMAN
> 3B—JIM BRETON
> SS—WOODY ENGLISH
> OF—CHARLIE MALAY
> OF—FRANK WELCH
> OF—DAN NORMAN
> C—JIM FRENCH
> P—LUCAS TURK

Or maybe even into Mickey Finn and Bill Roman.

CITIES

And while you're abroad you might visit . . .

> 1B—HAL DANZIG
> 2B—KELLY PARIS
> 3B—MIKE SHANNON
> SS—SAL MADRID
> OF—CLYDE MILAN
> OF—JOE HAGUE
> OF—GUS BERGAMO
> C—RUDY YORK
> P—LEE DELHI

Or even Bill Bergen, Al Naples, Jose Santiago or Tom Oran.

ADDRESSES

Ballplayers are on the road half of the time, but when they are home most live at one of the following:

1B—DAVE ROWE
2B—BOB WAY
3B—CY BLOCK
SS—GENE ALLEY
OF—MARVIN LANE
OF—PAUL STRAND
OF—DUSTY RHODES
 C—GABBY STREET
 P—PETE CENTER

Bob Walk is the backup pitcher.

THE HOUSE

And most of their houses have the following:

1B—LEE WALLS
2B—BOBBY DOERR
3B—BUDDY BELL
SS—ALAN BANNISTER
OF—DON LOCK
OF—HARLIN POOL
OF—GENE ROOF
 C—HOWIE STORIE
 P—KEN GABLES

And in the bullpen Alex Beam, Vallie Eaves and Dick Hall are being warmed up by Jack Rafter.

THE GARDEN

Outside you might find:

1B—FRED STEM
2B—JAKE FLOWERS
3B—LARRY GARDNER
SS—DONIE BUSH
OF—PETE ROSE
OF—BOB SEEDS
OF—GEORGE DAISEY
C—JIM LILLIE
P—DAVE VINEYARD

Or Charlie Root, Billy Bowers, Bob Vines and Bob Sprout.

THE MUSICAL ONES

If you are familiar with the careers of more than half of the following, you are a true trivia expert.

1B—LEW WHISTLER
2B—STEVE SAX
3B—JIM TABOR
SS—LEO BELL
OF—BILL SHARP
OF—JACK REED
OF—CHARLIE CHANT
C—FRED CARROLL
P—FRANK VIOLA

If Viola runs into trouble, there is always Bob Fife. And no, the Italian word for *band* isn't Bando.

TOOLS OF THE TRADE

They may not have great baseball players, but they could be counted on to do their share of the heavy labor.

1B—ALEX HOOKS
2B—SAM CRANE
3B—CHARLIE PICK
SS—CLAUDE DERRICK
OF—DALE GEAR
OF—JESSE PIKE
OF—JERRY MALLETT
C—LEW DRILL
P—BOB SPADE

Infielder Crane is a good example of the travails of the nineteenth-century player. Between 1873 and 1890, he managed to appear in box scores for portions of only nine years. In those nine seasons he played for ten different teams, was a member of two teams on two occasions, and played in four different leagues (National Association, American Association, Union Association and National League).

TRANSPORTATION

By virtue of their names, some players have been able to get to first base on more than their legs.

1B—CHARLIE CARR
2B—ED WHEELER
3B—STAN HACK
SS—PAT ROCKETT
OF—TY PICKUP
OF—CHARLIE METRO
OF—JOHNNY VANN
C—BILL SKIFF
P—VIRGIL TRUCKS

The mound staff would also include Jack Ferry and Cardell Camper, while any number of Walkers can come off the bench for pinch-hitting.

And executive? We'll take Ed Barrow.

TRANSACTIONS

Trades, sales, waiver purchases, free agents and everything else connected to the itinerant ways of major league players.

MOVING ON

A baseball wit once said that the answer to every trivia question was either Bob Miller or Dick Littlefield. Not so. Although both pitchers changed uniforms about as regularly as most people turn calendar pages, neither qualifies for this team of players who changed teams most, whether by trade, jumping leagues, or whatever.

1B—JACK DOYLE	12 teams
2B—JOE QUINN	12 teams
3B—JIM DONELY	11 teams
SS—BONES ELY	9 teams
OF—TOMMY DAVIS	12 teams
OF—TOM BROWN	10 teams
OF—DERON JOHNSON	10 teams
C—DEACON McGUIRE	14 teams
P—BOBO NEWSOM	17 teams

Doyle played for Columbus (AA); Baltimore, Washington (twice), Cleveland, the Dodgers, Phillies, Cubs and Giants (three times) in the National League; and the Yankees in the American.

Quinn labored for St. Louis (UA); the Cardinals (four times), Baltimore, Cleveland, the Braves (twice) and Reds in the National League; Boston (PL); and the Senators in the American League.

Donely started with Kansas City (UA); played with Indianapolis, St. Louis and Columbus in the American Association; and bounced around with Kansas City, Detroit, Washington, Baltimore, the Pirates, Giants and Cardinals in the National League.

Ely's itinerary included Louisville (AA) and Syracuse (AA); Buffalo, Baltimore, the Dodgers, Cardinals and Pirates in the NL; and the Athletics and Senators in the AL.

Davis spent eight years with the Dodgers and then in the next ten years played for the Mets, Astros and Cubs (twice) in the NL; and the White Sox, Pilots, A's (twice), Orioles, Angels and Royals.

Brown played for Columbus, Pittsburgh and Boston in the AA; Boston in the PL; and Indianapolis, Louisville, Washington, the Pirates, Braves and Cardinals in the NL.

Johnson wore the uniforms of the Yankees, Athletics (in both Kansas City and Oakland), Brewers, White Sox, Red Sox (twice), Reds, Braves and Phillies.

McGuire put in time with Toledo, Cleveland, Rochester and Washington in the AA; Detroit (twice), Washington, the Phillies and Dodgers in the NL; and the Tigers (twice), Yankees, Red Sox and Indians in the AL.

Newsom wins the prize, however, for his tenures with the Dodgers (twice), White Sox, Browns (three times), Senators (five times), Red Sox, Tigers, Athletics (twice), Yankees and Giants.

The manager is Bucky Harris, who was fired eight times—once each by the Red Sox, Phillies and Yankees; twice by the Tigers; and three times by the Senators.

UNDER ONE FLAG

Even before the advent of free agency, it was rare for a player to spend a lengthy career with a single team. These were the exceptions who proved the rule.

1B—CAP ANSON	22 years	Cubs
2B—CHARLIE GEHRINGER	19 years	Tigers
3B—BROOKS ROBINSON	23 years	Orioles
SS—LUKE APPLING	20 years	White Sox
OF—CARL YASTRZEMSKI	23 years	Red Sox
OF—MEL OTT	22 years	Giants
OF—AL KALINE	22 years	Tigers
C—BILL DICKEY	17 years	Yankees
P—WALTER JOHNSON	21 years	Senators

Robinson and Yastrzemski hold the major league record for most seasons with one club. Anson, who played only 19 of his 22 seasons at first base; Ott, who only pinch-hit in one season; and Stan Musial, who played only 19 of his 22 seasons in the outfield, share the NL record. Also, along these lines, Yastrzemski appeared in the outfield in all but one of his 23 seasons with the Sox.

Ted Lyons tied Walter Johnson for most years as a pitcher with one club, but Johnson pitched more games so we'll give him the nod.

The manager is Red Schoendienst, who led the Cardinals for twelve seasons (1965–76), the longest tenure for a manager who headed just one team in one city.

THE MILK RUN

All baseball players live out of a trunk, but some must have wondered whether they were actually living *in* one. The team below consists of players who appeared in the uniforms of four different teams in a single year or who were traded three times in a single season.

1B—DAVE KINGMAN	1977	Mets, Padres, Angels, Yankees
2B—GEORGE STREIF	1884	St. Louis (AA), Kansas City (UA), Chicago-Pittsburgh (UA), Cleveland
3B—TEX WESTERZIL	1915	Brooklyn (FL), Chicago (FL), St. Louis (FL), Chicago (FL)
SS—FRANK HUELSMAN	1904	White Sox, Tigers, White Sox, Browns, Senators
OF—WES COVINGTON	1961	Braves, White Sox, Athletics, Phillies
OF—PAUL LEHNER	1951	Athletics, White Sox, Browns, Indians
OF—HARRY WHEELER	1884	St. Louis (AA), Kansas City (UA), Chicago-Pittsburgh (UA), Baltimore (UA)
C—TOM DOWSE	1892	Louisville, Reds, Phillies, Washington
P—TED GRAY	1955	White Sox, Indians, Yankees, Orioles

Streif played second with only two of the teams for which he labored in 1884. And Huelsman played no shortstop at all in 1904, but was primarily a shortstop.

Wheeler and Streif bounced around together until the end of the season.

Huelsman, incidentally, landed five times in his marathon 1904 journey.

Other players who played for four teams were Willis Hudlin (1940), Mike Kilkenny (1972), Al Atkisson (1884), Doc Marshall (1904), Hal O'Hagen (1902) and Frank Fernandez (1971).

WORST TRADES

The most disastrous trade of all time? We like the 1900 deal in which Cincinnati obtained an over-the-hill Amos Rusie for a pitcher named Mathewson. Other boners involving non-active players:

1B—NORM CASH	1960 Indians to Tigers
2B—NELLIE FOX	1950 Athletics to White Sox
3B—GEORGE KELL	1946 Athletics to Tigers
SS—VERN STEPHENS	1948 Browns to Red Sox
OF—JOE JACKSON	1915 Indians to White Sox
OF—JACKIE JENSEN	1954 Senators to Red Sox
OF—LOU BROCK	1964 Cubs to Cardinals
C—JERRY GROTE	1966 Astros to Mets
P—CHRISTY MATHEWSON	1900 Reds to Giants

Cash went for utility man Steve Demeter. For Fox and Kell, the A's received catcher Joe Tipton and outfielder Barney McCoskey, respectively. The price tag for Stephens (and pitcher Jack Kramer) was people named Pellagrini, Widmar, Partee and Layden. The Shoeless One brought outfielders Bobby Roth and Larry Chappell and pitcher Ed Klepfer. Jensen went to Fenway Park for pitcher Mickey McDermott and outfielder Tom Umphlett. Brock for Ernie Broglio has become a standard trivia question. The Mets solved their catching problems for ten years when they obtained Grote for pitcher Tom Parsons.

Of all the players received for this nine, only McCoskey played up to expectations for more than one season.

Honorable mention to the 1929 Cubs for obtaining Rogers Hornsby from the Braves for infielder Fred Maguire and to the 1938 Dodgers for giving up .188 outfielder Eddie Morgan in exchange for Dolf Camilli.

WORST TRADES: ACTIVE PLAYERS

About 70 years after the Mathewson-Rusie swap, the Reds evened the score somewhat with the Giants by snatching away George Foster in exchange for Frank Duffy and Vern Geishert. Other one-sided deals involving active players include:

1B—JASON THOMPSON	1981 Angels to Pirates
2B—MANNY TRILLO	1979 Cubs to Phillies
3B—GRAIG NETTLES	1972 Indians to Yankees
SS—ALFREDO GRIFFIN	1978 Indians to Blue Jays
OF—GEORGE FOSTER	1971 Giants to Reds
OF—PEDRO GUERRERO	1974 Indians to Dodgers
OF—GEORGE HENDRICK	1978 Padres to Cardinals
C—DARRELL PORTER	1976 Brewers to Royals
P—NOLAN RYAN	1971 Mets to Angels

How one-sided were these deals? Thompson went for Mickey Mahler and Ed Ott; Trillo for Jerry Martin, Ted Sizemore, Barry Foote and two pitchers who never made it; Nettles for Charlie Spikes and John Ellis; Griffin for Victor Cruz; Guerrero for somebody named Bruce Ellingsen; Hendrick for Eric Rasmussen; Porter for Jim Wohlford and Jamie Quirk; and Ryan for Jim Fregosi.

UNPOPULAR DEALS

Or, deals that almost caused fans to lynch general managers.

1B—ORLANDO CEPEDA	1966 Giants to Cardinals
2B—ROGERS HORNSBY	1927 Cardinals to Giants
3B—BUDDY BELL	1979 Indians to Rangers
SS—BUCKY DENT	1982 Yankees to Rangers
OF—BABE RUTH	1920 Red Sox to Yankees
OF—CHUCK KLEIN	1934 Phillies to Cubs
OF—ROCKY COLAVITO	1960 Indians to Tigers
C—MICKEY COCHRANE	1934 Athletics to Tigers
P—TOM SEAVER	1977 Mets to Reds,
	1984 Mets to White Sox

Cepeda, San Francisco's most popular player, was traded for pitcher Ray Sadecki. Player-manager of a World Series winner or not, Hornsby's conflicts with the front office led to his exchange for fellow Hall of Famer Frankie Frisch. Bell, the only bright spot on the Indians, was dealt for Toby Harrah. Dent went for Lee Mazzilli in a miscalculation by George Steinbrenner that one teeny-bopper idol could be exchanged for another; Mazzilli was gone two months later, as well. Ruth was dealt to give Boston owner Harry Frazee a quick financial fix for his collapsing theatrical interests. The shambles that passed for a Philadelphia front office unloaded triple-crown winner Klein for the same reason that Frazee had sold Ruth. In a unique deal, home run champion Colavito was swapped for batting titlist Harvey Kuenn. Cochrane was just one of the many Philadelphia stars peddled by Connie Mack in two separate waves of dubious financial calculations. The first time Seaver went for Steve Henderson, Dan Norman, Pat Zachry and Doug Flynn; the second time he was left unprotected in the free agent compensation draft and was claimed by Chicago.

TRADED NOT TO PLAY

Baseball trades haven't always involved only active players; on occasion, managers, and even coaches, have been dealt from one franchise to another.

1B—GIL HODGES	1967 Senators to Mets
2B—JOE GORDON	1960 Indians to Tigers
3B—JIMMY DYKES	1960 Tigers to Indians
SS—LUKE APPLING	1960 Tigers to Indians
OF—JO JO WHITE	1960 Indians to Tigers
OF—CHUCK TANNER	1977 Athletics to Pirates
OF—BILLY SOUTHWORTH	1929 Cardinals to minors
C—WES WESTRUM	1963 Giants to Mets
P—CHRISTY MATHEWSON	1916 Giants to Reds

The Mets sent pitcher Bill Denehy to Washington for Hodges. Gordon, Dykes, Appling and White were swapped for one another in a mid-season attempt by general managers Frank Lane of Cleveland and Bill DeWitt of Detroit to revive interest in their also-ran clubs. Charlie Finley let manager Tanner go to Pittsburgh in exchange for catcher Manny Sanguillen. Southworth was farmed out to Rochester in a mid-season swap for Red Wings skipper Bill McKechnie. San Francisco sent Westrum to New York in a deal for Mets coach Cookie Lavagetto. Mathewson, McKechnie and Edd Roush went to Cincinnati for Buck Herzog, then player-manager of the Reds; Matty interrupted his new role as manager for only one more mound appearance.

ABRUPT DEPARTURES

Tempers, tact and tactlessness have accounted for the unexpected departure of more than one player from a team.

1B—BILL ABSTEIN	1909 Pirates
2B—MIKE ANDREWS	1973 Athletics
3B—ELLIOTT MADDOX	1980 Mets
SS—BOBBY MEACHAM	1984 Yankees
OF—CASEY STENGEL	1918 Dodgers
OF—GENE WOODLING	1962 Mets
OF—FREDDY LINDSTROM	1933 Giants
C—BOB BOONE	1981 Phillies
P—CHARLIE BUFFINTON	1892 Baltimore

Despite being the regular first baseman on a team just crowned world champions, Abstein was released three days after the World Series because owner Barney Dreyfuss thought he had endangered the championship with five errors and nine strikeouts. When Charlie Finley tried a similar tactic *during* the World Series because of errors by Andrews, he was stymied by the commissioner—but only until the Series was over. Maddox became an embarrassment to the Mets when he decided to pursue a suit against Shea Stadium for an old injury sustained as a Yankee in the park. Meacham was shipped to the Yankee Double A affiliate after making an error early in the season, a paradigm of George Steinbrenner's manner of dealing with his players. (Meacham did return later in the year, however.) Stengel was tossed to the Pirates when he clowned once too often for manager Wilbert Robinson's taste. Woodling walked out of the clubhouse into retirement after seeing the Mets cavort on the field once too often. Lindstrom was peddled to the Pirates because John McGraw had assured him he would be the next New York manager; when it was Bill Terry who succeeded McGraw, Lindstrom became an embarrassing presence. Boone's union activism during the strike year got him a quick ticket to the Angels. Buffinton was released when he would not accept a pay cut in mid-season.

FAST SHUFFLES

Or, how to sell the Brooklyn Bridge to rival general managers.

1B—MIKE CHARTAK	1942 Yankees to Senators
2B—JIMMY JORDAN	1933 Cardinals to Dodgers
3B—WES HAMNER	1947 Phillies to Browns
SS—CHICO CARRASQUEL	1950 Dodgers to White Sox
OF—DIXIE WALKER	1948 Dodgers to Pirates
OF—JOHNNY RIZZO	1938 Cardinals to Pirates
OF—JIM GREENGRASS	1955 Reds to Phillies
C—DON PADGETT	1941 Cardinals to Dodgers
P—DIZZY DEAN	1938 Cardinals to Cubs

Nobody has ever equaled Branch Rickey for unloading damaged or otherwise suspect goods. To wit—he sent Walker to Pittsburgh after persuading the Pirates that the outfielder's hostility to being on a team with black players not only made him available, but could also "hurt the game"; that Walker was over the hill and that the Dodgers received Preacher Roe and Billy Cox in return was apparently beside the point. The same Pirates fell for his story that the sore-armed Rizzo was healthy and that another Cardinal rookie named Slaughter actually had the sore arm. It was also Rickey who obtained $20,000 for Padgett without bothering to inform the Dodgers that the catcher had been drafted into the army; who picked up another $20,000 for Jordan with the argument that the weak-hitting scrub was available only because he was disliked by player-manager Frankie Firsch; and who dealt off the sore-armed Dean for pitchers Curt Davis and Clyde Shoun and a tidy $200,000.

The others: Hearing that the Yankees were about to sell Chartak to the Browns for $14,000, Clark Griffith sounded the patriotic note that wartime America needed a competent Washington team, got the outfielder-first baseman for only $12,000, and then turned around and sold him to the Browns anyway for the original $14,000. Occasionally, even Rickey got taken, as when Frank Lane held the Mahatma to a years-old remark about "take anyone you want" and got Carrasquel for people named Fred Hancock and Charlie Essenmann. In a particularly cunning record-keeping maneuver by the Phillies, the Browns drafted one "G. Hamner" from the Philadelphia organization under the assumption that they were acquiring Wesley Garvin's brother Granville; they weren't. When Cincinnati general manager Gabe Paul sent Greengrass to the Phillies, he neglected to send along the information that the outfielder had phlebitis and could hardly walk.

TRADED AND UNTRADED

Sometimes general managers have second thoughts, sometimes commissioners have first thoughts and sometimes players simply refuse to go along with the thoughts of others.

1B—JASON THOMPSON	Pirates to Yankees
2B—JACKIE ROBINSON	Dodgers to Giants
3B—DICK ALLEN	Phillies to Braves
SS—RICK AUERBACH	Reds to Rangers
OF—CURT FLOOD	Cardinals to Phillies
OF—JOE RUDI	Athletics to Red Sox
OF—PETE REISER	Dodgers to Cardinals
C—HARRY CHITI	Tigers to Mets
P—VIDA BLUE	Athletics to Red Sox, Athletics to Reds

Commissioner Bowie Kuhn scotched the intended trade of Thompson for Jim Spencer and Mike Griffin, and Pittsburgh fans have been grateful to him ever since. Kuhn also said no to Oakland owner Charles Finley's sale of Rudi and Blue to the Red Sox and to Finley's subsequent attempt to deal Blue to Cincinnati for Dave Revering. Robinson, Allen and Auerbach retired rather than report. Flood's refusal to go to Philadelphia set the wheels in motion for free agency, although Flood himself later made a brief appearance for the Washington Senators. Chiti was dealt to the Mets for the fabled "player to be named later." The player? Chiti himself. Reiser had originally been a key to the Brooklyn trade for Joe Medwick, but the Dodgers eventually persuaded the Cardinals to take money instead.

The greatest instance of a trade being undone? In 1941 Dodgers owner Larry McPhail was so incensed that his team had lost the World Series that he obtained waivers on the whole squad in order to sell it to the Browns. Cooler heads, and money shorts in St. Louis, prevailed.

HEALTHY CHANGES OF SCENERY

Some players have responded to trades as though given a new lease on life. For instance:

1B—ANDRE THORNTON	1977 Indians (from Expos)
2B—JOE MORGAN	1972 Reds (from Astros)
3B—GEORGE KELL	1946 Tigers (from Athletics)
SS—DAVE BANCROFT	1920 Giants (from Phillies)
OF—ROGER MARIS	1960 Yankees (from Athletics)
OF—MATTY ALOU	1966 Pirates (from Giants)
OF—LOU BROCK	1964 Cardinals (from Cubs)
C—WALLY SCHANG	1918 Red Sox (from Athletics)
P—RED RUFFING	1930 Yankees (from Red Sox)

Before joining Cleveland Thornton had never hit more than 18 home runs in a season; since then he has had seasons of 28, 33, 26, 32 and 33. Although always a fine fielder, Morgan went from being a .250 hitter to a two-time MVP. Kell hit over .300 in eight of his first nine Detroit seasons. Bancroft went from mediocrity to a .300 hitter. Maris had promised more than he delivered for the Indians and Athletics; for the Yankees he won two MVP titles and also did something else. In San Francisco Alou had years like .145 and .231; as soon as he put on a Pirate uniform he won the batting championship with .342 and followed up with .338, .332 and .331. As a Cardinal, Brock wasted little time in running away from his .250 career as a Cub. Schang discovered bats with .300 seasons in them as soon as he arrived in Boston. As a Bostonian, Ruffing, on the other hand, appeared well on his way to compiling the worst won-lost record (39-96) for a starting pitcher in the history of the game; as a New Yorker, he won 231 and lost only 124.

THE FINAL INGREDIENT

Sometimes the difference between a pennant winner and a second-place finisher can be one player. The following provided that final nudge to the World Series:

1B—VIC WERTZ	1954 Indians
2B—RED SCHOENDIENST	1957 Braves
3B—BILL WERBER	1939 Reds
SS—DICK BARTELL	1940 Tigers
OF—WILLIE MAYS	1951 Giants
OF—WALLY MOON	1959 Dodgers
OF—ROGER MARIS	1967 Cardinals
C—MICKEY COCHRANE	1934 Tigers
P—WILLIE HERNANDEZ	1984 Tigers

Wertz was obtained in a trade with the Browns. Schoendienst led Milwaukee to two pennants after a multiple-player swap with the New York Giants. Werber joined the Reds just in time to lead the NL in runs scored. Bartell provided both infield glue and clubhouse spark after Detroit had to find a replacement for the faded Billy Rogell. Mays was recalled from Minneapolis to become the symbol of the Giants' miracle overtaking of the Dodgers. Moon showed the Dodgers how to clear the left field screen in the Coliseum after he came over from the Cardinals in a deal for Gino Cimoli. When St. Louis acquired Maris for Charley Smith in a swap with the Yankees, they not only had a legitimate right fielder, but were also able to station Mike Shannon at third. Cochrane came to Detroit from the Athletics as manager, catcher and hitter, and the club went from a fifth-place finish in 1933 to two pennants. Hernandez saved 32 games in 33 opportunities and led Detroit from a 1983 finish of six games behind to a world championship season.

WAIVER SAVIORS

What farm systems and regular trade routes cannot provide, the waiver list often does. The following players were either much needed insurance behind the starter on a winning team or were themselves the final ingredient needed for winning.

1B—JOHNNY MIZE	1949 Yankees (Giants)
2B—DAL MAXVILL	1972 Athletics (Cardinals)
	1974 Athletics (Pirates)
3B—BILL MADLOCK	1979 Pirates (Giants)
SS—WILLIE MIRANDA	1953 Yankees (Browns)
OF—WALLY MOSES	1946 Red Sox (White Sox)
OF—ENOS SLAUGHTER	1956 Yankees (Athletics)
OF—JOHNNY HOPP	1950 Yankees (Pirates)
C—ELSTON HOWARD	1967 Red Sox (Yankees)
P—HANK BOROWY	1945 Cubs (Yankees)

Although the Madlock deal also involved pitchers Dave Roberts, Al Holland, Ed Whitson and Fred Breining, it required waivers because of being transacted two weeks after the June 15th trading deadline. Mize, probably the most famous waiver purchase of all, beefed up New York's left-handed power for five seasons. Maxvill and Miranda were purchased for their gloves, just as Howard was acquired to guide the Boston pitching staff into the World Series. Slaughter's second arrival in New York (he had been with the team three years before after a deal with the Cardinals) was the immediate occasion for the Yankees' release of Phil Rizzuto (on Old-Timers Day, yet!). The Yankees were also frequent purchasers of National League pitchers in September (Johnny Sain, Ewell Blackwell, etc.), but as successful as these men were, they can't compare with the 11-2 record (21-7 overall) Borowy contributed to the Chicago pennant.

LEAGUE LEADERS

Being traded in the middle of a season can be a disorienting experience. For both good and bad, however, a few players have managed to maintain league-leading paces even as they exchanged one uniform for another.

1B—DALE ALEXANDER	1932 Red Sox and Tigers
2B—RED SCHOENDIENST	1957 Giants and Braves
3B—HEINIE ZIMMERMAN	1916 Cubs and Giants
SS—POP SMITH	1889 Pirates and Braves
OF—HARRY WALKER	1947 Phillies and Cardinals
OF—GUS ZERNIAL	1951 White Sox and Athletics
OF—MINNIE MINOSO	1951 White Sox and Indians
C—FRANKIE HAYES	1945 Athletics and Indians
P—JIM HEARN	1950 Cardinals and Giants

First baseman Alexander and outfielder Walker are the only players to have won batting championships for combined teams. Schoendienst led the NL in hits. Zimmerman was the NL's runs batted in leader. On the negative side, Smith proved that it is possible to lead in strikeouts while switching uniforms. Zernial not only matched Zimmerman's feat in RBIs, but also led the AL in home runs (the only player to have accomplished this). Minoso led in both stolen bases and triples. Hayes was the AL leader for most double plays involving a catcher defensively. Hearn didn't allow his trade to the Giants to affect his league-leading ERA of 2.49.

Honorable mentions to (among others) Roy Cullenbine for the most walks in the AL in 1945 when he played for the Indians and Tigers; Pat Seercy who set the 1948 strikeout pace while dividing his time between the Indians and White Sox; Red Barrett who completed 24 games for the 1945 Braves and Cardinals; and Ron Herbel who appeared in 76 games as a pitcher for the 1970 Padres and Mets.

NEW YORK, NEW YORK . . . AND NEW YORK

Until Brooklyn is granted another major league franchise, it will be impossible for anyone to join the ranks of the very select company that played in at least three New York uniforms. So, for now we'll field the following:

1B—FRED MERKLE	Giants, Dodgers, Yankees
2B—TONY LAZZERI	Giants, Dodgers, Yankees
3B—DUDE ESTERBROOK	Giants, Dodgers, Mets (AA)
SS—CANDY NELSON	Troy Haymakers, Giants, Brooklyn (AA), Mets (AA)
OF—WILLIE KEELER	Giants, Dodgers, Yankees
OF—LEFTY O'DOUL	Giants, Dodgers, Yankees
OF—BENNY KAUFF	Giants, Yankees, Brooklyn (FL)
C—ZACK TAYLOR	Giants, Dodgers, Yankees
P—BURLEIGH GRIMES	Giants, Dodgers, Yankees

Sorry, Sal Maglie fans, but Grimes has better numbers.

Among the others who played for the Dodgers, Giants, and Yankees is first baseman Jack Doyle.

Honorable mention to some fine nineteenth-century ballplayers who played for three or more New York teams: Dan Brouthers (Giants, Dodgers, Buffalo and Troy); Dave Orr (Mets, Giants, Brooklyn of the American Association, and Brooklyn of the Players League); and Monte Ward (Giants, Dodgers and Brooklyn of the Players League).

Any doubt about the manager of such a team? Casey Stengel, of course, who managed the Dodgers, the Yankees and the modern Mets as well as having played for the Dodgers and Giants. Or for you really old-timers, there is John Montgomery Ward, who managed the Brooklyn franchise in the Players League as well as the Dodgers and Giants.

CALIFORNIA SPLIT

These players liked California so much that they have played for at least three teams in the state:

1B—WILLIE McCOVEY	Giants, Padres, Athletics
2B—TITO FUENTES	Giants, Padres, Athletics
3B—KEN McMULLEN	Dodgers, Angels, Athletics
SS—MARIO GUERRERO	Giants, Angels, Athletics
OF—DAVE KINGMAN	Giants, Padres, Angels and Athletics
OF—TOMMY DAVIS	Dodgers, Angels, Athletics
OF—WILLIE DAVIS	Dodgers, Angels, Padres
C—DERRELL THOMAS	Giants, Padres, Dodgers, Angels
P—ELIAS SOSA	Giants, Dodgers, Athletics and Padres

Both Dick Williams and John McNamara have managed the Athletics, Angels and Padres.

ENCORE, ENCORE

A small number of players traveled so much that they ended up doing service with the same team at least three times.

1B—JACK DOYLE	1892–95, 1898–1900, 1902 Giants
2B—JOE QUINN	1893–95, 1898, 1900 Cardinals
3B—BOB KENNEDY	1939–48, 1955–56, 1957 White Sox
SS—BUCK HERZOG	1908–09, 1911–13, 1916–17 Giants
OF—GOOSE GOSLIN	1921–30, 1933, 1938 Senators
OF—AL SIMMONS	1924–32, 1940–41, 1944 Athletics
OF—CHUCK KLEIN	1928–33, 1936–39, 1940–44 Phillies
C—JIM O'ROURKE	1885–89, 1891–92, 1904 Giants
P—BOBO NEWSOM	1935–37, 1942, 1943, 1946–47, 1952 Senators

Newsom also served three stints with the Browns (1934–35, 1938–39, 1943).

Quinn played with the Cardinals a fourth time (1885–86), but played only first, third and the outfield during those years.

Others who played on the same team three times are Bill Hallman (Phillies), Bill Pfeffer (Cubs), Hughie Jennings (Dodgers), Minnie Minoso (White Sox), Les Mann (Braves), Amos Strunk (Athletics), Bob Cerv (Yankees), Phil Weintraub (Giants) and Dick Williams (Orioles).

The manager is Danny Murtaugh, who piloted the Pirates four times (1957–64, 1967, 1970–71, 1973–75).

FREE AGENT SUCCESSES

No, it is *not* true that all free agents phone in their skills as soon as they have signed lucrative contracts. Some of them have even helped turn also-ran teams into leaders of the pack.

1B—PETE ROSE	Phillies
2B—BOBBY GRICH	Angels
3B—SAL BANDO	Brewers
SS—DERRELL THOMAS	Dodgers
OF—DON BAYLOR	Angels and Yankees
OF—REGGIE JACKSON	Yankees and Angels
OF—DAVE WINFIELD	Yankees
C—CARLTON FISK	White Sox
P—GOOSE GOSSAGE	Yankees and Padres

The contributions of Rose, Grich, Baylor, Jackson, Winfield and Gossage to the cited teams do not require much comment. It is worth pointing out, however, that the Angels and Yankees haven't signed *only* players like Bill Travers and Dave Collins, respectively. Prior to retiring in 1982, Bando made up for his slackening field performance by helping to instill a winning attitude in the Brewers. The same could be said of Fisk, although his contributions have also come from his bat and handling of the White Sox pitching staff. Thomas has had few equals as a utility man in recent years.

FREE AGENT BUSTS

On the other hand, some free agents haven't even had the change to phone in their skills. For example:

1B—DAVE COLLINS	Yankees
2B—RENNIE STENNETT	Giants
3B—MIKE CUBBAGE	Mets
SS—LUIS GOMEZ	Blue Jays
OF—JOE RUDI	Angels
OF—PAT KELLY	Indians
OF—ROWLAND OFFICE	Expos
C—DAVE ROBERTS	Astros
P—DON STANHOUSE	Dodgers

For the record, let it be said that Cubbage, Kelly, Office and Roberts were given big pacts to sit on the bench, and that Rudi was felled by an injury shortly after joining California. Still and all, it is also worth noting that, entering the 1985 season, only Collins was still listed on a major league roster.

THE ONES THAT GOT AWAY

Faulty scouting, faulty contracts and faulty preconceptions have cost teams the services of more than one subsequent diamond star. For example:

1B—GEORGE SISLER	Pirates
2B—NAP LAJOIE	Giants
3B—PIE TRAYNOR	Braves and Red Sox
SS—HONUS WAGNER	Phillies
OF—BABE RUTH	Reds
OF—HACK WILSON	Dodgers
OF—PAUL WANER	Dodgers
C—YOGI BERRA	Cardinals
P—TOM SEAVER	Indians

Sisler and Seaver had contracts with the indicated teams voided by the commissioner or league office. Traynor and Berra failed to impress during hasty tryouts. A Giant scout ruled out Lajoie although he was hitting more than .400 in the minors when seen. Disabled Phillies pitcher Con Lucid did the front office a "favor" by watching a minor league contest and recommending that Philadelphia draft Kid Elberfeld instead of the "clumsy" Wagner. Ruth never made it to Ohio because the Reds dispatched office hanger-on Harry Stevens to decide which two players they should take from Baltimore to conclude a deal; instead of Ruth (or Ernie Shore), Stevens urged the purchase of shortstop Claude Derrick and outfielder George Twombly. The Dodgers lost Wilson and Waner within a 48-hour period in 1925. First the team infuriated manager Wilbert Robinson by making the mistake of winning the final game of the season, and by so doing avoiding a last-place finish and ceding first draft rights to the Cubs for Wilson. The next day, Robinson's failure to reach owner Steve McKeever before an allotted deadline to get approval on the Waner purchase prompted the outfielder to go with Pittsburgh.

MET THIRD BASEMEN

Everybody knows that the Mets traded Nolan Ryan for Jim Fregosi and Amos Otis for Joey Foy in misguided attempts to solve their chronic third base problem. Well, those deals may have been the worst of it, but they were by no means all of it. The lineup below offers some of the other players the Mets gave away for a third sacker—along with the names of the infielders they received in exchange.

1B—DAVE KINGMAN	Bobby Valentine
2B—DON ZIMMER	Cliff Cook
3B—RICHIE HEBNER	Phil Mankowski
SS—FELIX MANTILLA	Pumpsie Green
OF—AMOS OTIS	Joey Foy
OF—LEE WALLS	Charley Neal
OF—FRANK THOMAS	Wayne Graham
C—JOE NOLAN	Leo Foster
P—NOLAN RYAN	Jim Fregosi

That's right—Wayne Graham.

THE RIVALS

The great American League rivalry between the Yankees and the Red Sox has made it more difficult in recent years for the teams to work out deals. But this was not always the case. Herein a lineup of players obtained by New York from Boston:

> 1B—BABE DAHLGREN
> 2B—MIKE McNALLY
> 3B—JOE DUGAN
> SS—EVERETT SCOTT
> OF—ROY JOHNSON
> OF—PATSY DOUGHERTY
> OF—BABE RUTH
> C—WALLY SCHANG
> P—RED RUFFING

Boston seems to have had a particular penchant for giving the Yankees prized pitchers. In addition to Ruffing, the New Yorkers have absconded from Fenway Park with Waite Hoyt, Joe Bush, Herb Pennock, Sam Jones, Carl Mays and Wilcy Moore. The last such acquisition was also the last major deal between the clubs—the 1972 trade which gave the Yankees future Cy Young winner Sparky Lyle in exchange for Danny Cater and Mario Guerrero.

One footnote. Although the two clubs haven't made direct swaps in recent years, they have gone after each other's free agents. Both Luis Tiant and Bob Watson donned pinstripes after playing for the Red Sox, while Mike Torrez went directly from New York to Boston.

THE KC CONNECTION

As often as George Steinbrenner is accused today of buying pennants by signing expensive free agents, the Yankees of the 1950s were accused of securing their flags by working out one-sided deals with the then-Kansas City Athletics. In truth, dozens of players moved between the two teams, some of them on round trips, with a suspicious regularity. Among those whom the New Yorkers obtained from the lowly A's were:

1B—HARRY SIMPSON
2B—JOE DeMAESTRI
3B—HECTOR LOPEZ
SS—CLETE BOYER
OF—ROGER MARIS
OF—BOB CERV
OF—ENOS SLAUGHTER
C—WILMER SHANTZ
P—RYNE DUREN

Boyer (mainly as a third baseman), Maris and Duren were vital components of Yankee winners in the late '50s and early '60s. Cerv and Slaughter were among the many who made round trips from the Bronx to Kansas City and back to the Bronx again. Offensively anyway, Lopez was a solid bench contributor, as, more briefly, were Simpson and DeMaestri. Only catcher Shantz was less than valuable, but then this was the era when New York had Yogi Berra, Elston Howard and Johnny Blanchard crowding the plate.

Among the others obtained from the A's were pitchers Art Ditmar, Bobby Shantz (Wilmer's more skilled brother), Bud Daley, Ralph Terry, Duke Maas, Virgil Trucks and Murry Dickson.

BLOCKED OUT

Sometimes even the most conspicuously talented young players have to be dealt away from a team because they play the position nailed down by an established star. For instance:

1B—JIM GENTILE	Dodgers
2B—WILLIE RANDOLPH	Pirates
3B—CURT FLOOD	Reds
SS—PEEWEE REESE	Red Sox
OF—ROBERTO CLEMENTE	Dodgers
OF—JACKIE JENSEN	Yankees
OF—WILLIE McGEE	Yankees
C—EARL BATTEY	White Sox
P—JIM BIBBY	Mets

Gentile was sold to the Orioles because of Gil Hodges. Rennie Stennett and Dave Cash both made Randolph available to the Yankees. Flood, who came into the majors as an infielder, went to the Cardinals because of Don Hoak and Johnny Temple. Reese ended up in Ebbets Field because player-manager Joe Cronin rejected some broad hints that his best shortstop days were behind him; fittingly enough, Reese ended up replacing another player-manager, Leo Durocher. Clemente went to the Pirates because of Carl Furillo. Jensen was only one of several outfielders blocked out by the DiMaggio-Bauer-Woodling Mantle picket in Yankee Stadium. In a later era, McGee faced the same problem and was packed off to the Cardinals as unwisely as Jensen had been dispatched to the Senators. Battey went to the Twins because of Sherman Lollar. Bibby barely got a look from the Mets in their Seaver-Koosman-Matlack-Ryan days and was sent off to the Cardinals.

FANCY MEETING YOU HERE

They were key players on teams that won consistently year after year. Then, toward the end of their careers, they found themselves on other teams with old friends. The trick here is to guess with whom the following were reunited:

1B—BOOG POWELL	1975 Indians
2B—JOE MORGAN	1983 Phillies
3B—EDDIE MATHEWS	1968 Tigers
SS—LEO DUROCHER	1940 Dodgers
OF—ENOS SLAUGHTER	1959 Braves
OF—DUKE SNIDER	1963 Mets
OF—REGGIE JACKSON	1977 Yankees
C—GENE TENACE	1977 Padres
P—GOOSE GOSSAGE	1984 Padres

Powell went to Cleveland at the behest of manager and former Oriole teammate Frank Robinson. Morgan, Pete Rose and Tony Perez were all Big Red Machine graduates on the pennant-winning Phillies. Mathews had a reunion in Detroit with the bullpen ace of the fine Milwaukee teams in the late 1950s, Don McMahon. Player-manager Durocher wasted little time in importing former Gashouse Gang teammate Joe Medwick into Brooklyn. When Slaughter was picked up by Milwaukee for the pennant stretch, he was reunited with former Cardinal mate Red Schoendienst. Snider returned to New York from Los Angeles just in time to suffer together with another boy of summer, Gil Hodges. Jackson and Catfish Hunter tried to revive their Charlie Finley glory years for George Steinbrenner. Another refugee from the championship Oakland clubs, Tenace met up in San Diego with Rollie Fingers. Gossage and third baseman Graig Nettles showed they could perform together as ably in San Diego as they had for the Yankees.

REMADE IN JAPAN

Not the best players who went East, but those who played best once they got there.

REMADE IN JAPAN

1B—GREG WELLS
2B—DON BLASINGAME
3B—CLETE BOYER
SS—DARYL SPENCER
OF—WILLIE KIRKLAND
OF—CLARENCE JONES
OF—GEORGE ALTMAN
C—BUCKY HARRIS
P—JOE STANKA

Blasingame, who also managed in Japan, and Boyer, the first player ever traded to Asia (from the Hawaii PCL franchise), were probably the most popular Americans ever to appear in the Japanese league. Jones has the most career homers of any "Gaijin." Wells had the best season—.355, 37 homers, 130 RBIs. Harris never played in the American majors, but won a Japanese MVP in 1937 (before being expelled because of the impending war). Stanka, a 1-0 hurler for the White Sox in 1959, won 29 games in the Japanese Pacific League in 1964 and also turned in a 1.89 ERA—good enough for the MVP title.

The first American to return to Japanese ball after WWII was Hawaiian-born Nisei Wally Yonamie, who played centerfield between 1951 and 1962 and shocked Japanese fans with his aggressive play. As for the origins of baseball in Japan, there are numerous contradictory accounts; as far back as 1908, however, Giant third baseman Tillie Shafer was a baseball coach at the University of Kyoto.

Among the players who have flopped in Japan: Don Zimmer, Dick Stuart, Jim Gentile, Zoilo Versalles, Don Money, Frank Howard and Joe Pepitone. Larry Doby and Don Newcombe went for the 1962 season, but more as a publicity stunt than anything else.

WILLIE MONTANEZ

Between 1966 and 1982, first baseman-outfielder Willie Montanez was a member of the Angels, Cardinals (for whom he never batted), Phillies, Giants, Braves, Rangers

93

(for a couple of hours), Mets, Rangers again, Padres, Expos, Pirates and Phillies again. Although even all these travels do not qualify him as the most traded player in baseball history, Montanez can certainly boast that the players exchanged for him during his career represent a very solid lineup.

```
1B—MIKE JORGENSEN
2B—MARTY PEREZ
3B—DICK ALLEN
 SS—DARRELL EVANS
 OF—EDDIE MILLER
 OF—JOHN MILNER
 OF—GARRY MADDOX
  C—TUCKER ASHFORD
  P—GAYLORD PERRY
```

The weak spot here is Ashford, who was an emergency receiver for the Mets in 1983. A southpaw alternative to Perry would be Jon Matlack.

One other note: Montanez was the player sent by the Cardinals to the Phillies in place of Curt Flood after the latter's challenge of the reserve clause in 1970.

ODDS AND ODDS

An assortment of transaction trivia:

```
1B—DICK GERNERT       1959 Red Sox to Cubs
2B—BUCK HERZOG        1916 Reds to Giants
3B—RON SANTO          1973 Cubs
 SS—MAURY WILLS       1959 Dodgers to Tigers
 OF—MAX FLACK         1922 Cubs to Cardinals
 OF—CLIFF HEATHCOTE   1922 Cardinals to Cubs
 OF—JOEL YOUNGBLOOD   1982 Mets to Expos
  C—JOE FERGUSON      1976 Dodgers to Cardinals
                      1976 Cardinals to Astros
  P—MURRAY WALL       1959 Red Sox to Senators
```

Gernert's swap for Jim Marshall and Dave Hillman was

the first modern interleague trade not requiring waivers. Herzog was traded for three future Hall of Famers (Christy Mathewson, Bill McKechnie and Edd Roush). Santo was the first "5-and-10" player to refuse a trade (from the Cubs to the Angels). Wills was sold conditionally to Detroit, then returned when the Tigers decided he wouldn't cut it in the majors. Flack and Heathcote were traded for each other between games of a doubleheader and played for both teams on the same day. Youngblood went them one better by getting a hit as a Met in an afternoon game in Chicago and two hits as an Expo in a night game at Philadelphia. Ferguson was dealt to the Cardinals with then-minor leaguer Bobby Detherage, then moved several months later to the Astros with the same Detherage. Wall was traded to Washington for Dick Hyde, immediately pitched an inning for the Nats, then received word that the exchange had been cancelled; in short, he pitched for a team he didn't belong to.

THE BEST

When all the numbers are in, these are the players who come out on top. Some teams have a ninth offensive player, a designated hitter; others have a pitcher who excelled at preventing opponents from accomplishing something similar to what their eight teammates on these teams did so well.

HIGHEST BATTING AVERAGE—CAREER

Hitting a baseball is probably the most difficult feat in sports. A batter must redirect a nine-inch sphere coming at him between 75 and 100 miles per hour. The ball may dip, drop, rise, or slant to either side. And the batter's only weapon is a cylindrical piece of wood. *And,* in order to be successful, he must hit the ball within a range of 90 degrees and have it elude nine opponents eager to stop it. No wonder then that hitting is the only pursuit in life in which failure two-thirds of the time amounts to incredible success. Here are the most successful:

1B—DAVE ORR	.353	
2B—ROGERS HORNSBY	.358	
3B—JOHN McGRAW	.334	
SS—HONUS WAGNER	.329	
OF—TY COBB	.367	
OF—JOE JACKSON	.356	
OF—PETE BROWNING	.355	
C—MICKEY COCHRANE	.320	
P—SPUD CHANDLER	.717 W-L Pct. (109-43)	

Incredibly, four of these players are not in the Hall of Fame—Orr, Jackson, Browning and Chandler. Orr played only eight seasons and is therefore ineligible. Jackson is tainted by the Black Sox episode. Chandler (109-43 career) simply did not have enough good seasons. But there is no rational reason for the omission of Browning.

The biggest surprise here is probably McGraw, whose managerial career has obscured his abilities as a player.

Honorable mention to the best hitting pitcher of all time, Babe Ruth, who compiled a respectable .304 average as a pitcher. And to Bill Terry (.341), Pie Traynor (.320) and Lefty O'Doul (.349), who would make this team if it included only twentieth-century players.

HIGHEST BATTING AVERAGE—SEASON

And here are the highest averages for a single year, as recognized under present rule 10.23 of the Official Baseball Rules.

1B—	GEORGE SISLER	.420	1922 Browns
2B—	ROGERS HORNSBY	.424	1924 Cardinals
3B—	DUDE ESTERBROOK	.408	1884 New York (AA)
SS—	HUGHIE JENNINGS	.397	1896 Baltimore
OF—	HUGH DUFFY	.438	1894 Braves
OF—	JESSE BURKETT	.423	1895 Cleveland
OF—	WILLIE KEELER	.432	1897 Baltimore
C—	BABE PHELPS	.367	1936 Dodgers
P—	ELROY FACE	.947 W-L Pct. (18-1)	1959 Pirates

For the purists who prefer an all-twentieth-century team, put George Brett (.390, 1980 Royals) at third, Luke Appling (.388, 1936 White Sox) at shortstop and Ty Cobb (.420, 1911 Tigers; .410, 1912 Tigers), Joe Jackson (.408, 1911 Indians) and Ted Williams (.406, 1941 Red Sox) in the outfield.

Phelps is the catcher here, even though he batted only 319 times, which was enough to qualify for the batting championship in those days.

Face's 1959 record of 18 wins and only 1 loss was all in relief. He also had 10 saves.

The best season at the plate by a pitcher? Walter Johnson batted .440 in 1925.

BEST HITTERS

The greatest hitter in the history of the game wasn't Babe Ruth or Ty Cobb or any of those early-century monsters who batted .400 as easily as most players swing and miss. The greatest hitter in the history of the game, based on cold statistics, was a Houston outfielder named John Paciorek, who went 3-for-3 in his only major league game. His teammates are:

1B—ROY GLEASON	1-1	1963 Dodgers
2B—STEVE BIRAS	2-2	1944 Indians
3B—HEINIE ODOM	1-1	1925 Yankees
SS—AL WRIGHT	1-1	1933 Braves
OF—JOHN PACIOREK	3-3	1963 Astros
OF—TY PICKUP	1-1	1918 Phillies
OF—JOHN MOHARDT	1-1	1922 Tigers
C—MIKE HOPKINS	2-2	1902 Pirates
P—BEN SHIELDS	4-0 (W-L)	1924–25 Yankees, 1930 Red Sox, 1931 Phillies

Perfection is difficult to beat—and each of these players was perfect for however brief a stretch.

Shields is interesting because it took him four seasons and 13 appearances to win his 4 games—and he did it with a lifetime earned run average of 8.34!

Honorable mention to the perfect hitting pitchers: Hal Deviney (1920 Red Sox), Fred Schemanske (1923 Senators), and Chet Kehn (1942 Dodgers), each of whom went two-for-two.

And most honorable mention to the player who achieved

perfection in two areas, John Kull of the 1909 Athletics, who was one-for-one as a batter and won one and lost none as a pitcher.

HIGHEST CAREER
AVERAGES—ACTIVE

Being limited to a nine-man team can be frustrating on occasion. Consider, for example, that the following lineup, based on players with at least 2000 plate appearances, has no room for Bill Madlock (.312).

1B—ROD CAREW	.330
2B—JOHNNY RAY	.209
3B—GEORGE BRETT	.314
SS—CAL RIPKEN	.293
OF—PETE ROSE	.305
OF—WILLIE WILSON	.305
OF—AL OLIVER	.305
C—TED SIMMONS	.288
P—RON GUIDRY	.680 (W-L Pct.)

Lineup jugglers could, of course, stick Madlock at second. Guidry's lifetime record is 132 wins and 62 losses.

BEST BATTING AVERAGE
OF THE DECADE

These are the players who have had the best batting averages—and the best won-lost percentage—over the past ten seasons.

1B—ROD CAREW	.388	1977 Twins
2B—RENNIE STENNETT	.336	1977 Pirates
3B—GEORGE BRETT	.390	1980 Royals
SS—ROBIN YOUNT	.331	1982 Brewers
OF—TONY GWYNN	.351	1984 Padres
OF—MIGUEL DILONE	.341	1980 Indians
OF—DAVE WINFIELD	.340	1984 Yankees
C—MANNY SANGUILLEN	.328	1975 Pirates
P—RON GUIDRY	.893 (25-3)	1978 Yankees

Curiously, only three of the position players on this team—Carew, Brett and Gwynn—won the batting championship in the year cited.

CHAMPIONS IN PLACE

From this list of players who won the most batting championships, try to guess the team that has won the most batting crowns in the twentieth century.

1B—ROD CAREW	3	1975, 1977–78 Twins
2B—ROGERS HORNSBY	7	1920–25 Cardinals, 1928 Braves
3B—BILL MADLOCK	4	1975–76 Cubs, 1981, 1983 Pirates
SS—HONUS WAGNER	7	1903–04, 1906–09, 1911 Pirates
OF—TY COBB	12	1907–15, 1917–19 Tigers
OF—TED WILLIAMS	6	1941–42, 1947–48, 1957–58 Red Sox
OF—STAN MUSIAL	6	1943, 1946, 1948, 1950–52 Cardinals
C—ERNIE LOMBARDI	2	1938 Reds, 1942 Braves
P—LEFTY GROVE	5	1929–31, 1933 Athletics, 1939 Red Sox

If you were seduced by all those big numbers next to Hornsby and Musial and picked the Cardinals, try again.

The Redbirds had only 19½ winners (including Harry Walker, who spent half of his title year with the 1947 Cards). The Pirates, with 23 championships, provide the correct answer. Besides Wagner and Madlock (two of whose batting crowns came with the Bucs), the Pirates also had Roberto Clemente (4), Paul Waner (3), Dave Parker (2), Ginger Beaumont, Arky Vaughan, Debs Garms, Dick Groat and Matty Alou.

Grove led the American League in W-L percentage in the years indicated.

Carew also won batting titles in 1969 and 1972–74 when he played only second base; Musial also won in 1957 when he played only first base.

Billy Goodman is the only utility player ever to win a batting crown. In his big year he batted .354 while playing 45 games in the outfield, 27 at third base, 21 at first, 5 at second, 1 at short and 11 as a pinch-hitter. In 1960 and 1962 another Boston jack-of-all-trades, Pete Runnels, won batting titles, but in those two years he was something of a fixture at first base.

MOST HOME RUNS—CAREER

The top power hitter at each position:

1B—LOU GEHRIG	493
2B—JOE MORGAN	265
3B—EDDIE MATHEWS	483
SS—ERNIE BANKS	293
OF—BABE RUTH	692
OF—HANK AARON	661
OF—WILLIE MAYS	643
C—JOHNNY BENCH	324
P—WES FERRELL	37

So the numbers don't look familiar. That's because the numbers shown above are for home runs hit while playing the indicated position. The full career totals for these players are: Gehrig, 493; Morgan, 268; Mathews, 512;

Banks, 512; Ruth, 714; Aaron, 755; Mays, 660; Bench, 389; Ferrell, 38.

HOMERS BY POSITION—SEASON

The only problem with making out this lineup is that two of its most deserving members can't make it. Take a look and then we'll explain.

1B—HANK GREENBERG	58	1938	Tigers
2B—DAVE JOHNSON	43	1973	Braves
3B—MIKE SCHMIDT	48	1980	Phillies
SS—ERNIE BANKS	47	1958	Cubs
OF—ROGER MARIS	61	1961	Yankees
OF—BABE RUTH	60	1927	Yankees
OF—HACK WILSON	56	1930	Cubs
C—ROY CAMPANELLA	41	1953	Dodgers
P—WES FERRELL	9	1931	Indians

By all rights, Ruth should be in this lineup twice—the second time for the 59 home runs he hit in 1921. Major league baseball rules state, however, that no player can occupy two positions in the lineup.

The second problem is Jimmie Foxx, who hit 58 homers in 1932, mostly as a first baseman—but he did play 13 games at third that year and hit a few of his homers while at that position, so Greenberg gets the nod here.

The third problem is that Johnny Bench hit 45 homers in 1970 and should thereby be the catcher. However, he hit six of them while playing the outfield and one while playing first base.

Honorable mention to Alan Sothoron (1921 Indians), who pitched 178 innings without giving up a home run.

MOST HOME RUNS—GAME

Ten players have hit four home runs in a game, but only six of them make this team.

1B—LOU GEHRIG	June 3, 1942	Yankees
2B—BOBBY LOWE	May 30, 1894	Braves
3B—MIKE SCHMIDT	April 17, 1976	Phillies
SS—ERNIE BANKS	Sept. 14, 1957	Cubs
OF—ED DELAHANTY	July 13, 1896	Phillies
OF—CHUCK KLEIN	July 10, 1936	Phillies
OF—ROCKY COLAVITO	June 10, 1959	Indians
C—BOB TILLMAN	July 30, 1969	Braves
P—JIM TOBIN	May 13, 1942	Braves

Gehrig, Lowe, Schmidt, Delahanty, Klein and Colavito hit their four homers each in four consecutive at bats. The other four players who connected four times in a game—Pat Seerey, Gil Hodges, Joe Adcock and Willie Mays—did not.

Banks is the only shortstop ever to hit three consecutive homers in a game.

Ditto Jim Tobin among pitchers.

Several catchers have hit three in a row; the choice of Tillman is arbitrary.

BEST HOME RUN RATIO

Among players who have had at least 4000 at bats, the ones with the highest long ball frequency are:

1B—HARMON KILLEBREW	14.22 at bats
2B—JOE GORDON	22.55 at bats
3B—MIKE SCHMIDT	14.56 at bats
SS—ERNIE BANKS	18.40 at bats
OF—BABE RUTH	11.76 at bats
OF—RALPH KINER	14.11 at bats
OF—DAVE KINGMAN	14.65 at bats
C—ROY CAMPANELLA	17.38 at bats
PH—JOE ADCOCK	12.75 at bats

The need to stick Killebrew somewhere overshadows Jimmie Foxx's ratio of one homer every 15.23 at bats.

Banks's total is for his entire career; if you calculate only his ratio while a shortstop, it would improve to 15.67.

Adcock's figure is strictly for his pinch-hitting appearances. If you include his at bats while in the starting lineup, his ratio would balloon to 19.66.

GRAND-SLAMS—CAREER

The only way to get four runs with one swipe of the bat is by hitting a home run with the bases loaded. These are the players who did that most often.

1B—LOU GEHRIG	23
2B—ROGERS HORNSBY	12
3B—HARMON KILLEBREW	11
SS—ERNIE BANKS	12
OF—TED WILLIAMS	17
OF—BABE RUTH	16
OF—HANK AARON	16
C—JOHNNY BENCH	11
P—JIM PALMER	0

Killebrew and Banks played more than one position, but there is no reason to move them off this squad.

In his 18 years in the big leagues Palmer never gave up a grand-slam.

MOST RUNS BATTED IN—CAREER

Driving in runs is what a clutch hitter is supposed to do. The highest lifetime totals belong to:

1B—LOU GEHRIG	1990	
2B—NAP LAJOIE	1599	
3B—EDDIE MATHEWS	1453	
SS—HONUS WAGNER	1732	
OF—HANK AARON	2297	
OF—BABE RUTH	2204	
OF—TY COBB	1960	
C—YOGI BERRA	1430	
P—JIM VAUGHN	2.33 ERA	

There are some suspect numbers here since RBIs weren't counted at all until 1907 and didn't become an official statistic until 1920. Lajoie's and Wagner's numbers are, therefore, the result of after-the-fact research. If you prefer RBIs counted as soon as they were driven in, you'll have to settle for Rogers Hornsby (1579) at second and Ernie Banks (1636) or (if you prefer a full-time shortstop) Joe Cronin (1423) at short. If you aren't fussy and will take Banks at short, you'll probably also want Harmon Killebrew (1584) at third.

ERA is the closest we could come to a pitching equivalent for runs batted in, so the ninth spot here goes to Vaughn, whose 2.33 ERA is the lowest career mark for all pitchers with 2000 or more innings pitched.

MOST RUNS BATTED IN—SEASON

And the high marks for a single season . . .

1B—LOU GEHRIG	184	1931 Yankees
2B—ROGERS HORNSBY	152	1922 Cardinals
3B—AL ROSEN	145	1953 Indians
SS—VERN STEPHENS	159	1949 Red Sox
OF—HACK WILSON	190	1930 Cubs
OF—BABE RUTH	170	1921 Yankees
OF—CHUCK KLEIN	170	1930 Phillies
C—ROY CAMPANELLA	142	1953 Dodgers
P—DUTCH LEONARD	1.01 ERA	1914 Red Sox

First basemen seem to hold all of the honorable mention spots on this team. Gehrig also had 175 RBIs in 1927 and

174 in 1930. Hank Greenberg is Gehrig's closest challenger, with 183 in 1937 and 170 in 1935. Then comes Jimmie Foxx with 175 in 1938 and 169 in 1932.

Leonard's incredible mark of giving up only one run for every nine innings is the best season ERA for pitchers with 200 or more innings pitched.

RBI PRODUCTION

Another unusual statistic, but an accurate indicator of run production is the number of RBIs recorded every 100 games for players with 4000 or more at bats.

1B—LOU GEHRIG	92
2B—ROGERS HORNSBY	70
3B—MIKE SCHMIDT	66
SS—JOE CRONIN	67
OF—SAM THOMPSON	92
OF—BABE RUTH	89
OF—JOE DiMAGGIO	89
C—ROY CAMPANELLA	70
P—CHRISTY MATHEWSON	.630

Gehrig's 92 edges Hank Greenberg's 91.5, the next highest figure recorded.

Schmidt just edges Harmon Killebrew's 65.

Ernie Banks drove in 75 runs for every 100 games he played at shortstop, but his years at first base dragged down his career figure to 65, so we'll put Cronin in the lineup.

Mathewson had the highest ratio of games won as a starter to games started (347 to 551), barely edging Mordecai Brown (208 to 332), among pitchers with 300 or more starts. To offer some context in which this statistic fits, consider the percentages of some rather great pitchers: Cy Young, .592; Lefty Grove, .586; Grover Cleveland Alexander, .585; Lefty Gomez, .575; Whitey Ford, .518; and Sandy Koufax, .506.

MOST HITS—CAREER

The 3000-hit club has received considerable attention in recent years, with seven of its fifteen members reaching that plateau within the memory span of even teenaged fans. Every position except catcher can claim at least one member. (Eight of the select fifteen are named on this page. If you can come up with the other seven names, go to the head of the class.)

1B—	STAN MUSIAL	3630
2B—	EDDIE COLLINS	3309
3B—	PETE ROSE	4097
SS—	HONUS WAGNER	3430
OF—	TY COBB	4191
OF—	HANK AARON	3771
OF—	TRIS SPEAKER	3515
C—	YOGI BERRA	2150
P—	MANNY MOTA	154

Rose had to be here *somewhere* on this team. So, too, did Musial. If you want a full-time first baseman and third baseman you will have to accept Cap Anson (3081) and Brooks Robinson (2848).

The most hits by a pitcher? Cy Young's 623.

MOST HITS—SEASON

Two hundred base hits in a season is considered to be a superior performance. By that standard the totals recorded here are up in the stratosphere.

1B—GEORGE SISLER	257	1920 Browns
2B—ROGERS HORNSBY	250	1922 Cardinals
3B—FREDDY LINDSTROM	231	1928 and 1930 Giants
SS—CECIL TRAVIS	218	1941 Senators
OF—LEFTY O'DOUL	254	1929 Phillies
OF—AL SIMMONS	253	1925 Athletics
OF—CHUCK KLEIN	250	1930 Phillies
C—TED SIMMONS	193	1975 Cardinals
P—JOSE MORALES	25	1976 Expos

The batting averages that went with these totals: Sisler, .407; Hornsby, .401; Lindstrom, .358 and .379; Travis, .359; O'Doul, .398; Al Simmons, .384; Klein, .386; Ted Simmons, .332; Morales, .321 as a pinch-hitter.

O'Doul is an interesting case. He started as a pitcher in the American League, slipped back to the minors for four seasons, then emerged as an outfielder with a potent bat for the Giants in 1928. After one season under John McGraw, for whom his antics proved too much, he bounced to the Phillies, then the Dodgers for two seasons each before returning to the Giants for two last years. For four seasons, 1929–1932, he was a ferocious hitter, batting a combined .373. Finally, The O'Doodle, as he liked to be called, slipped back to the Pacific Coast League where he became a fixture, as player and manager, for decades.

Honorable mention to first baseman Bill Terry (254 hits in 1930) and catcher Yogi Berra (192 in 1950) as the closest runners-up.

MOST HITS—GAME

There have been 122 games in which a player got six or more hits. These occasions stand out.

1B—JIM	Sept. 16, 1924	Cardinals
BOTTOMLEY	August 15, 1931	Cardinals
2B—RENNIE	Sept. 16, 1975	Pirates
STENNETT		
3B—COOKIE	Sept. 23, 1939	Reds
LAVAGETTO		
SS—JOHNNY	July 10, 1932	Indians
BURNETT		
OF—ROCKY	June 24, 1962	Tigers
COLAVITO		
OF—ED	June 2, 1890	Cleveland (PL)
DELAHANTY	June 16, 1894	Phillies
OF—DOC CRAMER	June 20, 1932	Athletics
	July 13, 1935	Athletics
C—WILBERT	June 10, 1892	Baltimore
ROBINSON		
P—GUY HECKER	August 15, 1886	Louisville (AA)

Bottomley, Delahanty and Cramer are the only players to go 6-for-6 twice.

Stennett and Robinson were 7-for-7 in nine-inning games.

Burnett went 9-for-11 in 18 innings and thereby keeps out of the lineup Cesar Gutierrez, the third player to go 7-for-7 (June 21, 1970, Tigers)—although his perfect day lasted 12 innings.

Colavito went 7-for-10 in 22 innings.

Hecker was 6-for-7.

Lavagetto was the most recent third baseman to go 6-for-6.

ON-BASE PERCENTAGE—CAREER

If any further barometer of Ted Williams's greatness be required, try the fact that his career on-base percentage, .483, was the highest in baseball history. The other leaders with a minimum of 1000 games are:

1B—LOU GEHRIG	.447	
2B—ROGERS HORNSBY	.434	
3B—JOHN McGRAW	.464	
SS—ARKY VAUGHAN	.406	
OF—TED WILLIAMS	.483	
OF—BABE RUTH	.474	
OF—BILLY HAMILTON	.455	
C—MICKEY COCHRANE	.419	
P—ADDIE JOSS	8.73 runners per 9 innings	

Joss, a relatively unknown star in the early part of this century, is significantly ahead of the next best pitcher at keeping runners off the bases, Ed Walsh (9.00). Joss gave up 1895 hits and 370 walks in 2336 innings over a nine-year career (1902–10) that was cut short by a fatal illness.

MOST TIMES ON BASE—SEASON

Hits, walks and times hit by a pitch combined equals times on base. These are the players who did it most often.

1B—JIMMIE FOXX	329	1932 Athletics
2B—ROGERS HORNSBY	318	1924 Cardinals
3B—EDDIE YOST	318	1950 Senators
SS—WOODY ENGLISH	320	1930 Cubs
OF—BABE RUTH	379	1923 Yankees
OF—TED WILLIAMS	358	1949 Red Sox
OF—TY COBB	336	1915 Tigers
C—DARRELL PORTER	284	1979 Royals
P—BILL WHITE	683 IP	1876 Cincinnati

English played as much third base as shortstop in 1930, so if you want to be a purist replace him with Arky Vaughan (313, 1936 Pirates).

White pitched more innings in the first season of what is now recognized as major league play than anyone else has since. Of course, he pitched in 75 games, almost the complete schedule. If you want a twentieth-century pitcher, take Ed Walsh of the 1908 White Sox, who pitched 464 innings in 66 games.

HIGHEST SLUGGING AVERAGE—CAREER

Slugging average is calculated by dividing at bats into total bases. Here are the best lifetime slugging averages for players with 4000 or more total bases.

1B—LOU GEHRIG	.632
2B—ROGERS HORNSBY	.577
3B—DICK ALLEN	.554
SS—ERNIE BANKS	.500
OF—BABE RUTH	.690
OF—TED WILLIAMS	.634
OF—STAN MUSIAL	.559
C—GABBY HARTNETT	.489
P—CY YOUNG	511 Wins

Musial edges out Willie Mays and Mickey Mantle, who both had .557 averages. Joe DiMaggio, despite a .579 average, just misses qualifying because he had only 3948 total bases.

And speaking of qualifying, no catcher has ever reached 4000 total bases. Hartnett's total was 3144. If you are willing to lower the cutoff level even further, you could replace Hartnett with Roy Campanella (.500 on 2101 total bases).

Honorable mention to Jimmie Foxx, whose .609 is the fourth highest.

Young is the pitcher with the most wins in the annals of baseball.

HIGHEST SLUGGING AVERAGE—SEASON

The eight hitters are very familiar and the pitcher should be equally so.

1B—LOU GEHRIG	.765	1927 Yankees
2B—ROGERS HORNSBY	.756	1925 Cardinals
3B—GEORGE BRETT	.664	1980 Royals
SS—ERNIE BANKS	.614	1958 Cubs
OF—BABE RUTH	.847	1920 Yankees
OF—TED WILLIAMS	.735	1941 Red Sox
OF—HACK WILSON	.723	1930 Cubs
C—GABBY HARTNETT	.630	1930 Cubs
P—CHARLIE RADBOURN	60 Wins	1884 Providence

Ruth slugged .700 or better nine times, including the astonishing season cited above and 1921 when he "slipped" to .846. Only seven other players have topped the .700 plateau: Gehrig five times, Williams and Jimmie Foxx three times each, Hornsby twice, and Wilson, Mickey Mantle and Stan Musial once apiece.

No one has ever—or is ever likely to—top Radbourn's number of victories.

MOST TOTAL BASES—CAREER

One for a single, two for a double, three for a triple, and four for a homer.

1B—STAN MUSIAL	6134
2B—ROGERS HORNSBY	4712
3B—PETE ROSE	5559
SS—HONUS WAGNER	4888
OF—HANK AARON	6856
OF—WILLIE MAYS	6066
OF—TY COBB	5860
C—YOGI BERRA	3643
P—SANDY KOUFAX	6.79 Hits per 9 Innings

For the pitcher we will include Koufax, whose stinginess with hits over his career puts him way ahead of the next best figure. The category is arbitrarily included, but Koufax certainly is not once the choice was made.

And honorable mention to the rest of the 5000+ club:

Babe Ruth (5793), Carl Yastrzemski (5539), Frank Robinson (5373), Tris Speaker (5101), Lou Gehrig (5059) and Mel Ott (5041).

MOST TOTAL BASES—SEASON

The standard of an exceptional season is 400 total bases. Surprisingly, some very fine power hitters never cracked the magic number.

1B—LOU GEHRIG	447		1927 Yankees
2B—ROGERS HORNSBY	450		1922 Cardinals
3B—EDDIE MATHEWS	363		1953 Braves
SS—ERNIE BANKS	379		1958 Cubs
OF—BABE RUTH	457		1921 Yankees
OF—CHUCK KLEIN	445		1930 Phillies
OF—STAN MUSIAL	429		1948 Cardinals
C—JOHNNY BENCH	355		1970 Reds
P—NOLAN RYAN	5.26 H/ 9 Inn.		1972 Angeles

There is no valid pitching equivalent here, so we arbitrarily choose Ryan's extraordinary mark of giving up only slightly more than five hits per complete game.

Jimmie Foxx not only had the highest total not qualifying for a position, but he also holds the distinction of being the only player to get 400 or more total bases twice and not make this team.

The other repeaters are Ruth (417, 1927 Yankees); Hornsby (409, 1929 Cubs); Klein (405, 1929 Phillies and 420, 1932 Phillies); and Lou Gehrig (419, 1930 Yankees; 410, 1931 Yankees; 409, 1934 Yankees; and 403, 1936 Yankees).

Seven additional players reached the 400 mark: Joe DiMaggio, Jim Rice and Hal Trosky in the American League; Hack Wilson, Babe Herman, Joe Medwick and Hank Aaron in the National.

MOST DOUBLES—CAREER

The two-base hit was a forgotten weapon for years until the Kansas City Royals started racking up high totals in the late 1970s and early 1980s.

1B—STAN MUSIAL	725	
2B—NAP LAJOIE	652	
3B—PETE ROSE	726	
SS—HONUS WAGNER	651	
OF—TRIS SPEAKER	793	
OF—TY COBB	723	
OF—CARL YASTRZEMSKI	646	
C—GABBY HARTNETT	396	
DH—HANK AARON	624	

Honorable mention to Paul Waner, whose 605 doubles make him the only player with 600 or more who is not on this team.

MOST DOUBLES—SEASON

"Take two" is the familiar cry of fans looking for aggressive base-running. These are the players who did just that most often in a single season.

1B—GEORGE BURNS	64	1926 Indians
2B—CHARLIE GEHRINGER	60	1936 Tigers
3B—GEORGE KELL	56	1950 Tigers
SS—JOE CRONIN	51	1938 Red Sox
OF—EARL WEBB	67	1931 Red Sox
OF—JOE MEDWICK	64	1936 Cardinals
OF—PAUL WANER	62	1932 Pirates
C—MICKEY COCHRANE	42	1930 Athletics
DH—HANK GREENBERG	63	1934 Tigers

Greenberg merits inclusion as the only player with 60 or more doubles in a season who is squeezed out of the eight positions.

MOST TRIPLES—CAREER

Someday a member of the Kansas City Royals or St. Louis Cardinals may join this team, but for the moment the most recent triple in the lineup dates back to the pre-Astroturf year of 1935.

1B—JAKE BECKLEY	246
2B—EDDIE COLLINS	186
3B—PIE TRAYNOR	164
SS—HONUS WAGNER	252
OF—SAM CRAWFORD	312
OF—TY COBB	298
OF—TRIS SPEAKER	222
C BUCK EWING	179
DH—ROGER CONNOR	227

Only two players with more than 200 triples don't make the team: outfielder Fred Clarke (219) and first baseman Dan Brouthers (212).

MOST TRIPLES—SEASON

The three-base hit is one of the most dynamic and exciting plays in baseball—with ball, runner, outfielder, third baseman and cutoff man all moving simultaneously in a kind of open air dance. These players choreographed that dance the most times in a season.

1B—PERRY WERDEN	33	1893 Cardinals
2B—HEINIE REITZ	29	1894 Baltimore
3B—JIMMY WILLIAMS	27	1899 Pirates
SS—HONUS WAGNER	22	1900 Pirates
OF—OWEN WILSON	36	1912 Pirates
OF—JOE JACKSON	26	1912 Indians
OF—SAM CRAWFORD	26	1914 Tigers
C—JOHNNY KLING	13	1903 Cubs
DH—KIKI CUYLER	26	1925 Pirates

Cuyler tied with Jackson and Crawford, so he gets the tenth spot.

The inclusion of four Pirates is no accident; the vast spaces of old Forbes Field made the three-base hit more frequent there than elsewhere.

MOST RUNS SCORED—CAREER

Runs scored is one of the few offensive statistics in which the singles hitters have an equal chance with the big sluggers at racking up impressive numbers.

1B—STAN MUSIAL	1949
2B—EDDIE COLLINS	1816
3B—PETE ROSE	2090
SS—HONUS WAGNER	1740
OF—TY COBB	2245
OF—BABE RUTH	2174
OF—HANK AARON	2174
C—YOGI BERRA	1175
P—WALTER JOHNSON	110 Shutouts

Pitchers try to stop runners from scoring, so for this team we will go with the pitcher with the most career shutouts.

Honorable mention to Willie Mays, whose 2062 runs scored make him the only player who crossed the plate more than 2000 times, but fails to make this team.

MOST RUNS SCORED—SEASON

And the players who crossed the plate the most times in a single season since 1900:

1B—LOU GEHRIG	167	1936 Yankees
2B—ROGERS HORNSBY	156	1929 Cubs
3B—WOODY ENGLISH	152	1930 Cubs
SS—PEEWEE REESE	132	1949 Dodgers
OF—BABE RUTH	177	1921 Yankees
OF—CHUCK KLEIN	158	1930 Phillies
OF—KIKI CUYLER	155	1930 Cubs
C—MICKEY COCHRANE	118	1932 Athletics
P—GROVER CLEVELAND ALEXANDER	16 ShO	1916 Phillies

English played a considerable amount of shortstop in 1930 and if that disqualifies him, you can insert Harlond Clift, who scored 145 runs for the St. Louis Browns in 1936.

Gehrig and Ruth are the only players since 1900 to score 160 or more runs in a season—and each of them did it twice. (Gehrig also had 163 in 1931. The Babe had the same number in 1927; he also scored 158 twice, in 1920 and 1926. A claim could be made that Ruth deserves all three outfield positions on this team.)

Left out are the many nineteenth-century players with numbers higher than what you see here. The highest ever was Billy Hamilton's 196 in 1894.

Alexander's 16 shutouts is the record for a single season.

MOST RUNS SCORED—GAME

Eight of the players on this team scored six runs in a game; the ninth player scored seven.

1B—FRANK TORRE	Sept. 2, 1957	Braves
2B—BOBBY LOWE	May 3, 1895	Braves
3B—EZRA SUTTON	August 27, 1887	Braves
SS—JOHNNY PESKY	May 8, 1946	Red Sox
OF—MEL OTT	August 4, 1934	Giants
	April 30, 1944	Giants
OF—GINGER BEAUMONT	July 22, 1899	Pirates
OF—JIMMY RYAN	July 25, 1894	Cubs
C—KING KELLY	August 27, 1887	Braves
P—GUY HECKER	August 15, 1886	Louisville (AA)

Hecker is the only player ever to score seven runs in one game.

Ott is the only player ever to score six times in a game twice.

Pesky is the only American Leaguer to cross the plate that many times in a game.

The others who scored six times in a game are Mike Tiernan, Cap Anson and Jim Whitney.

MOST WALKS—CAREER

If a walk is as good as a hit, these players are very good indeed.

1B—CARL YASTRZEMSKI	1737
2B—JOE MORGAN	1865
3B—EDDIE YOST	1614
SS—LUKE APPLING	1302
OF—BABE RUTH	2056
OF—TED WILLIAMS	2019
OF—MICKEY MANTLE	1734
C—JOHNNY BENCH	891
P—JUAN MARICHAL	3.27 K/BB Ratio

Yost, a lifetime .254 hitter, but the dominant leadoff man in the American League for years, is the only player here who will not end up with a lease in Cooperstown.

Only two pitchers in the history of baseball have pitched more than 3500 innings and managed to strike out three times as many batters as they walked. Marichal's ratio of 2302 strikeouts and 704 walks is approached only by Ferguson Jenkins' totals of 3192 strikeouts and 997 walks (3.20).

MOST WALKS—SEASON

It's a wonder that some of these players bothered to dig into the batter's box rather than go directly from the on-deck circle to first base. The pitcher, on the other hand, gave nothing away and holds the record for the fewest free passes issued in a season.

1B—WILLIE McCOVEY	137		1970 Giants
2B—EDDIE STANKY	148	·	1945 Dodgers
3B—EDDIE YOST	151		1956 Senators
SS—EDDIE JOOST	149		1949 Athletics
OF—BABE RUTH	170		1923 Yankees
OF—TED WILLIAMS	162		1947 Red Sox
			1949 Red Sox
OF—JIM WYNN	148		1969 Astros
C—GENE TENACE	125		1977 Padres
P—BABE ADAMS	18/263 inn.		1920 Pirates

Williams could also qualify for 1946 when he walked 156 times and Ruth for 1920 when he strolled to first base 148 times. A curious feature of this lineup is the number of players who set their records for teams mediocre or worse—the 1970 Giants, 1956 Senators, 1969 Astros and 1977 Padres having been anything but pennant contenders. It is also worth noting that Tenace batted a mere .233 and Yost .231 for the years cited.

Adams gave up the fewest walks per nine innings (.616) in the annals of the game. Christy Mathewson (1913 Giants) came close, though, with .618 walks per game.

HIGHEST BASE ON BALLS AVERAGE—CAREER

Base on balls average is computed by dividing a player's number of walks by the combined total of at bats and walks. These were the best at each position.

1B—EARL TORGESON	.165	
2B—MAX BISHOP	.204	
3B—EDDIE YOST	.180	
SS—EDDIE JOOST	.157	
OF—TED WILLIAMS	.208	
OF—BABE RUTH	.197	
OF—MICKEY MANTLE	.176	
C—GENE TENACE	.180	
P—DEACON PHILLIPPE	1.25 per 9 innings	

Torgeson is a surprise, but the real sleeper here is Joost, a .239 hitter whose walks bring his on-base percentage up to .358.

Phillippe has the lowest number of walks issued per 9 innings of all pitchers with 2500 or more innings pitched.

MOST STOLEN BASES—CAREER

A single isn't always a single; to some players it is merely the first stage of a double. For instance, these all-time thieves:

1B—FRANK CHANCE	405
2B—EDDIE COLLINS	743
3B—TOMMY LEACH	364
SS—BERT CAMPANERIS	620
OF—LOU BROCK	938
OF—TY COBB	892
OF—MAX CAREY	738
C—ROGER BRESNAHAN	211
PR—HERB WASHINGTON	31

You'll have to take our word on Washington, since no records are kept spelling out how many bases were stolen by a player in a pinch-running role. Washington, of course, never did anything else during his career with Oakland.

The odd man out on this team is Billy Hamilton, the nineteenth-century speedster who was officially credited with 937 stolen bases. In those days, however, a runner was given a stolen base if he advanced from first to third on a single, scored from second on a single, or crossed the plate from first on a double. There are no records of how many of Hamilton's steals resulted from these situations.

MOST STOLEN BASES—SEASON

The record-holders here reflect the fact that stealing bases was not regarded as an offensive priority between the Babe Ruth and Maury Wills eras.

1B—FRANK CHANCE	67	1903	Cubs
2B—EDDIE COLLINS	81	1910	Athletics
3B—FRITZ MAISEL	74	1914	Yankees
SS—MAURY WILLS	104	1962	Dodgers
OF—RICKEY HENDERSON	130	1982	Athletics
OF—LOU BROCK	118	1974	Cardinals
OF—RON LeFLORE	97	1980	Expos
C—JOHN WATHAN	36	1982	Royals
PR—HERB WASHINGTON	29	1974	Athletics

Henderson also had 100 stolen bases in 1980 and 108 in 1983. And Ty Cobb, whose 96 stolen bases in 1915 was long considered unapproachable, doesn't even make the team.

LOWEST STRIKEOUT
RATIO—CAREER

Nobody could top these players at putting the ball into play. On the basis of at least 4000 at bats, they struck out only once every . . .

1B—FRANK McCORMICK	30.28 at bats
2B—NELLIE FOX	42.74 at bats
3B—ANDY HIGH	33.85 at bats
SS—JOE SEWELL	62.56 at bats
OF—LLOYD WANER	44.92 at bats
OF—TOMMY HOLMES	40.92 at bats
OF—SAM RICE	33.71 at bats
C—MICKEY COCHRANE	23.82 at bats
P—NOLAN RYAN	9.40 K's per 9 innings

Since strikeouts weren't regularly recorded until 1913, such fabled contact hitters as Tris Speaker, Lave Cross, Stuffy McInnis and Willie Keeler must be excluded from consideration, although they had impressive percentages after that date.

Ryan's strikeout average is the best since 1913.

FEWEST STRIKEOUTS—SEASON

Maybe those fans in Chicago who recently formed an Emil Verban club know what they are talking about. Although he was a member of the Phillies at the time, their hero holds the mark for the fewest whiffs by a second baseman with at least 400 at bats in a season. Verban's teammates, their strikeouts, and their at bats are:

1B—STUFFY McINNIS	5—537	1922 Indians
2B—EMIL VERBAN	8—540	1947 Phillies
3B—JOE SEWELL	3—503	1932 Yankees
SS—LOU BOUDREAU	9—560	1948 Indians
OF—LLOYD WANER	5—414	1936 Pirates
OF—DON MUELLER	7—453	1956 Giants
OF—TRIS SPEAKER	8—523	1927 Senators
C—MICKEY COCHRANE	7—432	1927 Athletics
P—NOLAN RYAN	383 K's	1973 Angels

Sewell epitomizes the contact hitter. He also struck out fewer than ten times in 1925 (4—608), 1929 (4—578) and 1933 (4—524). The first of these years he was playing shortstop for the Indians, but we couldn't put him at two positions. In 1929 he was playing third for the Indians and in 1933 he was at third for the Yankees.

Other repeaters are McInnis with the 1921 Red Sox (9—584) and the 1924 Braves (6—581); Waner, 1933 Pirates (8—500); and Cochrane, 1929 Athletics (8—514).

Nolan Ryan is here for forcing others to do what the rest of the players on this team rarely did.

Actually, Matt Kilroy (1886 Baltimore) struck out 505 batters, but he had a few advantages Ryan never imagined. For one thing the mound was only 50 feet from home plate and for another it took seven balls to walk a batter.

ODDS AND ODDS

Some one-game record holders who would make an interesting team.

1B—DANNY MEYER	May 3, 1977	Mariners
2B—TITO FUENTES	Sept. 13, 1973	Giants
3B—BILL JOYCE	May 18, 1897	Giants
SS—RAY CHAPMAN	August 31, 1919	Indians
OF—MIKE GRIFFIN	June 23, 1890	Philadelphia (PL)
OF—PIGGY WARD	June 18, 1893	Reds
OF—MEL OTT	October 5, 1929	Giants
C—RUSS NIXON	August 31, 1965	Red Sox
P—NOLAN RYAN	August 12, 1974	Angels

Meyer reached first twice on catcher's interference. Fuentes is the most recent player to be hit by a pitch three times. Joyce is the most recent with four triples. Chapman is the most recent with four sacrifices. Griffin reached first on an error four times. Ward reached base 8 times (on 2 singles, 5 walks and being hit by a pitch). Ott had 5 intentional walks. Nixon is the most recent player to hit three sacrifice flies. Ryan is the most recent pitcher to strike out 19 batters in 9 innings.

Honorable mention to Walter Wilmot for his 7 walks

with the Cubs on August 22, 1891. (Wilmot also holds two other obscure records: 8 stolen bases in two consecutive games on August 6 and 7, 1894, and being called out twice in a game for getting hit by a batted ball on September 30, 1890.)

THE WORST

They tried, but they simply weren't up to it. Or they were up to it in most ways, but recorded big numbers in some categories that they might have preferred forgetting. As with the best, there is sometimes a DH, sometimes a pitching equivalent.

THE WORST—CAREER

Remember the name Bill Bergen. A catcher for Cincinnati and Brooklyn between 1901 and 1911, Bergen's lifetime average of .170 is the lowest in the history of baseball for any player having at least 1000 at bats. Here are his teammates, the years they played, their number of at bats, and their averages:

1B—JOHN BOCCABELLA	1462	.219
2B—RICH MORALES	1053	.195
3B—JACKIE HERNANDEZ	1480	.208
SS—RAY OYLER	1265	.175
OF—DAVE NICHOLSON	1419	.212
OF—RUSTY TORRES	1314	.212
OF—VIC HARRIS	1610	.217
C—BILL BERGEN	3028	.170
P—HUGH MULCAHY	45-89	(.336)

Keep this lineup handy for the next time somebody tries arguing that the league expansions in the 1960s had no effect on the quality of major league talent.

Among pitchers with at least 100 decisions, Rollie

Naylor (1917–24) is right behind Mulcahy with 42 wins and 83 losses for a similar .336 winning percentage.

For the record, the only other major leaguers with at least 1000 at bats who have ended up below .200 are catchers Fritz Buelow (.189) and Mike Ryan (.193).

THE WORST—SEASON

Although he regularly turned in such glamorous yearly averages as .132, .139 and .159, the earlier-mentioned Bill Bergen never quite managed the 400 at bats that would have qualified him for a batting title. The worst in this category are:

1B—DAVE KINGMAN	.204	1982 Mets
2B—PETE CHILDS	.194	1902 Phillies
3B—JERRY KENNEY	.193	1970 Yankees
SS—JOHN GOCHNAUR	.185	1902 Indians
OF—WILLIE KIRKLAND	.200	1962 Indians
OF—CURT BLEFARY	.200	1968 Orioles
OF—CHARLIE JAMIESON	.202	1918 Athletics
C—BILLY SULLIVAN	.191	1908 White Sox
P—JACK NABORS	1-21	1916 Athletics

As with the career worsts, the most pathetic season efforts all took place either at the beginning of the century or since the 1960s.

Gochnaur had the most competition. His average was .18519; Eddie Joost with the 1943 Braves hit .18527; and Eddie Brinkman batted .18547 for the 1965 Senators. Special mention should be made of Dal Maxvill, whose .175 average with the 1969 Cardinals fails to qualify since he batted only 372 times. (Cardinal pinch-hitters that year saw considerable duty since Maxvill's 372 at bats came in 132 games.)

Honorable mention to Joe Harris, who put together a record of 2 wins and 21 losses for the 1906 Red Sox.

The worst season with the bat for a pitcher belongs to Bob Buhl, who went 0-for-70 in 35 games with the Braves and Cubs in 1962.

WORST GAME

For these players the longest day had nothing to do with the invasion of Normandy.

1B—CECIL COOPER	June 14, 1974	Red Sox
2B—GLENN BECKERT	Sept. 16, 1972	Cubs
3B—CHARLIE PICK	May 1, 1920	Braves
SS—FRANK TAVERAS	May 1, 1979	Mets
OF—BENNY KAUFF	May 26, 1916	Giants
OF—GOOSE GOSLIN	April 28, 1934	Tigers
OF—MIKE KREEVICH	August 8, 1939	White Sox
C—GRANT BRIGGS	April 22, 1890	Syracuse (AA)
P—DAVE ROWE	July 24, 1882	Cleveland

Cooper struck out six times in a 15-inning game. Beckert left 12 runners stranded on base. In the historic 26-inning game played to a tie by the Braves and Dodgers, Pick went hitless in 11 plate appearances. Taveras is the most recent player to fan five consecutive times in a game. Kauff was picked off base three times. Goslin and Kreevich hit into four double plays each. (Joe Torre and Jim Rice later tied this record.) Briggs allowed 19 runners to steal on him. Rowe, apparently in need of work, gave up 35 runs in one game.

THE VERY WORST

These players hold the dubious distinction of being statistically the worst hitters (among non-pitchers) in the history of baseball.

1B—RED GUST	0-12	1911 Browns
2B—ED SAMCOFF	0-11	1951 Athletics
3B—RAMON CONDE	0-16	1962 White Sox
SS—CEYLON WRIGHT	0-18	1916 White Sox
OF—MIKE POTTER	0-23	1976–77 Cardinals
OF—JIM RILEY	0-14	1921 Browns, 1923 Senators
OF—DAVE COLEMAN	0-12	1977 Red Sox
C—ROY LUEBBE	0-15	1925 Yankees
P—TERRY FELTON	0-16	1979–82 Twins

Felton's numbers are a won-lost record. His ERA over this streak was 5.53 and no other pitcher has ever lost more games without winning one.

The rest of the squad is 0-for-121, which is a few innings shy of five no-hitters.

Honorable mention to Randy Tate, a pitcher, whose 0-for-41 as a member of the 1975 Mets establishes him as the worst hitting pitcher—and therefore player—in baseball history.

And to Paul Dicken, who compiled his 0-for-13 record (with the Indians in 1964 and 1966) entirely as a pinch-hitter.

POWER SHORTAGE

Not every hitter in the lineup is expected to produce the long ball, but there have been a few players who have abused the exemption. The following is a lineup of major leaguers who never hit a home run despite the ample number of at bats indicated.

1B—CHARLIE BABB	1180
2B—IRV HALL	1904
3B—MICK KELLEHER	1081
SS—TIM JOHNSON	1269
OF—TOM OLIVER	1931
OF—RIP CANNELL	913
OF—MARTY CALLAGHAN	767
C—ROXY WALTERS	1426
P—ROBIN ROBERTS	502 HR Allowed

Roberts gave up more home runs than any other pitcher. Other major leaguers who have come to bat at least 1000 times without hitting the ball out of the park are catcher Benny Bengough and infielders Luis Gomez, Red Shannon and Gil Torres.

WHAT DID THEY DO RIGHT?

Elsewhere in this book we have presented a lineup of career .000 hitters. The following is a lineup of players who, with one exception, batted higher than the absolute zero mark, but who have the equally dubious distinction of having racked up tremendous strikeout ratios.

1B—TOM BROWN	45-116	.388	1963 Senators
2B—AL LeFEVRE	13-27	.481	1920 Giants
3B—JIM WOODS	28-82	.341	1960–61 Phillies
SS—RAY BUSSE	54-155	.348	1971–74 Astros
OF—HORACE SPEED	46-135	.341	1975 Giants 1978 Indians
OF—JACKIE WARNER	55-123	.447	1966 Angels
OF—JAY VAN NOY	6-7	.857	1951 Cardinals
C—PAUL RATLIFF	119-297	.401	1963, 1970–71 Twins 1971–72 Brewers
P—BRUNO HAAS	28 BB/14 ⅓ IP		1915 Athletics

Keep in mind that those averages are not batting averages, but the percentage of times these players *struck out!* The actual career batting averages for the players cited are: Brown, .147; LeFevre, .148; Woods, .207; Busse, .148; Speed, .215; Warner, .211; Van Noy, .000; and Ratliff, .205.

Haas has the highest number of walks per innings pitched. He got off to a particularly fine start, walking 16 batters in his first game.

FEWEST RBIs—SEASON

Perhaps the most interesting thing about this team is the player who just misses making it. In 1907, while playing for the team now known as the Yankees, Wee Willie Keeler had only 17 runs batted in to show for 423 at bats. Also bad at driving in runs were:

1B—IRV GRIFFIN	20	467	1920 Athletics
2B—DON BLASINGAME	18	403	1965 Senators
3B—BOBBY BYRNE	14	439	1908 Cardinals
SS—ENZO HERNANDEZ	12	549	1971 Padres
OF—GOAT ANDERSON	12	413	1907 Pirates
OF—CLYDE MILAN	15	400	1909 Senators
OF—JACK SMITH	15	408	1919 Cardinals
C—OSCAR STANAGE	25	400	1914 Tigers
P—LES SWEETLAND	7.71 ERA		1930 Phillies

Many of these batters were leadoff men, but even at that they were extraordinarily unproductive. For the years cited their batting averages were: Griffin, .238; Blasingame, .223; Byrne, .191; Hernandez, .222; Anderson, .206; Milan, .200; Smith, .223; and Stanage, .193.

Sweetland had the highest earned run average of any pitcher who ever qualified for the league lead in ERA. He pitched 167 innings in 1930 and actually won 7 games while losing 15.

MOST STRIKEOUTS—CAREER

Striking out may kill a rally, but it certainly doesn't kill a career.

1B—WILLIE STARGELL	1936	
2B—BOBBY GRICH	1148	
3B—HARMON KILLEBREW	1699	
SS—ERNIE BANKS	1236	
OF—REGGIE JACKSON	2247	
OF—BOBBY BONDS	1757	
OF—LOU BROCK	1730	
C—JOHNNY BENCH	1278	
P—PHIL NIEKRO	202 Wild Pitches	

The most startling name here is Brock, who spent his career at the top of the lineup as a presumed table-setter.

Niekro's knuckleball obviously accounts for his record number of wild pitches.

MOST STRIKEOUTS—SEASON

In case you didn't believe that there have been more free swingers in the game in the last 25 years than ever before, note this array of whiffers of the year:

1B—DONN CLENDENON	163	1968 Pirates
2B—JUAN SAMUEL	168	1984 Phillies
3B—MIKE SCHMIDT	180	1975 Phillies
SS—ZOILO VERSALLES	122	1965 Twins
OF—BOBBY BONDS	189	1970 Giants
OF—DAVE NICHOLSON	175	1963 White Sox
OF—GORMAN THOMAS	175	1979 Brewers
C—GARY ALEXANDER	166	1978 Athletics-Indians
P—BILL STEMMEYER	64 WP	1886 Braves

Bonds holds the all-time record for most strikeouts in a season. The runner-up? The same Bonds who in 1969 held his strikeouts down to 187.

It's also worth noting that Versalles must have been doing something right whenever he managed to make contact since in the same 1965 season he was the American League's Most Valuable Player.

Stemmeyer uncorked his record number of wild pitches in 41 games.

HIGHEST STRIKEOUT AVERAGE

The numbers next to these players' names are their strikeout averages, the percentage of strikeouts to at bats. Among players with 4000 or more at bats, these struck out most often.

1B—DAVE KINGMAN	.285
2B—DICK GREEN	.196
3B—MIKE SCHMIDT	.249
SS—WOODIE HELD	.235
OF—REGGIE JACKSON	.260
OF—BOBBY BONDS	.249
OF—RICK MONDAY	.246
C—GENE TENACE	.227
P—TOM ZACHARY	.788

Only Kingman among these players has more strikeouts than hits, which means that his strikeout average is higher than his batting average—by 47 points.

Only five pitchers who have pitched more than 3000 innings have walked more men than they struck out. Zachary's ratio of 720 strikeouts and 914 walks in 3196 innings is by far the worst. The runners-up are Sad Sam Jones (.876), Earl Whitehill (.943), Ted Lyons (.957) and Bucky Walters (.988). Unlike Zachary, however, these four pitchers all won more games than they lost.

FEWEST WALKS—SEASON

Not all players believe that a walk is as good as a hit. Take, for instance, the following lineup, whose members walked the fewest times for at least 400 plate appearances in a season.

1B—GEORGE STOWELL	6-565	1909 Indians
2B—WHITEY ALPERMAN	2-420	1909 Dodgers
3B—OLLIE O'MARA	7-450	1918 Dodgers
SS—VIRGIL STALLCUP	6-428	1951 Reds
OF—RUBE OLDRING	7-441	1907 Athletics
OF—SHANO COLLINS	7-472	1922 Red Sox
OF—JESUS ALOU	7-419	1968 Giants
C—OSSEE SCHRECKENGOST	3-416	1905 Athletics
P—BOB FELLER	208 BB in 278 Inn.	1938 Indians

Some of these were good hitters who refused to lose an at bat, others were bad hitters whom pitchers refused to be cute with. The batting averages for these players in the cited years were: Stowell, .246; Alperman, .248; O'Mara, .213; Stallcup, .241; Oldring, .286; Collins, .271; Alou, .263; and Schreckengost, .272.

Feller walked more batters in one season than any other pitcher in this century.

LEAD FEET

Not every player is expected to be a speed demon, but a few have been slow enough to suggest that they have had difficulty walking, let alone running. The following is a lineup of players with the fewest stolen bases for 1000 games or more:

1B—DICK STUART	2-1112
2B—HAL LANIER	11-1196
3B—RICO PETROCELLI	10-1553
SS—DAL MAXVILL	7-1423
OF—WILLIE HORTON	8-2028
OF—FRANK HOWARD	8-1895
OF—DERON JOHNSON	11-1765
C—GUS TRIANDOS	1-1206
*PRD—SPUD DAVIS	6-1458

*Pinch Rundown

While Triandos is clearly in a class by himself, the most interesting thing about this team is the large number of shortstops and second basemen who barely miss qualifying for the starting infield. In addition to Lanier and Maxvill, Bobby Wine, Ron Hansen, Dick Groat and Eddie Bressoud (to name only four) stole fewer than 14 bases in their careers, thereby exploding the myth that middle infielders are usually fast on their feet.

Among those deserving honorable mention for other positions are first baseman Walt Dropo (5-1288), outfielder Gary Sutherland (11-1031) and catcher Ernie Lombardi (8-1853).

MOST EMBARRASSING MOMENTS

Even the most experienced major leaguers have had moments when they would have preferred being spectators in the bleachers.

1B—FRED MERKLE	1908 Giants
2B—CHICK FEWSTER	1926 Dodgers
3B—TOMMY GLAVIANO	1950 Cardinals
SS—LYN LARY	1931 Yankees
OF—EVAR SWANSON	1929 Reds
OF—HACK WILSON	1934 Dodgers
OF—GARY GEIGER	1961 Red Sox
C—YOGI BERRA	1951 Yankees
P—CATFISH HUNTER	1977 Yankees

Merkle's infamous boner in not touching second base ultimately cost the Giants a pennant. Fewster was the middle runner when Babe Herman "doubled into a double play" and was tagged out in right field after wandering away from all the confusion. Glaviano botched three consecutive ninth-inning grounders and turned a sure St. Louis win into a loss to the Dodgers. Lary cost Lou Gehrig sole possession of a home run title when he assumed that one of Gehrig's blasts was going to be caught and left the basepaths. In a game against the Cubs Swanson chased a drive into the bullpen, picked up a relief pitcher's jacket in his search for the ball, then stood in frustration while batter Norm McMillan rounded the bases for an inside-the-park grand-slammer; when he threw the jacket down in disgust, the ball rolled out of a sleeve. The hungover Wilson once chased another line drive into a corner and fired a bullet back to the infield—only to discover that the ball had been thrown by pitcher Boom Boom Beck in disgust for having been given the hook. Geiger tripled home the tying run in an extra-inning game, then walked to the dugout on the assumption that his hit had won the contest; he was tagged out, the rains came, and the game was declared a tie and ordered replayed. Berra dropped a Ted Williams foul with two out in the ninth inning to endanger Allie Reynolds's second no-hitter of the year; on the very next pitch Williams hit another foul that Berra held. In a game that appeared to mark the end of his fine career, Hunter was savaged for four homers in one inning by the Red Sox and reached the dugout only because a sympathetic Carl Yastrzemski deliberately made out. As it developed, Hunter made a comeback the following year.

OFF YEARS

Injuries, advancing age, or the need to adjust to a new team can cause even the best players to have bad seasons. What distinguishes these players is that they had no such excuses; they simply had bad years.

1B—JAKE BECKLEY	1892 Pirates
2B—JOE GORDON	1946 Yankees
3B—BOB ELLIOTT	1946 Pirates
SS—LUKE APPLING	1942 White Sox
OF—ZACK WHEAT	1915 Dodgers
OF—REGGIE JACKSON	1983 Angels
OF—AL SIMMONS	1935 White Sox
C—ERNIE LOMBARDI	1941 Reds
P—HOYT WILHELM	1955 Giants

Beckley, a lifetime .308 hitter, batted only .236. Gordon managed only 11 home runs and a .210 average. Elliott hit five home runs and hit a mere .263. Appling, the Hall of Fame shortstop who had a career mark of .310, could do no better than .262. Wheat checked in with a .258 year, while Jackson was down to .194 with 14 homers and Simmons to .267 with 16 homers. Lombardi, who went on to win the batting title the following year, turned in a .264 performance. Although he appeared in 59 games and won four of them, Wilhelm, the greatest relief pitcher in baseball history, failed to record a single save.

ODDS AND ODDS

A selection of season and career negative records.

1B—TOM McCRAW	1966 White Sox
2B—COOKIE ROJAS	1968 Phillies
3B—LARRY GARDNER	1920 Indians
SS—GEORGE McBRIDE	Career
OF—LOU BROCK	Career
OF—MICKEY RIVERS	1976 Yankees
OF—JIM RICE	1984 Red Sox
C—GENE TENACE	1974 Athletics
P—EARL WHITEHILL	Career

McCraw had the fewest at bats in 150 or more games, 389. Rojas went to bat 621 times without hitting a triple. Larry Gardner had the lowest stolen base percentage, .130 (three steals in 23 attempts). McBride had both the lowest lifetime batting average, .218, and the lowest lifetime slugging average, .264, among players with more than 4000 at bats. Brock was caught stealing more than anyone else, 307 times. Rivers walked fewer times, 13, than anyone else who played in 150 or more games. Rice grounded into more double plays in one season, 36, than anyone else. Tenace's 58 singles was the lowest total for a player who appeared in 150 or more games. Whitehill's 4.36 is not only the highest lifetime ERA for a pitcher who hurled in 3500 or more innings, it is also the only one over 4.00.

Special mention to a quartet of shortstops: Monte Cross (lowest batting average for a player in 150 or more games,

.182, 1904 Athletics); Rabbit Maranville (most at bats in a season without a home run, 672, 1922 Pirates); Tommy Thevenow (most career at bats without hitting the ball out of the park, 4164; Thevenow's only two homers were inside the park, but his two homers of any sort is still the lowest total among players with 4000 or more at bats); and Dal Maxvill (five doubles, seven extra base hits and 89 total bases—all low-water marks for players who appeared in 150 or more games—1970 Cardinals).

FROM A TO Z

The Sesame Street All-Stars. From A to Z, with a stopoff at Mc, some very bizarre lineups. And the most bizarre is the last.

A

A is for Astroturf, but there is nothing artificial about this team.

```
1B—CAP ANSON
2B—BOBBY AVILA
3B—DICK ALLEN
SS—LUKE APPLING
OF—HANK AARON
OF—EARL AVERILL
OF—RICHIE ASHBURN
 C—ALAN ASHBY
 P—GROVER CLEVELAND ALEXANDER
```

Manager: Walt Alston.

B

B as in bashing the ball.

B

1B—DAN BROUTHERS
2B—MAX BISHOP
3B—KEN BOYER
SS—ERNIE BANKS
OF—PETE BROWNING
OF—JESSE BURKETT
OF—LOU BROCK
C—JOHNNY BENCH
P—MORDECAI BROWN

Manager: Lou Boudreau.

C

Wait until you C this.

1B—ROD CAREW
2B—EDDIE COLLINS
3B—JIMMY COLLINS
SS—JOE CRONIN
OF—TY COBB
OF—KIKI CUYLER
OF—ROBERTO CLEMENTE
C—MICKEY COCHRANE
P—JOHN CLARKSON

Eight Hall of Famers and one active player who will eventually join the others in Cooperstown. And Fred Clarke to manage.

D

This team is dedicated to Joe D. His teammates are:

D

                1B—ED DELAHANTY
                2B—BOBBY DOERR
                3B—JIMMY DYKES
                SS—ALVIN DARK
                OF—JOE DiMAGGIO
                OF—HUGH DUFFY
                OF—ANDRE DAWSON
                 C—BILL DICKEY
                 P—DIZZY DEAN

Manager: Leo Durocher.

E

Easy enough.

                1B—LUKE EASTER
                2B—JOHNNY EVERS
                3B—BOB ELLIOTT
                SS—WOODY ENGLISH
                OF—DEL ENNIS
                OF—DWIGHT EVANS
                OF—MIKE EASLER
                 C—BUCK EWING
                 P—CARL ERSKINE

Manager: Cal Ermer.

F

Includes one of the game's most neglected hitters.

F

1B—JIMMIE FOXX
2B—FRANKIE FRISCH
3B—EDDIE FOSTER
SS—ART FLETCHER
OF—ELMER FLICK
OF—FATS FOTHERGILL
OF—CARL FURILLO
C—CARLTON FISK
P—WHITEY FORD

The generally overlooked Fothergill hammered out a career batting mark of .326 in tenures with the Tigers, White Sox and Red Sox between 1922 and 1933.

Frisch is the player-manager.

G

Three members of this lineup actually played together and were known as the G-Men.

1B—LOU GEHRIG
2B CHARLIE GEHRINGER
3B—BILLY GOODMAN
SS—DICK GROAT
OF—HANK GREENBERG
OF—GOOSE GOSLIN
OF—SID GORDON
C—FRANK GIBSON
P—LEFTY GROVE

Gehringer, Greenberg and Goslin were teammates on the Tigers of the 1930s.

Manager: Kid Gleason.

H

Herewith the honorees for the letter H:

H

```
1B—GIL HODGES
2B—ROGERS HORNSBY
3B—STAN HACK
SS—BUD HARRELSON
OF—BABE HERMAN
OF—CHICK HAFEY
OF—HARRY HEILMANN
 C—GABBY HARTNETT
 P—CARL HUBBELL
```

Ralph Houk would be honored to take the helm.

Hack is often forgotten when conversation turns to great third basemen. He shouldn't be, as his .301 average with the Cubs from 1932 to 1947 indicates.

I

In this instance the I's don't have it.

```
1B—FRANK ISBELL
2B—HAL IRELAN
3B—CHARLIE IRWIN
SS—ARTHUR IRWIN
OF—MONTE IRVIN
OF—DANE IORG
OF—MIKE IVIE
 C—HANK IZQUIERDO
 P—BERT INKS
```

Monte Irvin is in the Hall of Fame; the others aren't. Arthur Irwin would have trouble bringing this crew into the first division.

J

The Jacksons and Johnsons take over here.

J

           1B—JOE JUDGE
           2B—JULIAN JAVIER
           3B—WILLIE JONES
           SS—TRAVIS JACKSON
           OF—JOE JACKSON
           OF—REGGIE JACKSON
           OF—BABYDOLL JACOBSON
            C—CLIFF JOHNSON
            P—WALTER JOHNSON

A little weak behind the plate, but a splendid outfield
and pretty good pitching for manager Hughie Jennings.

K

K is for strikeout, and some members of this lineup certainly knew what it was to whiff. But most of them also
knew that not even three strikes too often necessarily
keeps you out of Cooperstown.

           1B—HARMON KILLEBREW
           2B—JOHNNY KERR
           3B—GEORGE KELL
           SS—HARVEY KUENN
           OF—WILLIE KEELER
           OF—CHUCK KLEIN
           OF—AL KALINE
            C—KING KELLY
            P—SANDY KOUFAX

Manager: shortstop Kuenn.

L

We'll go with:

1B—HENRY LARKIN
2B—NAP LAJOIE
3B—FREDDY LINDSTROM
SS—JOHNNY LOGAN
OF—FRED LEACH
OF—BUDDY LEWIS
OF—BILL LANGE
C—ERNIE LOMBARDI
P—BOB LEMON

And for being a real credit to their letter, let's not forget
Lew Llewellyn and Winston Llenas.
Manager: Al Lopez.

M

Many to pick from here. We'll go with:

1B—STAN MUSIAL
2B—JOE MORGAN
3B—EDDIE MATHEWS
SS—RABBIT MARANVILLE
OF—JOE MEDWICK
OF—MICKEY MANTLE
OF—WILLIE MAYS
C—THURMAN MUNSON
P—CHRISTY MATHEWSON

And manager Connie Mack can always call on the likes
of Johnny Mize and Heinie Manush to pinch-hit.

Mc

Not quite up to the previous team.

Mc

1B—FRANK McCORMICK
2B—GIL McDOUGALD
3B—JOHN McGRAW
SS—ED McKEAN
OF—HAL McRAE
OF—WILLIE McCOVEY
OF—BARNEY McCOSKEY
C—DEACON McGUIRE
P—JOE McGINNITY

Manager: Joe McCarthy.

N

Not necessarily negative.

1B—JOHNNY NEUN
2B—CHARLIE NEAL
3B—GRAIG NETTLES
SS—SKEETER NEWSOME
OF—BOB NIEMAN
OF—JIM NORTHRUP
OF—BILL NICHOLSON
C—RUSS NIXON
P—KID NICHOLS

Nichols, who led the Cardinals for a season and a half and finished fifth in his only full season, is also the manager.

O

A lot of left-handed hitting that could prevent too many O's on the scoreboard.

O

1B—DAVE ORR
2B—JORGE ORTA
3B—MARV OWEN
SS—IVY OLSON
OF—TIP O'NEILL
OF—LEFTY O'DOUL
OF—MEL OTT
C—JIM O'ROURKE
P—AL ORTH

Danny Ozark is the manager.

P

A better team than it appears to be at first peek.

1B—TONY PEREZ
2B—DEL PRATT
3B—RICO PETROCELLI
SS—JOHNNY PESKY
OF—VADA PINSON
OF—ANDY PAFKO
OF—DAVE PARKER
C—BABE PHELPS
P—EDDIE PLANK

Good hitters all around. Pratt (.292) and Phelps (.310) are pleasant surprises. Pilot Roger Peckinpaugh would also have plenty of reserve outfielders—Dave Philley, Jimmy Piersall, Lou Piniella and Jake Powell among them.

Q

It's hard to quarrel with these picks.

Q

                1B—JOE QUINN
                2B—FRANK QUILICI
                3B—LEE QUILLIN
                SS—JIM QUICK
                OF—JIM QUALLS
                OF—FINNERS QUINLAN
                OF—GEORGE QUELLICH
                 C—JAMIE QUIRK
                 P—DAN QUISENBERRY

About all one can say about this team, managed by Quilici, is that it is possible.

R

R is for runs and this lineup would produce more than a few.

                1B—PETE ROSE
                2B—JACKIE ROBINSON
                3B—BROOKS ROBINSON
                SS—PHIL RIZZUTO
                OF—BABE RUTH
                OF—FRANK ROBINSON
                OF—EDD ROUSH
                 C—MUDDY RUEL
                 P—CHARLIE RADBOURN

With Bill Rigney running things.

S

Perhaps the best team in this chapter.

> 1B—GEORGE SISLER
> 2B—RED SCHOENDIENST
> 3B—MIKE SCHMIDT
> SS—JOE SEWELL
> OF—TRIS SPEAKER
> OF—JAKE STENZEL
> OF—AL SIMMONS
> C—RAY SCHALK
> P—WARREN SPAHN

Only Stenzel, Schoendienst and Schmidt are not in the Hall of Fame, but the first two should be and the last will be. And who else but Casey Stengel to manage?

T

Take this team to town.

> 1B—BILL TERRY
> 2B—CESAR TOVAR
> 3B—PIE TRAYNOR
> SS—CECIL TRAVIS
> OF—SAM THOMPSON
> OF—JACK TOBIN
> OF—ROY THOMAS
> C—JOE TORRE
> P—LUIS TIANT

Manager: Birdie Tebbetts.

U

Unbelievable.

U

1B—BOB UNGLAUB
2B—AL UNSER
3B—BILLY URBANSKI
SS—TOM UPTON
OF—BOB USHER
OF—TOM UMPHLETT
OF—TED UHLAENDER
C—BOB UECKER
P—GEORGE UHLE

Uhle won 200 and lost 166 for the Indians, Tigers, Giants and Yankees between 1919 and 1936, but the rest of the lineup could be a headache for player-manager Unglaub.

V

V is for victory and this team might win a few.

1B—MICKEY VERNON
2B—EMIL VERBAN
3B—JOHNNY VERGEZ
SS—ARKY VAUGHAN
OF—BOBBY VEACH
OF—ELMER VALO
OF—JOE VOSMIK
C—ERNIE VICK
P—DAZZY VANCE

Vance is a Hall of Famer. Vernon was a legitimate star in the '50s. Vaughan (.318), Veach (.310) and Vosmik (.307) would provide considerable offense. And Vergez and Verban were solid performers for a few years.

Bill Virdon is the manager.

W

Wow!

W

1B—BILLY WILLIAMS
2B—BILLY WAMBSGANSS
3B—BILLY WERBER
SS—HONUS WAGNER
OF—HACK WILSON
OF—PAUL WANER
OF—TED WILLIAMS
C—WES WESTRUM
P—ED WALSH

Manager Earl Weaver would get the long ball from Wilson and the Williams boys; Wagner and Waner would get on base a lot; and Walsh was certainly a winner.

X

There has never been a major leaguer whose name began with an X, but the following lineup has enough x-major leaguers to qualify.

1B—JIMMIE FOXX
2B—NELLIE FOX
3B—BILLY COX
SS—JIM VIOX
OF—KEN LANDREAUX
OF—TIM HENDRYX
OF—GARRY MADDOX
C—JIM MATTOX
P—SANDY KOUFAX

Manager: Charlie Fox.

Y

Not such an unusual letter that it doesn't provide a lineup capable of winning more often than not.

1B—RUDY YORK
2B—STEVE YERKES
3B—EDDIE YOST
SS—ROBIN YOUNT
OF—ROSS YOUNGS
OF—CARL YASTRZEMSKI
OF—JOEL YOUNGBLOOD
C—STEVE YEAGER
P—CY YOUNG

Young (manager by default) and Youngs are Hall of Famers. Yaz will be. Yount, York and Yost have been bona fide stars. And the rest just fill out the lineup.

Z

Last in the alphabet—and perhaps close to that in quality as well.

1B—NORM ZAUCHIN
2B—ROLLIE ZEIDER
3B—HEINIE ZIMMERMAN
SS—DON ZIMMER
OF—RICHIE ZISK
OF—ZEKE ZARILLA
OF—GUS ZERNIAL
C—CHIEF ZIMMER
P—TOM ZACHARY

Not a single lifetime .300 hitter for manager Zimmer. Zimmerman, lifetime .295, did, however, lead the National League in hitting in 1912 with a .372 average.

LETTERS IN THE DIRT

Of course, a real all-star alphabet team would include none of the preceding, but would be made up of:

1B—JEWEL ENS
2B—FRANK EMMER
3B—ROY ELLAM
SS—SHORTY DEE
OF—WALTER KAY
OF—CHARLIE SEE
OF—TOMMIE AGEE
C—JOE AZCUE
P—JOHNNY GEE

The heavily stocked bullpen would include Joey Jay, Mark Esser and Horace Eller. For pinch-hitting there is always Mike Ivie. And when the team visits Japan, they can always sign on . . . Oh, no, don't say it!

IN THE SHADOWS

Players and their feats that have never been given proper attention. Even if you've heard of the players, you may have forgotten the accomplishments and misadventures they are cited for here.

SHOULD-BE HALL OF FAMERS

The 1984 induction of Luis Aparicio and Peewee Reese into Cooperstown raises hopes that the following will also be recognized for the stars they were:

> 1B—STUFFY McINNIS
> 2B—RED SCHOENDIENST
> 3B—STAN HACK
> SS—ARKY VAUGHAN
> OF—KEN WILLIAMS
> OF—BABYDOLL JACOBSON
> OF—JACK TOBIN
> C—ERNIE LOMBARDI
> P—HOYT WILHELM

Symptomatic of the neglect endured by the above is the fact that outfielders Williams, Jacobson and Tobin batted a combined .331 for the St. Louis Browns between 1920 and 1924. The other stories are better known, though it probably cannot be emphasized too often that Vaughan was a giant at his position. Aside from the small matter of having had a rocket for an arm, he had a lifetime batting average of .318 and a career on-base percentage of .406.

Rounding out the squad are the likes of Jim Bunning,

Phil Rizzuto, Riggs Stephenson, Pete Browning and Billy Williams.

MORE WHOLE THAN PARTS

What are the odds against a player compiling a lifetime average of .356 and never winning a batting championship? Whatever they are, take them. None of the players below was ever able to put a silver bat over the fireplace despite the career marks indicated after their names.

1B—HANK GREENBERG	.313	
2B—EDDIE COLLINS	.333	
3B—PIE TRAYNOR	.320	
SS—CECIL TRAVIS	.314	
OF—RIGGS STEPHENSON	.336	
OF—MIKE DONLIN	.334	
OF—JOE JACKSON	.356	
C—MICKEY COCHRANE	.320	
P—MORDECAI BROWN	.639 W-L Pct.	

The problem for most of these players was, of course, people named Cobb, Hornsby, Heilmann and Williams.

We've left out all the nineteenth-century players with remarkable averages simply because there were so many with even more remarkable averages.

Jackson is the twentieth-century player with the highest lifetime average *not* in the Hall of Fame, but his involvement in the Black Sox scandal explains that. How one explains the overlooking of Indians-Cubs star Stephenson is less easy.

MORE PARTS THAN A WHOLE

On the other hand, some players not only aren't in the Hall of Fame and don't have .300 lifetime averages—yet have won batting championships. The players, the years they won and their career marks:

1B—NORM CASH	.271	1961 Tigers
2B—GEORGE STIRNWEISS	.268	1945 Yankees
3B—HEINIE ZIMMERMAN	.295	1911 Cubs
SS—DICK GROAT	.286	1960 Pirates
OF—ALEX JOHNSON	.288	1970 Angels
OF—SHERRY MAGEE	.291	1910 Phillies
OF—DEBS GARMS	.293	1940 Pirates
C—JOE TORRE	.297	1971 Cardinals
P—BEN CANTWELL	.413	1933 Red Sox
	W-L Pct.	

And a special mention for Pete Runnels, who won *two* batting crowns—in 1960 and 1962—but had enough mediocre years to finish at .291.

Cantwell led the American League in won-lost percentage in 1933 with a 20-10 (.667) record, but he had only one other winning season, slipped to a 4-25 record in 1935, and ended his career with 76 wins and 108 losses.

CLOSE, BUT NO CIGAR

A close contest for a batting crown lends excitement to those last few dull games of the season when the pennant winners have been determined and there is little else at stake. The following players had the second best batting average in the season indicated—but only by the slimmest of margins.

1B—BILL TERRY	.34861 (.00028)	1931 Giants
2B—NAP LAJOIE	.38409 (.00097)	1910 Indians
3B—TONY CUCCINELLO	.30845 (.00009)	1945 White Sox
SS—ROBIN YOUNT	.33070 (.00092)	1982 Brewers
OF—TED WILLIAMS	.34275 (.00016)	1949 Red Sox
OF—JOE VOSMIK	.34839 (.00064)	1935 Indians
OF—CARL YASTRZEMSKI	.32862 (.00037)	1970 Red Sox
C—CHIEF MEYERS	.33248 (.00152)	1911 Giants
P—GAYLORD PERRY	1.9155 ERA (0.0049)	1972 Indians

The Indians seem particularly jinxed, but only five teams have players on this team.

Terry lost out to Chick Hafey (.34889), with Jim Bottomley third (.34817). Lajoie is still officially second to Ty Cobb (.38506) even though recent research has shown that Cobb's average was actually .38188 and Lajoie's .38344. (The infinitely wise Bowie Kuhn decided, however, that tradition has more weight than fact.) Cuccinello, in the closest race ever, was edged by Snuffy Stirnweiss (.30854). Yount was second to Willie Wilson (.33162). Williams was beaten by George Kell (.34291); Vosmik by Buddy Myer (.34903); and Yastrzemski by Alex Johnson (.32899). Meyers actually finished third, behind both Honus Wagner (.334) and Doc Miller (.32276). Perry's ERA was slightly higher than Luis Tiant's (1.9106).

WHAT DOES A GUY HAVE TO DO?

Over the past ten years, a period which has seen both Rod Carew and George Brett flirt with .400, the average seasonal batting champion has had to hit .345. Imagine, then, the chagrin of these players, who did *not* lead their leagues.

1B—LOU GEHRIG	.379	1930 Yankees
2B—NAP LAJOIE	.384	1910 Indians
3B—FRED LINDSTROM	.379	1930 Giants
SS—HONUS WAGNER	.363	1905 Pirates
OF—JOE JACKSON	.408	1911 Indians
OF—TY COBB	.401	1922 Tigers
OF—BABE RUTH	.393	1923 Yankees
C—BABE PHELPS	.367	1936 Dodgers
P—RALPH TERRY	.842	1961 Yankees
	W-L Pct.	

Jackson not only finished behind Cobb's .420 in 1911, but was a runner-up to the same Cobb in 1912 when the Tiger outfielder outhit him, .410 to .395.

The others: Gehrig bowed to Al Simmons's .381, Lajoie to Cobb's .385, Lindstrom to Bill Terry's .401, Wagner to Cy Seymour's .377, Cobb to George Sisler's .420, Ruth to Harry Heilmann's .403 and Phelps to Paul Waner's .373.

Terry's 16-3 record was only second best to fellow Yankee Whitey Ford's 25-4 (.862).

A tie for manager, since both Frank Chance of the 1909 Cubs and Leo Durocher of the 1942 Dodgers piloted teams that won 104 games and still finished in second place. Chance's Cubs wound up 6½ games behind Pittsburgh and Durocher's Dodgers finished two games behind St. Louis.

WHAT DOES A GUY REALLY HAVE TO DO?

They must have been better hitters in the old days because none of the following led the league in the year indicated—despite having batted over .400!

1B—DAN BROUTHERS	.419	1887 Detroit
2B—YANK ROBINSON	.426	1887 St. Louis (AA)
3B—DENNY LYONS	.469	1887 Philadelphia (AA)
SS—PAUL RADFORD	.404	1887 New York (AA)
OF—BOB CARUTHERS	.459	1887 St. Louis (AA)
OF—PETE BROWNING	.471	1887 Louisville (AA)
OF—TUCK TURNER	.423	1894 Phillies
C—GEORGE BAKER	.471	1884 St. Louis (UA)
P—CHARLIE BUFFINTON	47 Wins	1884 Braves

You're probably thinking that 1887 was a tough year for pitchers, but the catch is that in that year—and that year only—bases on balls were counted as hits, a rule which wildly inflated batting averages. (Also, it took four strikes to strike out in 1887, and that didn't hurt averages either.) Six other players—in addition to those named above and the two batting champions, Cap Anson (.421 in the National League) and Tip O'Neill (.492 in the American Association)—also recorded averages over .400 that year.

Real sympathy must be reserved for Turner and Baker. The former lost the NL batting crown to Hugh Duffy, who hit .438 under modern rules (although 1894 was the year the mound was moved from 50 feet to 60 feet, six inches away from the batter and pitchers had some difficulty adjusting). And the latter finished 51 points higher than the league leader, but failed to come to bat enough times. Had modern rules been in effect, and he would have been given enough at bats to qualify, and he would have won.

Buffinton's 47 victories were far behind Charlie Radbourn's league-leading total of 60.

REMARKABLE RUNNERS-UP

Sometimes an exceptional season just isn't enough because someone else bats higher, steals more bases, etc. The following players achieved remarkable totals, but couldn't do better than second place.

1B—LOU GEHRIG	.765 Slugging Average	1927 Yankees
2B—BILLY HERMAN	57 Doubles	1936 Cubs
3B—BILL BRADLEY	22 Triples	1903 Indians
SS—EDDIE JOOST	149 Walks	1949 Athletics
OF—OMAR MORENO	96 Stolen Bases	1980 Pirates
OF—MICKEY MANTLE	54 Home runs	1961 Yankees
OF—CHUCK KLEIN	250 Hits; 170 RBIs	1930 Phillies
C—ROY CAMPANELLA	41 Home runs	1953 Dodgers
P—CHRISTY MATHEWSON	33 Wins	1904 Giants

Gehrig's slugging average was the fourth highest ever, but Babe Ruth's .772 the same year was the third highest. Herman's 57 doubles have been beaten only 10 times, but Joe Medwick set the NL record that year with 64. Bradley's 22 triples would have been good enough to lead the league all but nine years in the twentieth century, but Sam Crawford hit 25 the same year. Joost's 149 walks was the sixth highest total in this century, but Ted Williams's 162 was second highest. Moreno's 96 stolen bases have only been matched or beaten six times since 1900, but that same year Ron LeFlore stole 97. Only ten players have hit as many as 54 home runs in a single season, but Mantle had the misfortune to do it the same year Roger Maris hit his record 61. Klein took two second spots: His hits, the seventh highest total ever, weren't enough to catch Bill Terry's NL record 254, and his RBI total, matched or beaten only nine times, lost out to Hack Wilson's record 190. Campanella, the only one ever to hit 40 or more homers as a catcher in a season, actually finished third behind both Eddie Mathews' 47 and Duke Snider's 42. Mathewson's 33 wins have been matched or beaten only nine times in this century, but teammate Joe McGinnity won 35 that year. (The following year Matty won 30 and lost out again to the Iron Man, who had 31.)

SO MANY, SO FEW

Some of the most renowned sluggers in the game never quite managed to hit enough homers in one season to lead the league. The following is a lineup of players who compiled 250 or more homers during their careers, but who always finished behind the Kiners and the Killebrews.

1B—NORM CASH	377	
2B—JOE GORDON	253	
3B—RON SANTO	342	
SS—RICO PETROCELLI	210	
OF—STAN MUSIAL	475	
OF—AL KALINE	399	
OF—BILLY WILLIAMS	426	
C—YOGI BERRA	358	
P—EDDIE PLANK	305 Wins	

The only shortstop ever to hit more than 250 homers was Ernie Banks and he led the league twice. Petrocelli's 210 is the highest total for a shortstop who did not lead the league.

Plank had some great years, but there always seemed to be someone who won more than he did.

SO FEW, SO MANY

Some unexpected names have sometimes appeared at the top of the list in the home run category for a season. For example:

1B—NICK ETTEN	22	1944 Yankees
2B—BOBBY GRICH	22	1981 Angels
3B—BILL MELTON	33	1971 White Sox
SS—VERN STEPHENS	24	1945 Browns
OF—BILL NICHOLSON	29	1943 Cubs
	33	1944 Cubs
OF—BOB MEUSEL	33	1925 Yankees
OF—TOMMY HOLMES	28	1945 Braves
C—BUCK EWING	10	1883 Giants
P—RED BARRETT	23 Wins	1945 Braves-Cardinals

Etten's career homer total was 89, Holmes's 88, and their titles clearly owed a great deal to the scarcity of the Greenbergs and Kiners during the war. The same could be argued for Stephens and Nicholson, although their career totals of 247 and 235, respectively, hardly indicate banjo hitters, either. Meusel (156) was barely into the lively ball era and Grich (202) tied with three other players in the strike-shortened season leaving Melton (160) as perhaps the most curious league leader since the 1920s. An honorable mention should also go to Jack Fournier (136), who led the NL in 1924 with 27 homers.

Johnny Bench is the only catcher of modern times to have led a league in round-trippers, and there is nothing odd about that. And Ewing is the only other catcher to lead a league in homers in any era.

Barrett had only 69 lifetime victories, the lowest total for any pitcher to lead the league in wins for a season. (He also had 69 losses.)

A SEASON DOES NOT A CAREER MAKE

Forty home runs in a season is quite an accomplishment. But to hit forty once and not reach 300 for an entire career is a genuine oddity. These are the players who managed it, along with their big years and their career totals.

1B—TED KLUSZEWSKI	49	1954 Reds	279
	47	1955 Reds	
2B—DAVE JOHNSON	43	1973 Braves	136
3B—DARRELL EVANS	41	1973 Braves	278
SS—RICO PETROCELLI	40	1969 Red Sox	210
OF—CY WILLIAMS	41	1923 Phillies	251
OF—WALLY POST	40	1955 Reds	210
OF—GUS ZERNIAL	42	1953 Athletics	237
C—ROY CAMPANELLA	41	1953 Dodgers	242
P—JACK CHESBRO	41 W	1904 Yankees	199 W

Campanella and Petrocelli had injury-plagued careers or they might have reached the magic 300. Evans is still active and has a shot at it. And the oddity of oddities here is Johnson, who was not a power hitter at all, except for that one year in the Atlanta launching pad when four members of the Braves had over 40 home runs.

Chesbro is the only pitcher to record over 40 victories in a single season and not get even 200 in his entire career.

THE GOOD AND
THE BAD—CAREER

Sometimes you have to be good enough to stick around long enough to be bad. If you can't figure that out, simply guess the negative career marks by these stars of the past.

     1B—JIMMIE FOXX
     2B—EDDIE COLLINS
     3B—BROOKS ROBINSON
     SS—HONUS WAGNER
     OF—TY COBB
     OF—HANK AARON
     OF—LOU BROCK
      C—ERNIE LOMBARDI
     P—WARREN SPAHN

Nobody ever led the AL more often in strikeouts than Foxx, who did it seven times. Collins stuck around long enough to make the most errors (435) by a second baseman, Wagner the same for shortstops (676). Robinson has the AL record for hitting into double plays (297). Cobb's 271 errors represent the career mark for outfielders. Aaron hit into more double plays than anybody else in the game's history (328). No NL outfielder has led the league more often in errors than Brock, who did it seven times. Lombardi led the NL in hitting into double plays a record four times. The most successful southpaw of all time, Spahn also gave up the most home runs by a NL pitcher (434).

THE GOOD AND
THE BAD—SEASON

These players all led their leagues in one category too many.

1B—DAVE KINGMAN	1982 Mets
2B—JAKE WOOD	1961 Tigers
3B—PETE ROSE	1975 Reds
SS—ZOILO VERSALLES	1965 Twins
OF—ROY JOHNSON	1929 Tigers
OF—BOBBY BONDS	1969 Giants
OF—GORMAN THOMAS	1979 Brewers
C—ERNIE LOMBARDI	1938 and 1942 Reds
P—NOLAN RYAN	1972–74 and
	1976–78 Angels

Kingman led in homers (37) and in compiling the worst batting average (.204). Wood topped all American Leaguers in triples (14) and in strikeouts (141). While he was showing the way in doubles (47) and in runs scored (112), Rose was also establishing the all-time NL mark for fewest steals (0) vis-a-vis games played. Versalles was elected the Most Valuable Player in the American League—but not for setting the all-time record for strikeouts by a shortstop (122). Johnson was first in plate appearances (640) and in doubles (45), but also in most outfield errors (31) for a league record. Bonds scored the most runs (120), but only when he hadn't walked back to the bench on his way to the most strikeouts (187). Thomas was the stereotypical slugger in leading in both homers (45) and strikeouts (175). Lombardi won two batting titles while leading National League catchers in passed balls. In six different seasons for California, Ryan led the American League in both strikeouts and walks.

GUESS AGAIN

The game here is to figure out what these players, their reputations notwithstanding, have *not* accomplished in their special talent areas.

1B—RUSTY STAUB
2B—JOHNNY EVERS
3B—FRANK BAKER
SS—LUIS APARICIO
OF—HANK AARON
OF—AL KALINE
OF—LOU BROCK
C—BILL DICKEY
P—JOHNNY VANDER MEER

Despite having collected at least 500 hits for four different teams (Astros, Expos, Mets, Tigers), Staub has never had a 200-hit season. Evers, fabled in poetry as part of that "Trio of bear cubs . . . Making a Giant hit into a double,/ Tinker to Evers to Chance," never turned more than 58 double plays in a season in which he played with Tinker and Chance. You should have known that "Home Run" Baker never hit more than 12 round-trippers in a season and had only 93 in his 13-year career. Brilliant leadoff man that he was, Aparicio never scored 100 runs in a season. Homer king Aaron never hit 50 in a season. Kaline never even reached 30. Brock never stole home while he was with the Cardinals; his only theft of the plate occurred in 1964 when he was with the Cubs and even that was part of a double steal with the catcher throwing down to second to get Billy Williams. Offensive threat that he was, Dickey never led the league in a single offensive category; nor did he ever lead in a defensive category except games played. Double no-hitters or not, Vander Meer never won 20 games in a season and concluded his career two games under .500 (119-121).

UNEXPECTED POWER SOURCES

Sometimes it's because of a new stance, sometimes because of a new coach, sometimes because of a new home park, and sometimes because of a new diet, but every once in a while a player will find himself in the unfamiliar territory of home run leaders. (The number in parentheses is the highest number of homers hit by the player in a year other than that indicated.)

1B—ED MORGAN	26 (11)	1930 Indians
2B—DAVE JOHNSON	43 (18)	1973 Braves
3B—CLETE BOYER	26 (18)	1967 Braves
SS—ROY SMALLEY, SR.	21 (8)	1950 Cubs
OF—TOMMY HOLMES	28 (13)	1945 Braves
OF—TOMMY HARPER	31 (18)	1970 Brewers
OF—WILLARD MARSHALL	36 (17)	1947 Giants
C—WALKER COOPER	35 (20)	1947 Giants
P—MONTE WEAVER	22 Wins (12)	1932 Senators

As we have noted elsewhere, Holmes's 28 homers were enough to lead the league. Marshall and Cooper clearly de-

rived their long-ball reputations from their contributions
to the explosive 1947 Polo Grounds team, which set the
National League mark for round-trippers (221), a record
subsequently tied by the 1956 Reds. Johnson and Boyer obviously benefited from the pitchers' nightmare that is Atlanta Stadium, a park that has come to be called "The
Launching Pad."

Weaver never won more than 12 games in a nine-year
career, except for his one big season.

ALWAYS A BRIDESMAID

Only 28 players have driven in 1425 or more runs in their
careers. And the eight position players on this team did so
without leading the league even once.

1B—TONY PEREZ	1590
2B—CHARLIE GEHRINGER	1427
3B—EDDIE MATHEWS	1453
SS—JOE CRONIN	1423
OF—AL KALINE	1583
OF—TRIS SPEAKER	1562
OF—WILLIE MAYS	1903
C—YOGI BERRA	1430
P—WILBUR COOPER	2.89 ERA

Mays is the standout. His RBI total is the seventh highest in history and few trivia experts would ever guess that
he always finished below the top.

Cooper has the lowest ERA of all hurlers with 3000 or
more innings pitched never to have led the league in that
category.

OUTSIDE THE MAGIC CIRCLE

A lot of hits produces a high batting average—but not always high enough. The following lineup consists of the
players with the most career hits who failed to maintain a
lifetime batting average over .300.

1B—CARL YASTRZEMSKI	3419	.285
2B—NELLIE FOX	2663	.288
3B—BROOKS ROBINSON	2848	.267
SS—GEORGE DAVIS	2683	.296
OF—LOU BROCK	3023	.293
OF—FRANK ROBINSON	2943	.294
OF—AL KALINE	3007	.297
C—YOGI BERRA	2150	.285
P—BOBO NEWSOM	211 Wins	.487

Newsom lost 222 games. The only other pitcher to win more than 200 and yet finish with a W-L Percentage below .500 is Jake Powell (247-254, .493).

NOT ENOUGH AT ANY ONE TIME

This team includes those players with the most career hits who never won a batting crown.

1B—JAKE BECKLEY	2930
2B—EDDIE COLLINS	3309
3B—BROOKS ROBINSON	2848
SS—GEORGE DAVIS	2683
OF—LOU BROCK	3023
OF—SAM RICE	2987
OF—SAM CRAWFORD	2964
C—YOGI BERRA	2150
P—EARLY WYNN	300 Wins

Collins and Brock are the only two members of the 15-member 3000-hit club without a batting crown to their credit.

And Wynn is the only pitcher in the 16-member 300-victory club who never led the league in Won-Lost Percentage.

LOW LEADERS

Occasionally events conspire to allow someone to lead the league in a major category with a figure that in other years would relegate him to a position low on the list. The following are record lows for league leaders.

1B—FRED MERKLE	71 RBIs	1918 Cubs
2B—PEDRO GARCIA	32 Doubles	1973 Brewers
3B—SAL BANDO	32 Doubles	1973 Athletics
SS—HONUS WAGNER	237 Total Bases	1906 Pirates
OF—CARL YASTRZEMSKI	.301 Average	1968 Red Sox
OF—DEL UNSER	8 Triples	1969 Senators
OF—HACK WILSON	21 Home runs, 69 Walks	1926 Cubs
C—FRANKIE PYTLAK	5 Hit by Pitch	1934 Indians
P—EARLY WYNN	3.20 ERA	1950 Indians

Merkle's league-leading total of RBIs came in the war-shortened 1918 season.

Wilson's 21 homers in 1926 is the lowest league-leading total since 1921 when the home run achieved prominence. Before that year anything was possible. For example, Tommy Leach led the National League with 6 in 1902, the absolute lowest—unless you want to go back to Orator Shaffer's 3 home runs in 1877.

Only four pitchers besides Wynn had ERAs over 3.00 that were the lowest in the league: Rosy Ryan, 3.00, 1922 Giants; Bill Walker, 3.08, 1929 Giants; Lefty Grove, 3.07, 1938 Red Sox; and Warren Spahn, 3.01, 1961 Braves.

NEAR MISSES

Great careers are measured by milestones—2000 hits, 3000 hits, 400 home runs, 500 home runs. The players in this lineup didn't quite make it to the next plateau.

1B—LOU GEHRIG	493 Home runs and 1990 RBIs
2B—ROGERS HORNSBY	2930 Hits
3B—EDDIE MATHEWS	1453 RBIs
SS—MAURY WILLS	586 Stolen Bases
OF—AL KALINE	399 Home runs and 498 Doubles
OF—SAM RICE	2987 Hits
OF—SAM CRAWFORD	2964 Hits
C—BILL DICKEY	1969 Hits
P—MILT PAPPAS	110 Wins (AL), 99 Wins (NL)

Most of these figures speak for themselves, but it is worth pointing out that Rice has the most career hits below the 3000-hit club; Crawford is next; Hornsby is tied (with Jake Beckley) for the fifth highest total.

Only two pitchers have won 100 or more games in both the National and the American Leagues—Cy Young and Jim Bunning. Pappas came as close as you can get. And, incidentally, he is the only pitcher who has won 200 or more in his career without ever winning 20 in a season.

MOMENTS IN THE SUN

Most winning teams have had journeymen or utilitymen come forward to contribute a season beyond all expectations. The following is a lineup of such players on division winners or pennant winners:

1B—RICH REESE	1969 Twins
2B—DENNY DOYLE	1975 Red Sox
3B—GENE FREESE	1961 Reds
SS—DICK SCHOFIELD	1960 Pirates
OF—BRANT ALYEA	1970 Twins
OF—LOU JOHNSON	1966 Dodgers
OF—ART SHAMSKY	1969 Mets
C—BRUCE EDWARDS	1947 Dodgers
P—NELSON POTTER	1944 Browns

Reese, a .253 career batter, hit 16 homers, had 69 RBIs and a .322 mark. Doyle hit .310 and was the infield glue after a mid-season move from California; his career mark was .250. Freese, who switched uniforms eight times in his career, hit 26 homers, drove in 87 runs and batted .277. Schofield hit better than .400 when called on to replace the injured Dick Groat in September; he batted .227 for nine teams. Alyea, despite a lifetime average of .247, had 16 homers, batted in 61 runs and hit .291 although starting only 75 games. Johnson, a .256 hitter for seven teams, batted .272 with 17 homers and 73 RBIs. Shamsky belied his .253 career mark by hitting 14 homers and compiling a .300 average. Edwards (.256 lifetime) narrowly missed being National League MVP with .296 and 80 runs batted in. Potter, who had a lifetime record of 92-97, won 19 and lost 7 for the miraculous Brownies. Honorable mention to Rocky Nelson, a .249 lifetime hitter, who batted .300 for the 1960 Pirates and who played pivotal defense at first behind Dick Stuart.

BEST SUPPORTING ACTORS

They weren't the center of the action, but they helped make the action possible.

BEST SUPPORTING ACTORS

1B—MONTE IRVIN	1951 Giants
2B—JOHNNY EVERS	1908 Cubs
3B—KEN KELTNER	1941 Indians
SS—FRED STANLEY	1982 Athletics
OF—WALTON CRUISE	1920 Braves
OF—JOE CHRISTOPHER	1964 Mets
OF—STEVE BRYE	1976 Twins
C—CURT BLEFARY	1968 Orioles
P—LEW BURDETTE	1959 Braves

Irvin's ability to play left field helped set in motion the dramatic lineup changes enacted by Leo Durocher in May 1951 that eventually gained the Giants a pennant; while Irvin and rookie Willie Mays went to the outfield, Whitey Lockman and Bobby Thomson came in to handle the infield corners. Evers was the second baseman who called attention to Fred Merkle's boner. Keltner robbed Joe DiMaggio of two hits on the evening Cleveland stopped the Yankee Clipper's record hitting streak. Stanley got himself picked off second base so trailing runner Rickey Henderson would have a clear field for the stolen base that would give him the major league record; Henderson made it on the next pitch. Cruise's triple led to the run that was to tie Boston and Brooklyn for 26 innings. Christopher's three-run homer produced the tying runs for the Mets-Giants game that was to last 23 innings (or 7 hours and 23 minutes). Brye's suspicious slowness after a looper hit by George Brett on the last day of the season drew criticism that he preferred the white third baseman to win the AL batting title rather than the black Hal McRae; as it turned out, Brett beat out his Kansas City teammate by one point. Blefary, normally an outfielder, was behind the plate when Tom Phoebus hurled a no-hitter. Harvey Haddix's memorable extra-inning perfect game would never have been possible without the zeroes put up on the board by his mound opponent, Burdette.

THE REST OF THE STORY

Forgotten aspects to memorable plays, games and events.

1B—FRED MERKLE	1908 Giants
2B—RENNIE STENNETT	1975 Pirates
3B—MIKE SCHMIDT	1976 Phillies
SS—PEEWEE REESE	1950 Dodgers
OF—BOBBY ROTH	1915 Indians
OF—DUKE SNIDER	1947 Dodgers
OF—HANK AARON	1974 Braves
C—MICKEY O'NEILL	1926 Dodgers
P—JACK CHESBRO	1904 Yankees

Merkle's infamous "boner" came in his very first full game as a starter for the Giants. When Stenett tied the big league record for most hits (7) in a nine-inning game on September 15, 1975, he also contributed to the most lopsided shutout (22-0) in baseball history. Schmidt's four homers on April 17, 1976, helped the Phillies overcome two 11-run deficits to the Cubs—the biggest comebacks for a team in a single game in major league annals. Although third base coach Milton Stock was given goat horns for getting Cal Abrams thrown out at home on the last day of the 1950 season, he probably would have created another mess by holding up Abrams since Reese had already motored around second and was halfway to third while Richie Ashburn's throw was still in flight. Roth's exchange for Joe Jackson will always be remembered as one of Cleveland's worst trades, but it should also be remembered that Roth led the league that year in homers. On the same day that Jackie Robinson broke baseball's color ban (April 15, 1947), Snider also made his debut with a pinch-single. On the same night that Aaron passed Babe Ruth for career homers (April 8, 1974), he also, in another at bat, set the National League record for most runs scored in a career. Third-string catcher O'Neill volunteered to coach at third base for an inning of a game for the Dodgers—the inning in which Babe Herman "doubled into a double play." Many years were to elapse before he was asked to coach again.

The year in which Chesbro set the modern record for most wins (41) in a season ended when the Yankee hurler wild-pitched across the pennant-deciding run in a game with Boston.

THE NOT-SO-GREAT SUCCESSORS

Hall of Famers are hard acts to follow, yet the following players were once considered ready to do just that. As you can see, some had a modicum of success, but most of them have been as forgettable as their predecessors were memorable.

1B—BABE DAHLGREN	1939 Yankees	Gehrig
2B—JIMMY BLOODWORTH	1942 Tigers	Gehringer
3B—TOMMY THEVENOW	1935 Pirates	Traynor
SS—CHUCK WARD	1917 Pirates	Wagner
OF—GEORGE SELKIRK	1935 Yankees	Ruth
OF—GARRY MADDOX	1972 Giants	Mays
OF—ROWLAND OFFICE	1974 Braves	Aaron
C—RAY LAMANNO	1942 Reds	Lombardi
P—HOD LISENBEE	1927 Senators	Johnson

The best in the batch is undoubtedly Maddox, but even he developed into one of the finest outfielders in the NL only after he had been traded to the Phillies.

For a manager we'll take Bill Rigney as the successor to Leo Durocher on the Giants. In four full seasons and part of a fifth, Rigney's best efforts were third place (twice).

THE NOT-SO-GREAT PREDECESSORS

And while we're at it, here are the players who held down the positions before the same eight future Hall of Famers and Lombardi came along.

1B—WALLY PIPP	1925 Yankees	Gehrig
2B—FRANK O'ROURKE	1925 Tigers	Gehringer
3B—CLYDE BARNHART	1921 Pirates	Traynor
SS—BONES ELY	1901 Pirates	Wagner
OF—SAMMY VICK	1919 Yankees	Ruth
OF—BOBBY THOMSON	1951 Giants	Mays
OF—BOBBY THOMSON	1954 Braves	Aaron
C—CLYDE SUKEFORTH	1931 Reds	Lombardi
P—FRANK KITSON	1906 Senators	Johnson

Purists might have an argument about Thomson being the lineup predecessor to Mays, since he was actually shifted to third base to make room for Willie, with Hank Thompson, the previous third baseman, consigned to the bench. Nevertheless, it remains a curiosity that the man responsible for the "shot heard 'round the world" had to get out of the way of two Hall of Famers.

Durocher's predecessor as Giants manager was Mel Ott, who from 1942 to 1948 never got his team closer than 13 games behind the leader.

IT DOESN'T RUN IN THE FAMILY

If you can't name the following players' more famous brothers, better not set yourself up as an expert on the Hall of Fame.

1B—TOMMIE AARON
2B—JIM DELAHANTY
3B—BUTTS WAGNER
SS—SAM WRIGHT
OF—JOSH CLARKE
OF—JOHN O'ROURKE
OF—VINCE DiMAGGIO
C—LUKE SEWELL
P—HENRY MATHEWSON

Aaron was a .229 hitter with the Braves. Delahanty hit .283 as a utility player. Wagner lasted only one season. Wright hung on for three seasons but played in only 12 games. Clarke had an odd career, playing in 223 games spread over five seasons in three different decades (1898, 1905, 1908–09 and 1911). O'Rourke batted .295 in his three years. DiMaggio, probably the most noted of the bunch, could hit the long ball (125 homers), but he was also one of the all-time strikeout kings (837 whiffs—more than twice as many as Joe and over 300 more than Dom). Sewell was a fixture in the AL for two decades, but had his best moments as the manager of the St. Louis Browns. In three games for the Giants in 1906 and 1907, Mathewson won none and lost one.

The Waners don't qualify for this team because they both made the mistake of getting into the Hall of Fame.

CADDIES

Caddies, a sub-class of utilitymen, are players kept around to back up a particular player with little prospect that the regular will miss more than a few innings a year. If you see a caddy on the field before the eighth inning of a 16-0 game, it probably means the rest of the bench has been blown away by a tornado.

1B—WAYNE BELARDI	Dodgers
2B—JIM BRIDEWESER	Several Teams
3B—SAMMY ESPOSITO	White Sox
SS—FRANK BAKER	Yankees and Orioles
OF—SAMMY BYRD	Yankees
OF—SAM MEJIAS	Reds
OF—JACK REED	Yankees
C—CHARLIE SILVERA	Yankees
P—MONTE KENNEDY	Giants

The most noted of these was undoubtedly Byrd, known throughout his career as "Babe Ruth's legs." Belardi, the very occasional backup for Gil Hodges at Ebbets Field, had a shot at a regular job with Detroit later in his career but made nothing of it. Kennedy came up to the Giants as a very promising pitcher, had a couple of modest years, then lingered as the epitome of the mopup man. The others in the lineup were never expected to be more than utility-men.

The player most identified with a caddying role, Gene Stephens of the Red Sox, was in fact much more than that. Although always available to back up Ted Williams, Stephens was a much-used pinch-hitter and saw service in more than 100 games in four different seasons. He is also known for banging out a record three hits in a single inning.

Honorable mention here to Matt Alexander, the speed-ster practically used as Willie Stargell's private pinch-runner.

OVERLOOKED FEATS

You know what these players are famous for. Or, do you?

1B—WILLIE McCOVEY	1969 Giants
2B—ROD CAREW	1969 Twins
3B—BOBBY THOMSON	1951 Giants
SS—CAL RIPKEN	1983 Orioles
OF—TED WILLIAMS	1941 Red Sox
OF—DUKE SNIDER	1949 and 1950 Dodgers
OF—LOU BROCK	1962 Cubs
C—GABBY STREET	1931 Cardinals
P—CY YOUNG	1904 Red Sox

Aside from hitting homers, McCovey holds the record for most intentional walks in a season (45). On the way to the first of seven batting titles, Carew also set a record for stealing home seven times in a season. On the last day of the regular season Thomson set the stage for his playoff dramatics by hitting a homer that got the Giants into their postseason duel with Brooklyn. In his MVP year Ripken set a record by playing in every inning of every game in the regular season, the divisional championship games and the World Series. While Joe DiMaggio was batting .406 during his 56-game hitting streak, Williams was bat-ting .412 over the same span! The slugger Snider singled in the tenth inning of the last game in 1949 to give the

Dodgers the flag; in the ninth inning of the last game one year later he hit another single that might have driven in the run to force a playoff against Philadelphia, but that led instead to Cal Abrams being thrown out at home. Brock used power, not speed, to join Joe Adcock and (later) Hank Aaron as the only players to hit balls into the Polo Grounds bleachers. Nineteen years after retiring, defensive specialist Street went behind the plate for a game and threw out a would-be base thief. All-time winner Young also pitched a record 24 consecutive hitless innings for Boston.

NOT IN THE BIGS

Some remarkable feats—never matched in the majors—have taken place in the minor leagues.

1B—JOE BAUMAN	1954 Roswell, Longhorn League
2B—BILL ALEXANDER	June 15, 1902 Corsicana, Texas League
3B—AL ROSEN	July 26–27, 1948 Kansas City, American Association
SS—BUZZY WARES	1910 Oakland, Pacific Coast League
OF—WALTER MALMQUIST	1913 York, Nebraska State League
OF—FRENCHY BORDAGARAY	July 9–12, 1940 Kansas City, American Association
OF—JOE WILHOIT	1920 Wichita, Western League
C—NIG CLARKE	June 15, 1902 Corsicana, Texas League
P—RON NECCIAI	May 13, 1952 Bristol, Appalachian League

Bauman hit 72 home runs, the highest season total in any professional league. (His stats for the year were a .400 batting average, 224 RBIs, and a .916 slugging average in 138 games.) Alexander went 8-for-8 in a game against

Texarkana. Rosen hit five consecutive home runs. Wares had 72 sacrifices. Walter Malmquist's .477 batting average is the highest ever in a professional league; Bordagaray hit safely in 13 consecutive turns at bat. Wilhoit had a 69-game hitting streak. Clarke, in the same game in which Alexander went 8-for-8, hit 8 home runs in 8 at bats, and drove in 16 runs. (The final score was 51-3.) Necciai struck out 27 batters in a 9-inning no-hitter.

Honorable mention to Buzz Arlett, who hit four home runs in one game on two separate occasions in 1932 for the International League Baltimore Orioles; Joe Cantley, who hit three grand-slams in one game for the Opelika franchise of the Georgia-Alabama League in 1914; Bob Crues, whose 254 RBIs (Amarillo, West Texas-New Mexico League, 1948) is the most ever in a professional season; Gene Rye, who hit three homers in one inning for Waco of the Texas League; Bob Riesener, who had 20 wins and no losses for Alexandria of the Evangeline League in 1957; and Necciai's teammate, Bill Bell, who pitched three no-hitters in 1952, two of them back-to-back.

ODDS AND ODDS

A mixed bag of the dimly remembered and the better forgotten.

1B—JACK HARSHMAN	Career
2B—MEL ROACH	Career
3B—HAL BEVAN	Career
SS—BERNIE JAMES	Career
OF—BOB COULSON	1911 Dodgers
OF—RICO CARTY	1970 Braves
OF—CLAUDELL WASHINGTON	Career
C—GROVER HARTLEY	1928 Indians
P—LARRY JASTER	1966 Cardinals

With 21 home runs in his 76 hits, Harshman has the highest ratio of homers to safeties for any player with 400 at bats. Roach defied mathematical probability by playing eight seasons in the 1950s without once batting in the

.200s (he was always above or below). In the same decade Bevan played for four franchises and hit a composite .292—but appeared in only 15 games. James had three big league seasons—1929 when he batted .307 right-handed, 1930 when he batted .182 left-handed and 1933 when he batted .224 as a switch-hitter. Coulson doubled off Cy Young, who watched the ball land, walked off the field and called it a career. Carty's .366 has been the highest National League batting average since 1948. Along with Johnny Mize and Dick Stuart, Washington is the only player to have hit three homers in a game in both leagues. Along with pitchers Joe Heving (1935 White Sox) and Tom Qualters (1954 Phillies), Hartley is the only uninjured or unsuspended player to be on a team an entire year without appearing in a single game. Jaster shut out one team (Los Angeles) five times in a season, equaling the mark held by Tom Hughes in 1905 and Grover Cleveland Alexander in 1916.

WHAT'S IN A NAME? II

Some more fun.

THE BEST NAMES

Baseball seems to have had more than its share of ridiculous names. Herewith some of the most memorable:

```
1B—PEEK-A-BOO VEACH
2B—CREEPY CRESPI
3B—COCO LABOY
SS—YATS WUESTLING
OF—BEVO LE BOURVEAU
OF—BINGO BINKS
OF—GAVVY CRAVATH
 C—YAM YARYAN
 P—HEINIE MEINE
```

Honorable mention to infielders Putsy Caballero and Rivington Bisland; catchers Pickles Dilhoeffer and Clyde Kluttz; and pitchers Orval Overall, Boots Poffenberger, Sig Jakucki, Cannonball Titcomb, Emil Bildilli, Garland Buckeye, Dooley Womack and the ever lyrical Van Lingle Mungo.

WHO???

If Alfred Pesano were to choose an all-star team, he could do far worse than:

WHO???

1B—HAROLD TROYAVESKY
2B—CASIMIR KWIETNIEWSKI
3B—ANDREW NORDSTROM
SS—JOHN PAVESKOVICH
OF—MAXIMILLIAN CARNARIUS
OF—LEOPOLD HOERNSCHMEYER
OF—ALOYSIUS SZYMANSKI
C—CORNELIUS McGILLICUDDY
P—SANFORD BRAUN

Pesano, better known as Billy Martin, would have in fact selected a team of Hal Trosky (1B), Cass Michaels (2B), Andy Carey (3B), Johnny Pesky (SS), Max Carey (OF), Lee Magee (OF), Al Simmons (OF), Connie Mack (C) and Sandy Koufax (P).

THE CALENDAR

For those who wish the baseball season would last all year.

1B—LUKE EASTER
2B—BOBBY VALENTINE
3B—PINKY MAY
SS—HENRY ESTERDAY
OF—JOHNNY WEEKLY
OF—BILLY SUNDAY
OF—CHAMP SUMMERS
C—STEVE CHRISTMAS
P—SASSAFRAS WINTER

Backup pitchers include Jack Spring, Bill Faul and Skipper Friday. Bug Holliday plays when one of the starting outfielders takes a day off.

COLORS

The most colorful team in this book is unquestionably:

COLORS

                1B—LU BLUE
                2B—FRANK WHITE
                3B—BOBBY BROWN
                SS—BOBBY WINE
                OF—PETE GRAY
                OF—PETE ROSE
                OF—JIM LEMON
                  C—GENE GREEN
                  P—JIMMY LAVENDER

With Joe Black in the bullpen and Darryl Motley on the bench. And honorable mention to the St. Louis Browns and Cincinnati Reds.

DIRECTIONS

No matter which way you turn, this lineup has you covered.

                1B—LOU NORTH
                2B—BILL WEST
                3B—HARRY EAST
                SS—AL WEST
                OF—SAMMY WEST
                OF—BILLY NORTH
                OF—MAX WEST
                  C—DICK WEST
                  P—JAMIE EASTERLY

And Billy Southworth to manage.

THE WOODS

You could get lost in the middle of this team.

THE WOODS

    1B—ESTEL CRABTREE
    2B—JAKE WOOD
    3B—GRAIG NETTLES
    SS—ED HOLLY
    OF—HOWIE MOSS
    OF—BOB HAZLE
    OF—KEN ASH
     C—HOWARD MAPLE
     P—MIKE PALM

In the bullpen Walt Linden is available to warm up the rest of the staff—Red Branch, Lefty Grove, Jim Stump and Fred Glade.

NATURAL FORMATIONS

And on the eighth day there was created this team:

    1B—LESTER ROCK
    2B—ELIAS PEAK
    3B—HUNTER HILL
    SS—IVAN MESA
    OF—JOHN STONE
    OF—TOM GULLEY
    OF—JACK BEACH
     C—GEORGE LAND
     P—FRANK MOUNTAIN

And a solid team it is—especially with Whitey Ford, Ernie Shore, Hub Knolls and Luis Arroyo to round out the pitching staff, and Moe Berg as the backup catcher.

WATER, WATER EVERYWHERE

We may be all wet with this one, but . . .

1B—BOOMER WELLS
2B—KURT BEVACQUA
3B—HUBIE BROOKS
SS—FREDDY MARSH
OF—HARRY BAY
OF—CURT FLOOD
OF—MICKEY RIVERS
C—FRED LAKE
P—JACK SPRING

For reserves there are outfielder Harlin Pool and pitchers Arlie Pond and Fred Waters—but this isn't a very deep squad.

ON TRIAL

This lineup must be considered innocent until proven guilty:

1B—JOE JUDGE
2B—CHUCK SCRIVENER
3B—JOHNNY BENCH
SS—VANCE LAW
OF—BOB BAILEY
OF—GEORGE CASE
OF—FRANK FOREMAN
C—JOE JUST
P—BARRY CORT

If Cort needs a recess, Smoke Justis can be called on for relief.

ROYALTY

This team could build a dynasty and rule the game for years.

ROYALTY

1B—WALTER PRINCE
2B—LEE KING
3B—HARRY LORD
SS—MARK KOENIG
OF—BOB MARQUIS
OF—AL KAISER
OF—MEL QUEEN
C—BILLY EARL
P—MARTIN DUKE

Edgar Baron is the relief pitcher. Art Rebel just wouldn't fit in at this team's home park, the Kingdome. And honorable mention to all the Royals of Kansas City.

AROUND THE CASTLE

This lineup is secondary to the previous one.

1B—MIKE SQUIRES
2B—JIMMY STEWART
3B—RAY KNIGHT
SS—JOE CHAMBERLIN
OF—MIKE PAGE
OF—BRETT BUTLER
OF—BOB USHER
C—DARRELL PORTER
P—VIRGIL JESTER

Gary Gentry and Bob Groom throw to Smokey Burgess in the bullpen. But shortstop Joe Tinker and outfielder Tom Poorman can't break in.

THE GOD SQUAD

If prayer helps, this team might never lose a game.

THE GOD SQUAD

        1B—FRED ABBOTT
        2B—JOHNNY PRIEST
        3B—JIMMY SEXTON
        SS—MAX BISHOP
        OF—MAURICE ARCHDEACON
        OF—DAVE POPE
        OF—BOB CHRISTIAN
         C—BERT CHAPLIN
         P—HOWIE NUNN

Jiggs Parson is in the bullpen; Harry Shriver is the manager and Johnny Podres the pitching coach. Honorable mention to all the St. Louis Cardinals and San Diego Padres. Could Jose Pagan make this team? Bless our souls, no.

PLAYERS OF WORSHIP

This team would provide a peaceful place for contemplation.

          1B—AMOS CROSS
          2B—JOHNNY TEMPLE
          3B—LARRY PARRISH
          SS—CHRIS SPEIER
          OF—LARRY CHAPPELL
          OF—CHARLIE ABBEY
          OF—BEN PASCHAL
           C—EARL GRACE
           P—BUBBA CHURCH

We wanted to choose between Tony Faeth and Ralph Works as the pitcher, but we decided not to get into *that*.

READING AND WRITING

You're more likely to run into this team in a bookstore than at an All-Star game.

1B—MITCHELL PAGE
2B—BILLY REED
3B—STAN HACK
SS—GLENN WRIGHT
OF—CHARLEY MANUEL
OF—GEORGE TOMER
OF—JOE FRAZIER
C—BUDDY BOOKER
P—KEN PENNER

The relief corps would be headed by Judge Works and Fred Worden.

THE OLD TESTAMENT

You can imagine the genesis of this team.

1B—JAKE DANIEL
2B—MIKE EDEN
3B—STAN BENJAMIN
SS—AMADO SAMUEL
OF—BABE RUTH
OF—HANK AARON
OF—MOE SOLOMON
C—GERRY MOSES
P—BOB CAIN

The slugging of Ruth and Aaron would undoubtedly attract a lot of fans and provide the owners of the team with a tidy prophet.

COPS AND ROBBERS

This squad might steal a few games—or catch itself trying.

COPS AND ROBBERS

1B—DAN BRIGGS
2B—BERT CONN
3B—JOHN CROOKS
SS—TOM LAWLESS
OF—JIMMY OUTLAW
OF—EMIL FRISK
OF—AL HEIST
C—JABBER LYNCH
P—JIM CONSTABLE

The bullpen would include Josh Swindell, Don Hood and Jon Warden. Of course, Buck Hooker would also have to be careful not to end up in a Wayne Cage.

THE BODY

Unfortunately, the various parts of this lineup don't add up to one ballplayer.

1B—JACK LAPP
2B—JOHNNY TEMPLE
3B—DAVE BRAIN
SS—GEORGE BONE
OF—BOB PATE
OF—TED BEARD
OF—JIM RAY HART
C—HARRY CHEEK
P—ED HEAD

Activity in the bullpen with Bill Hands, Rollie Fingers, Elroy Face and Buck Marrow taking turns tossing them to Barry Foote.

HEADS UP

If baseball is a game played with the head as much as the arms and legs, this team should be able to do it all.

1B—JAKE MUNCH
2B—BOBBY LOWE
3B—JIMMY SAY
SS—TONY SUCK
OF—CHARLIE SEE
OF—DEAN LOOK
OF—BOB SPEAKE
C—ARCHIE YELLE
P—STEVE PEEK

Clarence Bray might make more noise than any of the starting outfielders and Elmer Ponder might prove to be a more thoughtful pitcher than Peek.

STOP AND GO

We put together this lineup in fits and starts.

1B—JOE START
2B—SAM TROTT
3B—AL HALT
SS—JIM QUICK
OF—JOHNNY HOPP
OF—CHARLIE WAITT
OF—HORACE SPEED
C—BOB SWIFT
P—ROD SCURRY

The bullpen is staffed by Bob Rush, Bob Hasty, Bob Walk, Bob Trice and Darcy Fast.

THE BARD

Name the plays in which appear the characters with the same names as these players and you win the literary trivia prize.

THE BARD

1B—RUDY YORK
2B—BILL REGAN
3B—FRED LEAR
 SS—WILLIE MIRANDA
OF—JOHN TITUS
OF—CARL WARWICK
OF—PAT DUNCAN
  C—BRUCE BENEDICT
  P—FRANK BUSHEY

Now our revels are ended.

NATIONALITIES

Italian Americans and Polish Americans have their ethnic halls of fame. But they're not the only ones entitled to them. These teams' players would be a good place for some ethnic groups to start. On the other hand, the pickings are pretty slim for some groups, but at least sufficient to field a team.

THE BLACKS

Jackie Robinson opened the door in 1947 and hordes of talent rushed in behind him.

<pre>
1B—WILLIE McCOVEY
2B—JOE MORGAN
3B—JACKIE ROBINSON
SS—ERNIE BANKS
OF—FRANK ROBINSON
OF—WILLIE MAYS
OF—HANK AARON
 C—ROY CAMPANELLA
 P—BOB GIBSON
</pre>

This is perhaps the best team in the book, certainly the best in this chapter. The players who don't make it—Willie Stargell, Bill Madlock, Lou Brock, Reggie Jackson and Ferguson Jenkins—would make the beginnings of a respectable entry.

THE ITALIANS

The first Italian-American to reach the major leagues was Ed Abbaticchio, a respectable infielder with the Phillies, Braves and Pirates in 1897–98, 1903–05 and 1907–10. Abbaticchio batted a career .254. His successors were rather better.

> 1B—DOLF CAMILLI
> 2B—TONY LAZZERI
> 3B—JOE TORRE
> SS—PHIL RIZZUTO
> OF—JOE DiMAGGIO
> OF—DOM DiMAGGIO
> OF—CARL FURILLO
> C—YOGI BERRA
> P—ED CICOTTE

Billy Martin would have to manage.

The least familiar name here is Cicotte, perhaps because he was one of the infamous Black Sox. Nonetheless, his career record of 211-147 qualifies him.

And why were so many Italian-American ballplayers catchers? Besides Berra there were Ernie Lombardi, Phil Masi, Joe Garagiola, Gus and Frank Mancuso, Ray Lamanno, Joe Pignatano, Chris Cannizzaro, Johnny Romano and even Roy Campanella.

JEWISH STARS

In the beginning there was Lip Pike, the first Jewish player, who started in the National League in 1876. Since then there have been:

JEWISH STARS

1B—HANK GREENBERG
2B—ROD CAREW
3B—AL ROSEN
SS—BUDDY MYER
OF—SID GORDON
OF—BENNY KAUFF
OF—GEORGE STONE
C—JOHNNY KLING
P—SANDY KOUFAX

Carew, like some other recent players such as Elliot Maddox and Lenny Randle, is a convert. Ken Holtzman could be in the bullpen.

THE POLES

No Polish jokes here.

1B—TED KLUSZEWSKI
2B—BILL MAZEROSKI
3B—WHITEY KUROWSKI
SS—TONY KUBEK
OF—STAN MUSIAL
OF—AL SIMMONS
OF—CARL YASTRZEMSKI
C—CARL SAWATSKI
P—STAN COVELESKI

Simmons's real name was Aloysius Syzmanski.

THE FRENCH

Franco-Americans are not one of the significant ethnic groups in baseball, but French pride would not be offended by these selections.

1B—DEL BISSONETTE
2B—NAP LAJOIE
3B—JIM LEFEBVRE
SS—LOU BOUDREAU
OF—FRENCHY BORDAGARAY
OF—BRUCE BOISCLAIR
OF—JACK FOURNIER
C—BRUCE BOCHY
P—BILL VOISELLE

For a manager we'll take Leo Durocher.

Lajoie and Boudreau are Hall of Famers. Fournier was mostly a first baseman, but we had to get Bissonette's .305 lifetime average into the lineup without losing Fournier's .313. Bochy is the only native-born Frenchman here. Voiselle had a losing record lifetime (74-84), but he had one fine year with the Giants, 21-16 in 1944.

THE PUERTO RICANS

This team comes very close to being an all-star team for any occasion.

1B—VIC POWER
2B—FELIX MILLAN
3B—JOSE PAGAN
SS—IVAN DeJESUS
OF—ROBERTO CLEMENTE
OF—ORLANDO CEDEDA
OF—JOSE CRUZ
C—TONY PENA
P—ED FIGUEROA

The bench would include Sixto Lezcano, Felix Torres and Fernando Gonzales.

NATIVE AMERICANS

Baseball may be the American game, but it is not the native Americans' game.

       1B—WILLIE STARGELL
       2B—BOB JOHNSON
       3B—ROY JOHNSON
       SS—MARK CHRISTMAN
       OF—LOU SOCKALEXIS
       OF—JIM THORPE
       OF—GENE LOCKLEAR
        C—CHIEF MEYERS
        P—CHIEF BENDER

Stargell (half-Indian), Meyers and Bender were all authentic stars. The Johnson brothers were primarily outfielders, but both played a bit of infield. (And both ended their careers with identical .296 averages.) Christman and Locklear were journeymen. Thorpe, the greatest Indian athlete, was less than that. So was Sockalexis, the first Indian major leaguer.

Honorable mention to Allie Reynolds.

THE IRISH IRISH

That's right. Not an Irish-American team but the real McCoy (or McHale) from the Emerald Isle itself. Most of the candidates played in the early days of the century and an unusual number were catchers (big hands?), but at least one was good enough to be remembered for Hall of Fame induction.

1B—ROGER BRESNAHAN
2B—REDDY MACK
3B—JIM HALLINAN
SS—ANDY LEONARD
OF—JACK DOYLE
OF—JIM WALSH
OF—MIKE O'NEILL
C—JIMMY ARCHER
P—TONY MULLANE

Two position notes here. Bresnahan, the Hall of Famer, was of course better known as a catcher than as a first baseman, though he was said to have acquitted himself equally well at the latter position. O'Neill, who also played under the name Mike Joyce, was moved to the outfield from the pitcher's mound for the 1902 season by the St. Louis Cardinals. He might not have been Babe Ruth, but he managed to bat a fine .318.

THE MOTHER COUNTRY

Considering the fact that baseball is at least in part derived from the British game of rounders, a better team might have been expected here.

1B—ED COGSWELL	England
2B—DICK HIGHAM	England
3B—JIMMY AUSTIN	Wales
SS—DAVE BRAIN	England
OF—HUGH NICOL	Scotland
OF—BOBBY THOMSON	Scotland
OF—TOM BROWN	England
C—AL SHAW	England
P—PARSON LEWIS	Wales

Journeymen prevail here. The exceptions are Austin (.246 in 21 seasons), Brain (.252 in seven seasons), Brown (.264 in 16 seasons), and Thomson (.270 in 15 seasons). Lewis won 91 and lost 63 in the late 1890s and early 1900s.

ON THE CONTINENT

Very few Europeans have made it to the major leagues. In the absence of anyone better we'll offer:

1B—JOHNNY REDER	Poland
2B—JOE STRAUSS	Hungary
3B—RENO BERTOIA	Italy
SS—WILLIE KUEHNE	Germany
OF—ELMER VALO	Czechoslovakia
OF—JAKE GETTMAN	Russia
OF—OLAF HENDRIKSEN	Denmark
C—ART JORGENS	Norway
P—BERT BLYLEVEN	Netherlands

No two players from the same country—but only because Joe Strauss managed to squeeze in two games at second base back in 1884.

And honorable mention to Switzerland's contribution to major league ball, pitcher Otto Hess.

CANADIAN IMPORTS

It is a strange but true fact that baseball spread south across the Caribbean and the Rio Grande and west across the Pacific more readily than to Canada. The following are the best of those who managed to slip across the world's longest undefended border.

1B—TERRY PUHL
2B—SHERRY ROBERTSON
3B—PETE WARD
SS—BLACKIE O'ROURKE
OF—TIP O'NEILL
OF—GEORGE SELKIRK
OF—GOODY ROSEN
C—MOON GIBSON
P—FERGUSON JENKINS

Jenkins and the outfield are particularly noteworthy. In fact, honorable mention also goes to two other outfielders, Jack Graney and Jeff Heath.

THE CUBANS

Most early Latins in professional baseball were Cubans, and black Cubans were prominent in the old Negro Leagues. Most of this team, however, comes from the post-Castro refugee generation.

1B—TONY PEREZ
2B—COOKIE ROJAS
3B—TITO FUENTES
SS—ZOILO VERSALLES
OF—MINNIE MINOSO
OF—TONY OLIVA
OF—JOSE CARDENAL
C—MIKE GONZALEZ
P—MIKE CUELLAR

The exceptions are Gonzalez, who bounced around the National League from 1912 to 1932; Minoso, who starred with the Indians and the White Sox in the 1950s and early 1960s; and the manager, Preston Gomez.

And honorable mention to Frank Bancroft, a nineteenth-century manager, who introduced baseball to Cuba.

THE DOMINICANS

The Dominicans may come from a banana republic, but there are few bananas in this bunch.

THE DOMINICANS

1B—FELIPE ALOU
2B—JULIAN JAVIER
3B—PEDRO GUERRERO
SS—FRANK TAVERAS
OF—RICO CARTY
OF—CESAR CEDENO
OF—MANNY MOTA
C—OZZIE VIRGIL, JR.
P—JUAN MARICHAL

The scouting report: weak at short and catcher, good bats at first and third and the outfield, a fancy fielding second baseman, weak defense in Mota and Carty and a pitcher second to none.

SOUTH OF THE BORDER

Mexico simply does not send its best players north—probably because the domestic leagues are so good. Until something better comes along, we'll stick with:

1B—MEL ALMADA
2B—BOBBY AVILA
3B—AURELIO RODRIGUEZ
SS—RUBEN AMARO
OF—JORGE ORTA
OF—MANUEL CUETO
OF—CELERINO SANCHEZ
C—ALEX TREVINO
P—FERNANDO VALENZUELA

Except for Avila and Valenzuela there are no real stars here, even though Rodriguez was a fine fielder and Orta swings a decent bat. The rest were hardly exciting. And if you think Sanchez was a poor choice in the outfield, just grab the nearest encyclopedia and look up the alternatives—Bobby Trevino, Carlos Lopez and Felipe Montemayor.

THE PANAMANIANS

There are no teams from Honduras, Costa Rica, Nicaragua, Guatemala or Belize. Baseball seems to have skipped them on the way down the Central American isthmus to Panama, where it arrived via the Canal Zone.

> 1B—ROD CAREW
> 2B—RENNIE STENNETT
> 3B—HECTOR LOPEZ
> SS—CHICO SALMON
> OF—BEN OGLIVIE
> OF—OMAR MORENO
> OF—ADOLFO PHILLIPS
> C—MANNY SANGUILLEN
> P—HAL HAYDEL

Carew anchors this team. But Oglivie, Moreno and Sanguillen are all fine ballplayers. And even Stennett and Lopez, while not exactly Gold Glovers, provide some punch. The weak spot is pitching. Haydel, a reliever with Minnesota in 1970 and 1971, compiled a lifetime record of 6-2 with 1 save and a 4.04 ERA. The only major leaguers born between Mexico and Panama are Dennis Martinez and David Green, both from Nicaragua.

THE VENEZUELANS

Venezuela is baseball's South American outpost. Hundreds of North American ballplayers flock there for the winter leagues, braving the heat and the water for a chance to play year round. Also, Venezuela has been kind enough to send some pretty good players the other way to take part in our summer leagues.

1B—OSSIE BLANCO
2B—MANNY TRILLO
3B—DAVE CONCEPCION
SS—LUIS APARICIO
OF—CESAR TOVAR
OF—VIC DAVALILLO
OF—TONY ARMAS
C—BO DIAZ
P—LUIS LEAL

Venezuela seems to specialize in shortstops. Aparicio is the best of them. Concepcion can move over to third. But Chico Carrasquel gets squeezed out.

THE ANTILLES

Cricket is more to be expected from the islands of these players' origins, but a baseball team is also possible.

1B—JOSE MORALES	Virgin Islands
2B—HORACE CLARKE	Virgin Islands
3B—VALMY THOMAS	Virgin Islands
SS—ANDRE RODGERS	Bahamas
OF—ED ARMBRISTER	Bahamas
OF—TONY CURRY	Bahamas
OF—JOE CHRISTOPHER	Virgin Islands
C—ELLIE HENDRICKS	Virgin Islands
P—WENTY FORD	Bahamas

An infield that lacks defense, an outfield without offensive punch, and that's Wenty—not Whitey—on the mound.

Third baseman Thomas was, of course, primarily a catcher, but if he could play the hot corner in one game for the 1959 Giants, he can do it for us, too.

PACIFIC ISLANDERS

It's simply not true that out there in the Pacific there's no America except the Marines.

PACIFIC ISLANDERS

1B—	TONY SOLAITA	American Samoa
2B—	BOBBY FENWICK	Okinawa
3B—	JOE QUINN	Australia
SS—	LENN SAKATA	Hawaii
OF—	MIKE LUM	Hawaii
OF—	PRINCE OANA	Hawaii
OF—	JOHN MATIAS	Hawaii
C—	TONY REGO	Hawaii
P—	MASANORI MURAKAMI	Japan

Murakami is the only native Japanese to make the jump across the Pacific. He pitched well in relief for the Giants in 1964 and 1965, but went back to the Land of the Rising Sun for the honor of his family, which demanded that he exhibit his skills in his native land.

Honorable mention to Bobby Balcena, the only Filipino to play in the major leagues. Unfortunately, he was born in California and therefore doesn't qualify.

THE BEST II

The numbers are there to support our opinions—but these selections of the choicest of the choice remain opinions.

GREATEST CAREERS

Perhaps the most worked-over entry in this book, The All-Time All-Star Team. So much so that it has become a cliché. But here goes . . .

> 1B—LOU GEHRIG
> 2B—ROGERS HORNSBY
> 3B—PIE TRAYNOR
> SS—HONUS WAGNER
> OF—TY COBB
> OF—BABE RUTH
> OF—WILLIE MAYS
> C—BILL DICKEY
> P—WALTER JOHNSON

Gehrig over Jimmie Foxx, George Sisler and Cap Anson. Hornsby over Nap Lajoie, Frankie Frisch, Eddie Collins and Charlie Gehringer. Traynor over John McGraw. Mays over Ted Williams, Pete Browning, Jesse Burkett, Hank Aaron, Joe DiMaggio, Mickey Mantle, Stan Musial and Ed Delahanty. Dickey over King Kelly and Mickey Cochrane. And Johnson over Cy Young, Grover Cleveland Alexander, Christy Mathewson, Lefty Grove, Warren Spahn, Whitey Ford and Sandy Koufax.

Wagner, Cobb and Ruth are uncontestable members of this team.

Casey Stengel is the manager over John McGraw and Joe McCarthy.

GREATEST SEASONS

Everyone has a personal choice for an All-Time All-Star team, but how about the greatest single season by a player at each position?

1B—LOU GEHRIG	1927 Yankees
2B—ROGERS HORNSBY	1924 Cardinals
3B—GEORGE BRETT	1980 Royals
SS—ERNIE BANKS	1958 Cubs
OF—TY COBB	1911 Tigers
OF—BABE RUTH	1921 Yankees
OF—HACK WILSON	1930 Cubs
C—JOHNNY BENCH	1970 Reds
P—WALTER JOHNSON	1913 Senators

The batting order? Cobb (.420 BA, 83 SB), Hornsby (.424), Ruth (59 HR, .846 SA), Gehrig (47 HR, 175 RBI), Wilson (56 HR, 190 RBI), Bench (45 HR, 148 RBI), Banks (47 HR), Brett (.390), Johnson (36-7, 1.09 ERA).

Honorable mention to Tip O'Neill (1887 St. Louis, AA), who batted .492 (when walks were counted as hits) and also led the league in doubles, triples, home runs, runs, slugging average, total bases and hits. He is the only player who ever led his league in doubles, triples and homers in the same year.

GREATEST GAMES

Every player has his day, but some have compressed a week of achievement into a single game.

1B—JIM BOTTOMLEY	Sept. 16, 1924	Cardinals
2B—RENNIE STENNETT	Sept. 16, 1975	Pirates
3B—BILL JOYCE	May 18, 1897	Giants
SS—JOHNNY BURNETT	July 10, 1932	Indians
OF—TY COBB	May 5, 1925	Tigers
OF—ROCKY COLAVITO	June 10, 1959	Indians
OF—GEORGE GORE	June 25, 1881	Cubs
C—DUKE FARRELL	May 11, 1897	Washington
P—HARVEY HADDIX	May 26, 1959	Pirates

Bottomley drove in 12 runs. Stennett stroked four singles, two doubles and a triple in a nine-inning game. Joyce legged out four triples. Burnett made the best of an 18-inning game by collecting seven singles and two doubles. Cobb responded to a dare that he couldn't hit the long ball by bashing three homers and adding three singles for a 6-for-6 afternoon. Colavito joined the select group of players who have hit four homers in a game. Gore swiped seven bases. Farrell threw out a record eight would-be base thieves. Haddix pitched a perfect game for 12⅓ innings before losing everything on an error, an intentional walk and a home run—sort of. The home run was, in fact, scored as a double when the batter passed a runner on the bases. The batter who ended Haddix's evening? Joe Adcock, who deserves an honorable mention here for the afternoon in 1954 when, as a member of the Milwaukee Braves, he racked up a record 18 total bases with four homers and a double. Another honorable mention to catcher Wilbert Robinson, who set the precedent for Stennett by banging out seven hits (six singles and a double) in an 1892 nine-inning contest.

GREATEST DAYS

These players had no reason to regret a scheduled doubleheader—or in one case even a tripleheader.

1B—NATE COLBERT	August 1, 1972	Padres
2B—MAX BISHOP	May 21, 1930	Athletics
	July 8, 1934	Red Sox
3B—CLYDE BARNHART	October 2, 1920	Pirates
SS—HERMAN LONG	May 30, 1894	Braves
OF—STAN MUSIAL	May 2, 1954	Cardinals
OF—TED WILLIAMS	Sept. 28, 1941	Red Sox
OF—JOE KELLEY	Sept. 3, 1894	Baltimore
C—JOHN BATEMAN	Sept. 10, 1968	Astros
P—ED REULBACH	Sept. 26, 1908	Cubs

Both Colbert and Musial cracked five home runs in a double bill. Colbert also set records by driving in 13 runs and amassing 22 total bases. On two occasions five years apart Bishop walked eight times. Barnhart is the only player in major league history to get at least one hit in three games on the same day. Long had a lot of hitting behind him, as evidenced by the nine runs he tallied in the course of a doubleheader. Going into the final day of the season with a batting average half a hair below .400, Williams refused to let rounded-off numbers push him into the magic circle; he went 4-for-5 in the first game and 2-for-3 in the second, ending up at .406. Kelly cracked out nine consecutive hits. Bateman shares the record of most putouts by a catcher in a doubleheader (25) with Hank Severeid, registering 22 of them through strikeouts. Reulbach pitched two complete game shutouts against the Dodgers.

Honorable mention to Tim Keefe, who won both ends of a doubleheader for the American Association New York Mets in 1883. He gave up only three hits in doing so, but managed to give up a run in the process.

GREATEST INNINGS

And some players did a full day's work in a single inning.

1B—ED CARTWRIGHT	3rd inn. Sept. 23, 1890	St. Louis (AA)
2B—FRED PFEFFER	7th inn. Sept. 6, 1883	Cubs
3B—NED WILLIAMSON	7th inn. Sept. 6, 1883	Cubs
SS—TOM BURNS	7th inn. Sept. 6, 1883	Cubs
OF—GENE STEPHENS	7th inn. June 18, 1953	Red Sox
OF—JIM LEMON	3rd inn. Sept. 5, 1959	Senators
OF—JOSH DEVORE	9th inn. June 20, 1912	Giants
C—SAMMY WHITE	7th inn. June 18, 1953	Red Sox
P—BRUCE SUTTER	9th inn. Sept. 8, 1977	Cubs

Cartwright hit two home runs and drove in seven runs. Pfeffer had two singles and a double. Williamson had two singles, a double, and three runs scored. Burns had two doubles, a homer and three runs scored. Stephens had two singles and a double. Lemon hit two homers and had six RBIs. Devore stole four bases. White scored three runs. And Sutter is the most recent pitcher to strike out the side on nine pitches.

Other players who reached base three times in one inning are Herman Long, Hugh Duffy and Bobby Lowe (first inning, June 18, 1894, Braves); and Peewee Reese (first inning, May 21, 1952, Dodgers).

GREATEST STREAKS

You should know what most of these seasonal marks are:

1B—DALE LONG	1956 Pirates
2B—DAVEY LOPES	1975 Dodgers
3B—PINKY HIGGINS	1938 Red Sox
SS—BILLY ROGELL	1938 Tigers
OF—BILLY HAMILTON	1894 Phillies
OF—JOE DiMAGGIO	1941 Yankees
OF—TED WILLIAMS	1957 Red Sox
C—BUDDY ROSAR	1946 Yankees
P—RUBE MARQUARD	1912 Giants

Major league records all:

Long homered in eight straight games. Lopes stole 38 bases without being caught. Higgins (and later Walt Dropo) rapped out 12 straight hits. Rogell (and later Mel Ott and Eddie Stanky) walked seven consecutive times. Hamilton scored at least one run in 24 straight games. DiMaggio hit safely in 56 games in a row. Williams reached base safely 16 consecutive times (four homers, two singles, nine walks, one hit by pitch). Rosar went 117 games without an error for a season fielding average of 1.000. Marquard won 19 games in a row to tie him with Tim Keefe of the 1888 New York Mets.

Honorable mentions to: Oscar Grimes, for batting in at least one run in 17 consecutive games; Elmer Smith and Earl Sheely, for seven consecutive extra base blows; Paul Waner, for getting one or more extra base hits in 14 consecutive games; and Dave Philley and Rusty Staub, for eight consecutive pinch-hits.

DRAMATIC MOMENTS

When these players succeeded, they affected more than their individual statistics.

1B—JOE ADCOCK	May 26, 1959	Braves
2B—JACKIE ROBINSON	Sept. 30, 1951	Dodgers
3B—MIKE SCHMIDT	October 4–5, 1980	Phillies
SS—PHIL RIZZUTO	Sept. 17, 1951	Yankees
OF—DICK SISLER	October 1, 1950	Phillies
OF—CHET LAABS	October 1, 1944	Browns
OF—HANK GREENBERG	Sept. 30, 1945	Tigers
C—GABBY HARTNETT	Sept. 28, 1938	Cubs
P—FLOYD GIEBELL	Sept. 27, 1940	Tigers

Adcock broke up Harvey Haddix's perfect game in the 14th inning with a drive over the wall that defeated the Pirates' lefty, but that was ruled a double because of sloppy base-running. Robinson's 14th-inning homer against the Phillies on the last day of the season kept the Dodgers around to suffer at the hands of Bobby Thomson. Schmidt's two homers on the final weekend of the season paved the way toward a Philadelphia championship. Rizzuto squeezed home Joe DiMaggio with the winning run in the ninth inning and put the Yankees in first place to stay. Sisler kept the Phils out of a playoff with a three-run homer in the tenth inning of the final game of the season. Laabs hit two home runs against the Yankees on the final day to clinch the St. Louis miracle. Greenberg's grand-slam—in the ninth inning of the final game—was the margin of Detroit's pennant. Hartnett's "homer in the gloamin' " assured a Chicago pennant. Giebell, whose season record was a mere 2-0, beat Bob Feller with a 6-hit shutout by a score of 2-0 to clinch the Detroit pennant on the last weekend.

AS TIME GOES BY

Some players managed to set standards for themselves that they met year in and year out.

AS TIME GOES BY

1B—JIMMIE FOXX
2B—ROGERS HORNSBY
3B—JOE SEWELL
SS—HONUS WAGNER
OF—BABE RUTH
OF—TY COBB
OF—HANK AARON
C—BILL DICKEY
P—TOM SEAVER

Foxx hit 30 or more home runs for 12 consecutive years (1929–40). Hornsby batted .380 or better for five consecutive years (1921–25). Sewell struck out six or fewer times in five consecutive years (1929–33) as a third baseman and seven years in a row if you count 1927 and 1928 when he was a shortstop. Wagner batted .300 or better for the first 17 years he played (1897–1913). Ruth hit 40 or more homers seven straight seasons (1926–32). Cobb batted .300 or better for 23 consecutive years (1906–28). Aaron hit 20 or more home runs in 20 straight years (1955–74). Dickey caught 100 or more games for 13 straight years (1929–41), a mark later tied by Johnny Bench (1968–80). Seaver struck out 200 or more batters for nine straight years (1968–76).

Honorable mention to Willie Keeler (200 or more hits for eight consecutive years, 1894–1901); Lou Brock (50 or more stolen bases for 12 straight years, 1965–76); Cy Young (20 or more wins in 14 straight seasons, 1891–1904); Kid Nichols (30 or more wins in 4 straight seasons, 1891–94); and Foxx (1929–41) and Lou Gehrig (1926–38) for 100 or more RBIs in 13 straight seasons.

YOU'RE THE TOP

Some players seem to stake out certain batting categories and lead the league year after year.

1B—WILLIE McCOVEY	1969–71, 1973
2B—NELLIE FOX	1954–60
3B—BROOKS ROBINSON	1962, 1964, 1967–68
SS—HONUS WAGNER	1900–02, 1904, 1906–09
OF—TY COBB	1907–15, 1917–19
OF—BABE RUTH	1918–21, 1923–24, 1926–31
OF—DOC CRAMER	1933–35, 1938, 1940–42
C—YOGI BERRA	1950–57
P—WARREN SPAHN	1949–50, 1953, 1957–61

McCovey led the league in intentional walks four times. (Frank Robinson also did this in 1961–64.) Fox led in singles eight times. Brooks Robinson led in sacrifice flies four times. Wagner led in doubles eight times. Cobb led in batting twelve times. (Cobb also led in hits eight times: 1907–09, 1911–12, 1915, 1917 and 1919.) Ruth led in homers twelve times. (Sometimes it must have seemed that Ruth staked out *every* batting category as his own private domain. He also led the American League in walks eleven times, runs scored eight times, and RBIs six times.) Cramer led in at bats seven times. Berra led all catchers in games played eight times. And Spahn led in wins eight times.

TRIPLE CROWNS

The Triple Crown belongs to a player who leads his league in batting average, home runs and RBIs. Most of these players did it once. Some of them did it twice. And some only came close.

1B—LOU GEHRIG	1934 Yankees
2B—ROGERS HORNSBY	1922 and 1925 Cardinals
3B—HEINIE ZIMMERMAN	1912 Cubs
SS—HONUS WAGNER	1908 Pirates
OF—TED WILLIAMS	1942 and 1947 Red Sox
OF—JOE MEDWICK	1937 Cardinals
OF—TY COBB	1909 Tigers
C—JOHNNY BENCH	1970 and 1972 Reds
P—LEFTY GROVE	1929, 1930 and 1931 Athletics

Hornsby and Williams are the only players to win two Triple Crowns.

Gehrig gets the nod over Jimmie Foxx (1933 Athletics) because Gehrig's numbers were better in his Triple Crown year.

Williams gets a spot in the lineup for winning twice, Medwick and Cobb for leading the league in five additional categories. Other outfielders to win the Crown were Chuck Klein (1933 Phillies), Mickey Mantle (1956 Yankees), Frank Robinson (1966 Orioles) and Carl Yastrzemski (1967 Red Sox).

Wagner led the league in batting and RBIs but not homers, but he also led in six other categories. Bench won two-thirds of a triple crown twice, leading in homers and RBIs in the years indicated.

Only seven pitchers have ever led the league in Won-Lost Percentage, ERA and strikeouts in the same year. Grove, who did it three consecutive years, is the only one to do it more than once. The others are Walter Johnson (1913 Senators), Grover Cleveland Alexander (1915 Phillies), Lefty Gomez (1934 Yankees), Hal Newhouser (1945 Tigers), Harry Brecheen (1948 Cardinals) and Sandy Koufax (1965 Dodgers).

LEADER OF THE PACK

Sometimes one player can carry a whole team but sometimes, no matter how well the player does, he can't carry it very far.

1B—JIMMIE FOXX	1935 Athletics
2B—ROGERS HORNSBY	1928 Braves
3B—BOB DILLINGER	1947 Browns
SS—ERNIE BANKS	1958 Cubs
OF—WALLY BERGER	1930 Braves
OF—RALPH KINER	1949–52 Pirates
OF—HANK SAUER	1952 Cubs
C—ERNIE LOMBARDI	1942 Braves
P—STEVE CARLTON	1972 Phillies

Foxx tied for the league lead in homers with 36, and led the league in RBIs (115) and slugging (.636); the Athletics finished last. Hornsby led the league in batting with a .387 average and hit 21 homers with 94 RBIs; the Braves finished seventh. Dillinger batted .294 and led the league in stolen bases with 34; the Browns finished last. Banks led the league in homers (47), RBIs (129) and slugging (.614) while batting .313; with all that hitting the Cubs could do no better than fifth. Berger hit a league-leading 38 homers; the rest of the Braves could manage only 28 more and ended in sixth place. Kiner led the league (or tied for the lead) in home runs in all four seasons noted while the Pirates finished sixth, last, seventh and last. Sauer's MVP year was based on a .270 average and league-leading totals in home runs (37) and RBIs (121); the Cubs finished fifth. Lombardi led the league in hitting (.330); the next highest average on the team was .278 and the Braves ended in seventh place. Carlton—27-10, a 1.98 ERA, and 310 strikeouts, all league-leading figures—was the entire franchise as the Phils won only 59 games and finished last.

ROUND AND ROUND

Since 1900 there have only been 32 occasions on which a player has hit two inside-the-park home runs in one game. The most recent are:

1B—DICK ALLEN	July 31, 1972	White Sox
2B—MORRIE RATH	Sept. 20, 1920	Reds
3B—HANK THOMPSON	August 16, 1950	Giants
SS—RABBIT MARANVILLE	July 1, 1919	Braves
OF—TERRY MOORE	August 16, 1939	Cardinals
OF—BEN CHAPMAN	July 9, 1932	Yankees
OF—CARL REYNOLDS	July 2, 1930	White Sox
C—ROGER BRESNAHAN	May 30, 1902	Orioles
P—CHIEF BENDER	May 8, 1906	Athletics

Bresnahan is the only player to do this twice in this century. Ed Delahanty hit four inside-the-park homers on July 13, 1896.

GREAT SUCCESSORS

When Carl Yastrzemski is inducted into the Hall of Fame, he will become only the second player in major league history who followed his immediate predecessor on a team into Cooperstown. The other pair? Shame on you if you don't know.

1B—RUDY YORK	Hank Greenberg
2B—JOE GORDON	Tony Lazzeri
3B—EDDIE MATHEWS	Bob Elliott
SS—LUIS APARICIO	Chico Carrasquel
OF—CARL YASTRZEMSKI	Ted Williams
OF—MICKEY MANTLE	Joe DiMaggio
OF—CHUCK KLEIN	Cy Williams
C—ELSTON HOWARD	Yogi Berra
P—MICKEY LOLICH	Jim Bunning

A manager? How about Ralph Houk as the immediate successor to Casey Stengel?

IN THE PINCH

Every manager dreams of having someone who can come off the bench in the late innings and win a ball game with one swipe of the bat. The best of those who could do that were:

1B—GEORGE CROWE
2B—RED SCHOENDIENST
3B—FRENCHY BORDAGARAY
SS—JIMMY STEWART
OF—GATES BROWN
OF—JERRY LYNCH
OF—MANNY MOTA
 C—SMOKEY BURGESS
P—RED LUCAS

Crowe hit 14 home runs off the bench and beats out Willie McCovey, who had 16, because the former had a significantly higher batting average. Schoendienst hit .303. Bordagaray batted .312, the all-time high. Stewart, a utility player, beats out Joe Cronin and Arky Vaughan, who had higher averages, but didn't pinch-hit as often. Brown (16 home runs), Lynch (18 home runs) and Mota (a record 154 hits) make it over some high average hitters (Frankie Baumholtz, Tommy Davis, Fats Fothergill, Rusty Staub and Dave Philley) and some long ball hitters (Bob Cerv, Cy Williams, Fred Whitfield, Gus Zernial and Wally Post). Although Cliff Johnson holds the record for most pinch homers (19), Burgess is perhaps the greatest pinch-hitter of all time: 145 hits, a .286 average and 16 homers. Lucas's 114 hits puts him in an elite group even though his pinch-hitting average (.261) is lower than his overall average, .281.

DESIGNATED HITTERS

If these players had been standout fielders, they wouldn't have become designated hitters in the first place, so we'll leave it to the reader to assign them positions. Hint: The order corresponds to the lineup order in the rest of the book, with the ninth spot that of a pinch-hitter.

DH—RUSTY STAUB
DH—JACK BROHAMER
DH—TOMMY DAVIS
DH—DON MONEY
DH—HAL McRAE
DH—DON BAYLOR
DH—GREG LUZINSKI
DH—CLIFF JOHNSON
DH—LOU PINIELLA

Some DH trivia:

Orlando Cepeda was the first player ever signed to a contract exclusively for DH duty, by the Red Sox in 1973. Ron Blomberg of the Yankees was the first DH to appear at the plate, on April 6, 1973. Tony Oliva hit the first home run as a DH, in 1973. Hal McRae is the only DH to have led the American League in important offensive categories—tying for the lead in doubles in 1977 and 1982 and leading in runs batted in in 1982. Roric Harrison of the Orioles hit the last home run by an AL pitcher on October 3, 1972.

Note: Although Don Baylor is often cited as the only DH to be named MVP, he did play 97 games in the outfield in the year in question, 1979.

ALL-TIME RIGHTIES

Right-handed hitters are supposed to have a half-step disadvantage going to first base, but somehow we don't think this lineup would be hindered by the difference.

1B—JIMMIE FOXX
2B—ROGERS HORNSBY
3B—PIE TRAYNOR
SS—HONUS WAGNER
OF—WILLIE MAYS
OF—HANK AARON
OF—JOE DiMAGGIO
C—KING KELLY
P—WES FERRELL

The only criticism of this lineup we can imagine is that there is no room in it for Frank Robinson.

ALL-TIME LEFTIES

The best from the other side of the plate are:

1B—LOU GEHRIG
2B—EDDIE COLLINS
3B—EDDIE MATHEWS
SS—JOHNNY PESKY
OF—TED WILLIAMS
OF—TY COBB
OF—TRIS SPEAKER
C—BILL DICKEY
P—BABE RUTH

Pesky is usually not mentioned in such exalted company, but the fact is that his .307 lifetime average qualifies him for this otherwise Hall of Fame team.

Any suggestions for a pinch-hitter for the pitcher?

ALL-TIME SWITCHERS

These players both switched *and* fought.

ALL-TIME SWITCHERS

1B—RIP COLLINS
2B—FRANKIE FRISCH
3B—PETE ROSE
SS—MAURY WILLS
OF—MICKEY MANTLE
OF—REGGIE SMITH
OF—MAX CAREY
C—TED SIMMONS
P—VIDA BLUE

Switch-hitting records held by these players include most extra base hits in a season (87) Collins (1934 Cardinals); highest lifetime average (.316) Frisch; most hits in a season (230) Rose with the Reds in 1973; most runs scored in a season (140) Carey (1922 Pirates); and most home runs by a National League switch-hitter (172) Simmons.

Mantle, of course, holds many switch-hitting power records: 536 lifetime homers, 54 home runs in a season (1961); 130 RBIs in a season (1956) and a .705 slugging average (1956).

Some notables who fail to make this team are George Davis (most triples in a season, 26, with the 1893 Giants); Tommy Tucker (highest season batting average, .375, with the American Association Baltimore team); and Willie Wilson and Garry Templeton (the only players to collect 100 or more hits from each side of the plate in a single season). Templeton had 111 hits left-handed and 100 right-handed with the Cardinals in 1979; Wilson had 130 from the left side and 100 from the right with the Royals in 1980.

SWITCH ARMERS

Why have some of the best left-handed hitters been righties when it came to throwing? We don't know either, but here are some of them:

SWITCH ARMERS

1B—ROD CAREW
2B—EDDIE COLLINS
3B—JOHN McGRAW
SS—JOHNNY PESKY
OF—TED WILLIAMS
OF—JOE JACKSON
OF—TY COBB
C—BILL DICKEY
P—RED LUCAS

Lucas was good enough to compile a lifetime average of .281, including 437 pinch-hitting appearances.

BATS RIGHT, THROWS LEFT

Batting left-handed and throwing right-handed is commonplace. The opposite, for some unexplainable reason, isn't at all. In fact, there have probably been fewer than two dozen players in the history of the game who possessed this combination. The best of them are:

1B—HAL CHASE
2B—BILL GREENWOOD
3B—HICK CARPENTER
SS—JIMMY MACULLAR
OF—PATSY DONOVAN
OF—JIMMY RYAN
OF—RICKEY HENDERSON
C—POP TATE
P—JOHNNY COONEY

Chase was a fancy-fielding first baseman whose unsavory associations led to his unwilling exit from baseball. Greenwood played over 150 games at second for five teams in the old American Association. Carpenter played over 100 games at third—mostly for Cincinnati in the American Association—between 1879 and 1892. Macullar played short over 300 times in six seasons in the 1870s and 1880s. (Carpenter and Macullar were teammates with Cincinnati in 1882 and 1883 and while Macullar didn't become a full-time shortstop until he moved to the Orioles in 1884, he did play short for Cincinnati once in 1883. There exists, therefore, the possibility that Cincinnati fielded a left-handed shortstop *and* a left-handed third baseman in the same game.)

Donovan and Ryan were established players; both had lifetime averages over .300. Henderson holds the record for most stolen bases in a season. Tate caught over 200 games—left-handed—in both the NL and the AA from 1885 to 1890. And Cooney was a fair pitcher with the Braves (1921–30) before becoming an outfielder—and a pretty good hitter—with the Braves, Dodgers and Yankees from 1935 to 1944.

SOUTHPAW ALL THE WAY

Players who bat left-handed *and* throw left-handed, on the other hand, are quite common—except at certain positions.

       1B—LOU GEHRIG
       2B—LIP PIKE
       3B—LEFTY MARR
       SS—BILL HULEN
       OF—STAN MUSIAL
       OF—TRIS SPEAKER
       OF—JESSE BURKETT
        C—JACK CLEMENTS
        P—BABE RUTH

Ruth, Gehrig and the outfielders are all Hall of Famers; the others are virtually unknown. The reason, of course, is that left-handed players aren't usually assigned to catch or play second, third or short. A number have, though, and here we have chosen those who played those positions most often. Pike was primarily an outfielder (1876–78, 1881, 1887), but he did play second 29 times, 22 of them with Cincinnati in 1877. Marr appeared at a number of positions in his four years (1886, 1889–91); his 129 appearances at third came with Columbus of the American Association (66 games in 1889) and Cincinnati in the National League (63 games in 1890). Hulen played 73 games at short for Philadelphia in 1896 and 19 more for Washington in 1899. And Clements caught over 1000 games between 1884 and 1900, most of them with the Phillies.

Mike Squires of the White Sox played a few games at third in 1984, making him the most recent lefty to do so.

The most recent left-handed shortstop was Nino Escalera, who ended up at shortstop—or rather short field—in one of the more bizarre defensive alignments designed to stop Stan Musial. The year was 1954 and the shift was about as successful as more conventional defenses, which is to say not very.

ODDS AND ODDS

A potpourri of lifetime and seasonal records.

1B—JIM GENTILE	1961 Orioles
2B—RON HUNT	1971 Expos and Career
3B—BILL BRADLEY	1907 Indians
SS—DALE BERRA	1983 Pirates
OF—AUGIE GALAN	1935 Cubs
OF—DON BUFORD	Career
OF—BOBBY BONDS	1971 Giants and Career
C—RAY SCHALK	Career
P—ROLLIE FINGERS	Career

Gentile hit five grand-slams in 1961 (to tie Ernie Banks' record with the 1955 Cubs). Hunt was hit by a pitch 50 times in 1971 and 243 times in his career. Bradley moved a runner along 46 times on a sacrifice. Berra reached first seven times on catcher's interference. Galan went to bat 646 times without hitting into a double play. Buford hit into a double play only every 138 at bats (33 GIDP in 4553 at bats). Bonds hit 11 homers as a lead-off batter in 1971 and 35 in his career. Schalk called the signals in four no-hitters. Fingers holds the lifetime record for saves, 324.

Honorable mention to Sam Crawford for his 50 career

inside-the-park homers, Max Carey for a stolen base percentage of .961 with the 1922 Pirates (the highest percentage for 50 or more attempts (51 out of 53), and Dan Quisenberry (1983 Royals) and Bruce Sutter (1984 Cardinals) for their joint season record of 45 saves.

POSITIONS

Some very unexpected players have turned over the double play and some even less expected ones have hurled shutout innings. This section is all about the positions major leaguers have played and how long they played them.

POSITION SWITCHERS

The names are familiar, but not at the positions assigned. Nevertheless, it was at these positions they started off in the majors.

1B—JACKIE ROBINSON	1947 Dodgers
2B—LARRY DOBY	1947 Indians
3B—STEVE GARVEY	1970 Dodgers
SS—BOBBY MURCER	1965 Yankees
OF—HONUS WAGNER	1897 Louisville
OF GRAIG NETTLES	1967 Twins
OF BILL RUSSELL	1969 Dodgers
C—GIL HODGES	1947 Dodgers
P—LEFTY O'DOUL	1919 Giants

Hodges actually made his debut in 1943 as a third baseman, but only for one game.

POSITION SWITCHERS II

The players on the previous team had modest careers at

their first positions, then starred at the second. Those in this lineup were *stars* at both positions.

1B—BABE HERMAN	To OF	
2B—PETE ROSE	To OF, to 3B, to 1B	
3B—TONY PEREZ	To 1B	
SS—ERNIE BANKS	To 1B	
OF—STAN MUSIAL	To 1B, to OF, to 1B, to OF	
OF—BOB ELLIOTT	To 3B	
OF—BOOG POWELL	To 1B	
C—JOE TORRE	To 1B, to 3B	
P—BABE RUTH	To OF	

Honorable mention to Freddy Lindstrom (third to outfield), Buddy Lewis (third to outfield), Bucky Walters (third to pitcher), Joe Sewell (shortstop to third base), Harvey Kuenn (short to the outfield), Travis Jackson (short to third), Lonnie Frey (short to second), Billy Cox (short to third), Rico Petrocelli (short to third), Ray Boone (short to third), Hal Jeffcoat (the outfield to pitcher) and Joe Wood (pitcher to outfield).

FROM THE FIELD TO THE MOUND

No, Bob Lemon *isn't* the only player converted to pitching from another position. Here are some of his teammates:

1B—JACK HARSHMAN
2B—BOB SMITH
3B—BUCKY WALTERS
SS—GENE LILLARD
OF—BOB LEMON
OF—HAL JEFFCOAT
OF—WOODIE WHEATON
C—MOOSE DAHL
P—ERNIE WHITE

White makes the team because he went to the mound from the coaching lines after National League president

Ford Frick gave the Braves special permission to start the right-hander in a September 1947 contest.

FROM THE MOUND TO THE FIELD

And no, Babe Ruth *isn't* the only player converted from pitching to another position. Here are some of his teammates:

      1B—GEORGE SISLER
      2B—KID GLEASON
      3B—JOE YEAGER
      SS—BOBBY WALLACE
      OF—BABE RUTH
      OF—JOE WOOD
      OF—ELMER SMITH
       C—CHARLIE MORAN
       P—WHITEY FORD

Ford makes the team by virtue of his 1964 season, when he was asked to double as the ace of the Yankee staff and pitching coach.

FILLING IN

This team consists of pitchers who have been called on to see how their teammates make a living. It excludes pitchers who seriously, even if semi-regularly, played another position.

      1B—LEFTY TYLER
      2B—RED LUCAS
      3B—HAL BROWN
      SS—BOBBY MATHEWS
      OF—JOE BUSH
      OF—GEORGE MULLIN
      OF—WALTER JOHNSON
       C—GEORGE UHLE
      PH—RICK LANGFORD

Tyler (127-118 won-lost record) played 11 games at first, Lucas (157-135) 12 at second, Brown (85-92) two at third and Mathews (166-138) two at short. Bush (193-184) played in the outfield nine times, Mullin (232-192) 11 times and Johnson (414-282) 15 times. Uhle (200-166) went behind the plate for one game. As a member of the 1982 Athletics, Langford became that rarest of American League species—a pitcher in the batter's box. After playing the outfield for an inning, the right-hander made out in the only plate appearance by a pitcher in the junior circuit that year.

CONSECUTIVE GAME STREAKS

Every baseball fan knows that Lou Gehrig played in 2130 consecutive games. What a whole lot fewer know is that he did not play all of those games at first base. The members of this team played the most consecutive games at their respective positions.

1B—LOU GEHRIG	885	1925–30
2B—NELLIE FOX	798	1955–60
3B—EDDIE YOST	576	1951–55
SS—EVERETT SCOTT	1307	1916–25
OF—BILLY WILLIAMS	897	1963–69
OF—RICHIE ASHBURN	694	1950–54
OF—WALTER BRODIE	574	1893–97
C—BLIMP HAYES	312	1943–46
P—MIKE MARSHALL	13	1974

Gehrig's streak was interrupted when he was ill and was placed in the lineup at shortstop—just long enough to single in the top of the first.

Scott holds the all-time record for most consecutive games at a single position.

Marshall appeared in 13 consecutive games as a relief pitcher.

MOST SEASONS

Longevity is the mark of consistency. These are the players who appeared in the most seasons at each position.

1B—WILLIE McCOVEY	22
2B—EDDIE COLLINS	21
3B—BROOKS ROBINSON	23
SS—LUKE APPLING	20
OF—TY COBB	24
OF—HANK AARON	23
OF—WILLIE MAYS	22
C—DEACON McGUIRE	25
P—JIM KAAT	25

Collins played in 25 seasons, but only 21 of them at second base. Bobby Wallace and Bill Dahlen also played 20 years at shortstop, but Appling appeared in more games there than either of them. Similarly, Al Kaline, Tris Speaker and Carl Yastrzemski tied Mays at 22 years, but Mays played the most games in the outfield. McGuire played in a 26th season in which he did not catch.

The manager is Connie Mack, who headed various teams for 53 years.

MOST GAMES

Games played is a measure of both how long a player lasts and how frequently he plays while he is on the roster. This team consists of those players who appeared in the most games at each position.

1B—JAKE BECKLEY	2247
2B—EDDIE COLLINS	2651
3B—BROOKS ROBINSON	2870
SS—LUIS APARICIO	2581
OF—WILLIE MAYS	2843
OF—TY COBB	2938
OF—HANK AARON	2760
C—AL LOPEZ	1918
P—HOYT WILHELM	1070

Wilhelm, of course, is the only pitcher who has ever appeared in over 1000 games. He started 52 times and relieved 1018 times, which also gives him the most relief appearances. The most starts belong to Cy Young, 818.

Honorable mention to Carl Yastrzemski and Pete Rose, who have played in more games than anyone else (3308 and 3371, respectively) but who never played enough games at any one position to qualify here.

STAYING PUT

This lineup may lack maneuverability, but the players in it—those who appeared in the most games at their positions without ever playing anywhere else—had a lot of experience.

1B—JAKE DAUBERT	2001
2B—BOBBY DOERR	1852
3B—RON CEY	1783
SS—LUIS APARICIO	2581
OF—LOU BROCK	2507
OF—MAX CAREY	2422
OF—ZACK WHEAT	2350
C—RICK FERRELL	1806
P—SPARKY LYLE	899

Lyle has the most relief appearances for any pitcher who has never started a game.

PERMANENT FIXTURES

Some players seem never to move at all. These entries played the most games at their positions without ever playing another position and without ever changing teams.

1B—DEL BISSONETTE	598	Dodgers
2B—BOBBY DOERR	1852	Red Sox
3B—BUDDY BLAIR	126	Phillies
SS—ALAN TRAMMELL	960	Tigers
OF—CLYDE MILAN	1901	Senators
OF—EARLE COMBS	1386	Yankees
OF—DWIGHT EVANS	1539	Red Sox
C—BILL DICKEY	1712	Yankees
P—RED FABER	669	White Sox

Pinch-hitting doesn't count. Neither does serving as designated hitter, which is not a position by any stretch of the imagination.

Third basemen seem to be the most mobile of fielders.

Honorable mention to Carl Furillo, who played 1739 games in the outfield for the Dodgers without ever playing anywhere else and without playing for anyone else. Unfortunately the Dodgers moved from Brooklyn to Los Angeles for the last two years of his career, thus keeping him off this team. Yet another sin to be laid at the doorstep of Walter O'Malley.

THREE-WAY REGULARS

A player who has held down a regular berth at three positions is either incredibly versatile or has a bat so potent that managers want him in the lineup no matter how badly he fields. Each of the following has played 100 or more games in a single season at three different positions.

THREE-WAY REGULARS

1B—PETE RUNNELS
2B—BILLY GOODMAN
3B—RAY BOONE
SS—GIL McDOUGALD
OF—PETE ROSE
OF—HARMON KILLEBREW
OF—DICK ALLEN
C—JOE TORRE
P—NIXEY CALLAHAN

Runnels also played second and short; Goodman, first and third; Boone, first and short; McDougald, second and third; Rose, the only one to play *four* different positions 100 times in a season, first, second and third; Killebrew, first and third; Allen, first and third; Torre, first and third; and Callahan, third and the outfield.

QUADRUPLE THREATS

The players in this lineup exhibited their versatility in a different way. In the course of their careers, each of them played 100 or more games at four different positions.

1B—JACK DOYLE
2B—JACKIE ROBINSON
3B—JIMMY DYKES
SS—HONUS WAGNER
OF—PETE ROSE
OF—HOWARD SHANKS
OF—JIM O'ROURKE
C—DEACON WHITE
P—JOHN MONTGOMERY WARD

Their other positions are: Doyle—second, outfield and catcher; Robinson—first, third and the outfield; Dykes—first, second and short; Wagner—first, third and the outfield; Rose—first, second and third; Shanks—second, third and short; O'Rourke—first, third and catcher; White—first, third and the outfield; and Ward—second, short and the outfield.

Surprisingly few players have ever accomplished this. Among the few others are Woodie Held, Roy Hartzell, Billy Goodman, Denis Menke, George Davis, Eddie Miksis, Joe Quinn, Chico Salmon, Rollie Zeider and John Knight.

FIELDERS' CHOICES

The following players appeared at every position in the season indicated.

1B—GENE PAULETTE	1918	Browns
2B—JIMMY WALSH	1911	Phillies
3B—CESAR TOVAR	1968	Twins
SS—BERT CAMPANERIS	1965	Athletics
OF—SPORT McALLISTER	1899	Cleveland
OF—SAM MERTES	1902	White Sox
OF—JACK ROTHROCK	1928	Red Sox
C—KING KELLY	1891	Cincinnati (AA)— Boston (AA)— Braves
P—CHARLIE GETTIG	1898	Giants

Gettig and Kelly did not play all three outfield positions, but they did appear in the outfield.

Tovar and Campaneris played all nine positions in the same game, one position for each inning.

Others who pitched, caught, played all four infield positions and appeared in at least one outfield position in one season are Mike Dorgan (1879 Syracuse), John Grim (1890 Rochester, AA), Spider Clark (1890 Buffalo, PL) and Barney Friberg (1925 Cubs and Phillies).

900/700

Having illustrated versatility in a variety of ways, we would be remiss if we did not include a lineup of players who played the most games at two positions.

1B—TONY PEREZ	1673	760—3B
2B—ROD CAREW	1128	1065—1B
3B—JIMMY DYKES	1253	726—2B
SS—ERNIE BANKS	1125	1259—1B
OF—STAN MUSIAL	1896	1016—1B
OF—CARL YASTRZEMSKI	2076	763—1B
OF—PETE ROSE	1327	768—1B
		634—3B
		628—2B
C—JOE TORRE	903	797—1B
		515—3B
P—KID GLEASON	251	1574—2B

Musial, Banks and Carew are the only players in the history of the game to appear in 1000 or more games at two different positions.

Rose is the only player ever to appear in 500 or more games at four different positions, and Torre is the only other player to appear in that many games at three positions. (Pete Runnels just misses. He played 644 games at first, 642 at second and 463 at short.)

Gleason is the pitcher who played the most games, combining a regular fielding position with his mound work.

Honorable mention to Harry Stovey (945 in the outfield, 550 at first); Tommy Leach (1078 in the outfield, 955 at third); Willie Stargell (1293 in the outfield, 848 at first); Harmon Killebrew (930 at first, 792 at third); Phil Cavarretta (1254 at first, 536 in the outfield); Jim Gilliam (1046 at second, 761 at third); Ron Fairly (964 in the outfield, 935 at first); Joe Sewell (1221 at short, 642 at third); and Roy Sievers (888 in the outfield, 838 at first).

TEMPORARY RELIEF

Sometimes a game will get so far out of hand that a manager will go to the field rather than to the bullpen for a rested arm. Among the non-active regulars who have been called to the mound are:

1B—JIMMIE FOXX	1939 Red Sox, 1945 Phillies
2B—COOKIE ROJAS	1967 Phillies
3B—WHITEY WIETELMANN	1945–46 Braves
SS—ALVIN DARK	1953 Giants
OF—ROCKY COLAVITO	1958 Indians, 1968 Yankees
OF—MATTY ALOU	1965 Giants
OF—JIM HICKMAN	1967 Dodgers
C—AL LAKEMAN	1948 Phillies
PH—JULIO BECQUER	1960 Senators, 1961 Twins

Rojas pitched for 1 inning and gave up nothing. Wietelmann appeared in 4 games (7⅔ innings), but had no decisions. Dark started his lone mound appearance, yielded 2 runs, and called it a pitching career with an ERA of 18.00. Colavito pitched twice for a total of 5⅔ innings, gave up no runs, and was credited with a win for the Yankees. Alou pitched 2 innings without giving up a run. Hickman hurled for 2 innings and gave up 1 run for a 4.50 ERA. Lakeman was knocked around for several hits and 1 run in 1 inning (9.00). Becquer gave up 1 run in 1 inning in 1960 and 3 more runs in another inning the following year for a career ERA of 27.00. Foxx pitched 1 inning for the Red Sox, setting the side down in order, then later appeared in 9 more games for the Phillies, 2 of them as a starter, and gave up 13 hits and 14 walks but only 4 earned runs (1.52 lifetime). He also struck out 11 and won a game.

CATCH AS CATCH CAN

Some major leaguers have been so eager to help their team that they have made the ultimate sacrifice of donning a chest protector and shinguards for an inning or two until help arrived from the nearest farm club. Among the established players (at other positions) who have done this have been:

1B—WILLIE AIKENS	1977 Angels
2B—COOKIE ROJAS	1967 and 1968 Phillies
3B—LENNY RANDLE	1975 Rangers
SS—LOU BOUDREAU	1948 Indians
OF—BOB WATSON	1970–73 Astros
OF—MANNY MOTA	1964 Pirates
OF—HANK BAUER	1955 Yankees
C—GIL HODGES	1956 and 1958 Dodgers
PH—JERRY LYNCH	1955 Pirates, 1957 Reds

Hodges makes the team because, although he began his career as a catcher, he went back behind the plate for only two games during the 15 seasons in which he was establishing himself as one of the game's greatest fielding first basemen. On the other hand, Watson barely makes it because his nine games in the tools of ignorance almost qualify him as a bona fide catcher.

Special mention, of course, must go to Dale Long (two games for the 1958 Cubs) and Mike Squires (two games for the 1980 White Sox) for being that rarity among baseball rarities—left-handed catchers.

OTHER LEAGUES

The National and American Leagues aren't the only circuits that can put together impressive all-star teams. Here are the very best in other loops—major, minor and miscellaneous.

THE NEGRO LEAGUES

The old Negro Leagues are but a dim memory now, although in the opinion of many people the quality of play there was every bit as good as that in the all-white major leagues of the day. Statistics are sketchy and questionable; the abilities of this lineup are not.

> 1B—BUCK LEONARD
> 2B—BINGO DeMOSS
> 3B—JUDY JOHNSON
> SS—JOHN HENRY LLOYD
> OF—OSCAR CHARLESTON
> OF—COOL PAPA BELL
> OF—MARTIN DIHIGO
> C—JOSH GIBSON
> P—SATCHEL PAIGE

Eight Hall of Famers here (all but DeMoss), but only Paige made it to the majors and he only at some advanced—however indeterminate—age. Leonard and Gibson were the Gehrig and Ruth of the Negro Leagues; Honus Wagner once said that he was proud to be compared to John Henry Lloyd; Cool Papa Bell was so fast he could go from first to third on a sacrifice; Dihigo was a star at every position; and Satchel Paige was—well—Satchel Paige.

THE AMERICAN ASSOCIATION

The American Association, the first challenger to the monopoly of the National League, lasted ten seasons, from 1882 to 1891. The Association was formed because Cincinnati, St. Louis and Louisville had been dropped from the National League. It permitted Sunday baseball, sold beer at the parks and charged only 25¢ admission instead of the NL's 50¢. After one year the two leagues signed the reserve clause agreement that allowed teams to bind players for life. The two leagues even played an inter-league championship series from 1884 to 1890. But by 1891 weak leadership (as opposed to the early glory days of such colorful owners as Chris Von der Ahe of the St. Louis Browns), financial difficulties resulting from the Players' League War, and arguments over players weakened the Association to the point where several of its teams joined the National League and the rest disbanded.

> 1B—DAVE ORR
> 2B—BID McPHEE
> 3B—DENNY LYONS
> SS—BILL GLEASON
> OF—PETE BROWNING
> OF—TIP O'NEILL
> OF—HARRY STOVEY
> C—JACK MILLIGAN
> P—BOB CARUTHERS

The manager is Charlie Comiskey, who won four pennants and finished second twice with St. Louis.

Orr had a .353 lifetime average, most of it in the Association. O'Neill batted .492 in 1887, that strange year when walks were counted as hits. Caruthers won 168 games in five seasons. But the hero of the Association was Pete Browning, "The Old Gladiator," who hit like Ted Williams, played like Pete Rose, and talked like Dizzy Dean.

He drank. He boasted. But he hit .355. And there is no plaque for him in Cooperstown.

THE UNION ASSOCIATION

Assuming that the success of the American Association meant that there was room for yet a *third* major league, Henry V. Lucas, a St. Louis millionaire with egalitarian tendencies, formed the Union Association for the 1884 season in order to advance the rights of the players. (The most prestigious of the players who jumped to the new league, George Wright, did so in order to sell the baseballs his sporting goods company manufactured.) The "Onions" lasted but one season and folded when Lucas, who lost a considerable amount of money on the venture, refused to support a second season. But the UA did produce two oddities: the smallest city ever to hold a major league franchise, Altoona, PA; and the briefest franchise, St. Paul, MN, which dropped out after winning only two of its eight games.

1B—JUMBO SHOENECK
2B—FRED DUNLAP
3B—JACK GLEASON
SS—GERMANY SMITH
OF—ORATOR SCHAFFER
OF—HARRY MOORE
OF—EMMETT SEERY
C—CANNONBALL CRANE
P—BILLY TAYLOR

Shoeneck batted .308 with the combined Chicago-Pittsburgh franchise and with Baltimore. Dunlap, the star of the league, led in batting (.420) as well as in home runs, hits and runs scored; he also managed the St. Louis team to the pennant by a wide margin but by the end of a season, which saw so many cities get into the act, very few cared. Gleason batted .312 for St. Louis. Smith batted .307 for Altoona in 25 games, but then the team folded and he wandered off to play for Cleveland in the National League.

Schaffer finished second in batting (.354) for St. Louis. Moore batted .337 for Washington in his only season in the majors. Seery hit .309 for Baltimore and in one game for Kansas City, which replaced Altoona. Crane played more in the outfield than behind the plate for Boston and batted only .231, but he was second in home runs behind Dunlap. And Taylor won 24 and lost only 2 for St. Louis—then jumped to Philadelphia in the American Association, where he was 18-12.

THE PLAYERS LEAGUE

The Players League arose out of labor unrest among players in the late 1880s, stemming most immediately from an attempt by owners to impose a classification system (based on deportment rather than performance) for establishing salaries. Led by star pitcher-shortstop-attorney Monte Ward, numerous members of the Players' Brotherhood bolted from the National League and American Association to form their own league for the 1890 season. Everyone ended up losing money, with the National League in particular forced to the edge of ruin. The revolt came to an end when the players were outsmarted at a peace conference and agreed to merge with the National League.

> 1B—ROGER CONNOR
> 2B—LOU BIERBAUER
> 3B—BILL JOYCE
> SS—JOHN MONTGOMERY WARD
> OF—PETE BROWNING
> OF—HARDY RICHARDSON
> OF—JIM O'ROURKE
> C—BUCK EWING
> P—CHARLIE RADBOURN

Connor batted .372 for New York and led the league in home runs. Bierbauer hit .319 for Brooklyn. Joyce hit .269 for the same club and led the league in walks. Ward completed an exceptional infield for Brooklyn by batting .371. (Dave Orr, the first baseman, hit .387.)

Browning led the league for Cleveland with a .391 average, while Richardson of Boston hit .332 and was second in homers and O'Rourke of New York came in at .366. Ewing hit .349 for New York and Radbourn led Boston to the pennant with a record of 26-12.

The hero of the league was Boston manager King Kelly, who refused a $10,000 bonus and a blank contract from Boston's National League team in order to remain with the Brotherhood. (He also hit .324 as a catcher and shortstop.)

THE FEDERAL LEAGUE

Unlike the Union Association and the Players League, the Federal League was a capitalist venture. Millionaire James A. Gilmore took over a regional minor league in 1913 and persuaded other like-minded tycoons to challenge the National and American leagues. The league lasted for two seasons, 1914 and 1915, during which it attracted a number of star players and missed out on some others only because National and American league franchise owners dramatically increased salaries to dissuade would-be defectors. The Feds seemed to weaken in their second year, but still represented a strong enough threat to their older rivals that a contemplated move of their Newark franchise to New York set the scene for both sides to agree to peace talks. The terms included the purchase of the Chicago Cubs and St. Louis Browns by Federal owners, long-term buyouts for other owners and the assumption of $385,000 in player contracts by the older leagues.

1B—HAL CHASE
2B—DUKE KENWORTHY
3B—JIMMY WALSH
SS—JIMMY ESMOND
OF—BENNY KAUFF
OF—DUTCH ZWILLING
OF—VIN CAMPBELL
C—TED EASTERLY
P—GENE PACKARD

Chase hit .354 and .284 for Buffalo. Kenworthy batted .317 and .298 and also led the league in homers with 15 in 1914 for Kansas City. Walsh batted .310 and .304 for Baltimore. Esmond was .295 with Indianapolis in 1914 and .258 with Newark in 1915. Kauff, "the Ty Cobb of the Feds," led the league in batting both seasons—.366 for Indianapolis and then .344 for Brooklyn. Campbell hit .315 for Kansas City in 1914 and followed up with a .314 average for Newark the next year. Zwilling hit .308 and .291 and finished among the leaders in homers while with Chicago. Easterly was .331 and .267 for Kansas City. The same team's Packard was the only pitcher to win 20 games both years, compiling a 20-14 record in 1914 and a 20-12 mark in 1915.

The manager is Joe Tinker for bringing Chicago home second the first year and winning the pennant the next.

THE MINORS

Once upon a time players actually made careers in the minors. These were the best.

THE MINORS

1B—JOE HAUSER
2B—EDDIE MULLIGAN
3B—FRITZ MAISEL
SS—JOE BOLEY
OF—JIGGER STATZ
OF—SPENCER HARRIS
OF—IKE BOONE
C—ERNIE LOMBARDI
P—FRANK SHELLENBACK

Hauser hit 399 minor league home runs and 79 in the majors; his best years were 1930 (63 with Baltimore) and 1933 (69 with Minneapolis). Mulligan was a smart and scrappy mainstay of eight different Pacific Coast League teams from 1919 to 1938. Maisel and Boley were the backbone of the Baltimore Orioles teams that won seven consecutive pennants in the International League (1919–25); they were the only ones to play for all seven championship teams. Statz collected 3356 hits during his 18 years with the Pacific Coast League Los Angeles Angels (1920–21, 1925–26 and 1929–42); in 1926 he led the PCL with 291 hits. Harris had 3617 hits in his 26 years in the minors; his lifetime average was .318. Boone won five batting championships in three different leagues, his highest average being .407 with Mission of the PCL in 1929; after 83 games in 1930 he was batting .448 and was called up to the Dodgers. Lombardi spent only four seasons in the minors but never batted below .366. Shellenback won 295 and lost 178 for four Pacific Coast League teams between 1920 and 1938; he also won 20 and lost 14 in the International League.

Honorable mention to switch-hitting outfielder-first baseman Buzz Arlett, who spent 13 years with the Oakland Oaks of the Pacific Coast League (1918–1930) and hit 251 homers.

MEXICAN JUMPING BEANS

The last mass defection from the established major leagues occurred in 1946, when 20-odd players accepted big money offers to jump to the Mexican League. Among them were:

1B—NAP REYES
2B—GEORGE HAUSMANN
3B—LOU KLEIN
SS—VERN STEPHENS
OF—LUIS OLMO
OF—DANNY GARDELLA
OF—ROY ZIMMERMAN
C—MICKEY OWEN
P—MAX LANIER

Other jumpers included Roland Gladu and pitchers Sal Maglie, Fred Martin, Alex Carrasquel, Ace Adams, Harry Feldman and Jean Pierre Roy.

The shortest-lived expatriate was Stephens, who only played two games in Mexico before caving in to blackball threats. The others were, in fact, blacklisted until a 1949 agreement allowed for their reinstatement.

The overwhelming majority of the defectors came from the Cardinal (Klein, Lanier and Martin), Dodger (Olmo, Owen, Gladu and Roy) and Giant (Reyes, Hausmann, Gardella, Zimmerman, Maglie, Adams and Feldman) organizations. Stephens belonged to the Browns and Carrasquel to the White Sox.

SUN DEVILS

Arizona State University is one of the great baseball institutions. The best of the 37 players ASU has sent to the major leagues are:

1B—RICK MONDAY
2B—BUMP WILLS
3B—SAL BANDO
SS—ALAN BANNISTER
OF—REGGIE JACKSON
OF—KEN LANDREAUX
OF—HUBIE BROOKS
C—DUFFY DYER
P—LARRY GURA

Brooks is, of course, a third baseman, but he played shortstop and the outfield in college.

Honorable mention to Gary Allenson, Chris Bando, Floyd Bannister, Gary Gentry, Bob Horner, Lerrin La-Grow, Gary Rajsich, Lenny Randle, Craig Swan and Ed Vande Berg.

Bobby Winkles is the only college coach to become a major league manager, jumping from ASU to the Oakland A's in 1977.

THE JAPANESE LEAGUES

Baseball is no longer exclusively an American sport and no book of this sort would be complete without this Samurai selection.

1B—SADAHARU OH	Yomiuri Giants
2B—SHIGERU CHIBA	Yomiuri Giants
3B—SHIGEO NAGASHIMA	Yomiuri Giants
SS—YOSHIO YOSHIDA	Hanshin Tigers
OF—SHINICHI ETO	Chunichi Dragons
OF—SHIGERU TAKADA	Yomiuri Giants
OF—ISAO HARIMOTO	Toei Flyers
C—KATSUYA NOMURA	Nankai Hawks
P—MASAICHI KANEDA	Kokutetsu Swallows

The Giants dominate here, which should be no surprise since they have won more Japan Series than any other team.

Oh hit more home runs than Hank Aaron. Nagashima

was the most popular player in the history of Japanese baseball and once hit a famous home run to break up a tie game and allow the Emperor to catch a train. Harimoto holds the Japanese record for highest lifetime average, .383. And Kaneda won 400 games (including 20 or more for 14 consecutive seasons), struck out 4490 batters and once fanned Mickey Mantle three straight times.

ROOKIES

Everything you ever wanted to know about greenhorns—
the ones who succeeded and the ones who didn't.

BEST ROOKIE YEARS

Every spring managers look over a fresh crop of rookies.
Their hope is that they will find a kid who will have a year
like these did.

1B—DALE ALEXANDER	1929 Tigers
2B—TONY LAZZERI	1926 Yankees
3B—JIMMY WILLIAMS	1899 Pirates
SS—JOHNNY PESKY	1942 Red Sox
OF—JOE JACKSON	1911 Indians
OF—GEORGE WATKINS	1930 Cardinals
OF—TED WILLIAMS	1939 Red Sox
C—BILL DICKEY	1929 Yankees
P—GROVER CLEVELAND ALEXANDER	1911 Phillies

Dale Alexander hit .343 with 25 home runs. Lazzeri had
18 homers and 114 RBIs. Jimmy Williams batted .355 and
had a 27-game hitting streak. Pesky finished with a .331
average. Jackson, who appeared in 30 games between
1908 and 1910, hit an astonishing .408 in his first full season. Watkins' .373 is the highest average ever for a rookie
after Jackson. Ted Williams batted .327 with 31 homers
and a record 145 RBIs. Dickey's rookie batting average
was .324. And Alexander holds several rookie pitching

records—most wins (28 as opposed to 13 losses), most complete games (31) and most shutouts (7).

Honorable mention to Wally Berger (1930 Braves) and Frank Robinson (1956 Reds), who hold the major league record for most home runs as a rookie, 38; Al Rosen (1950 Indians), who holds the AL record, 37; Tony Oliva (1964 Twins), whose .323 average made him the only rookie ever to win a batting championship; Lloyd Waner (1927 Pirates), whose record 223 hits gave him a .355 average; and Dwight Gooden (1984 Mets), whose 276 strikeouts is a rookie record and whose 11.39 strikeouts per nine innings established a major league record.

BEST DEBUTS

Talk about getting off to a good start!

1B—WILLIE McCOVEY	July 30, 1959	Giants
2B—SPOOK JACOBS	April 13, 1954	Athletics
3B—CECIL TRAVIS	May 16, 1933	Senators
SS—BERT CAMPANERIS	July 23, 1964	Athletics
OF—BOB NIEMAN	Sept. 14, 1951	Browns
OF—FRED CLARKE	June 30, 1894	Louisville
OF—BOBBY BONDS	June 25, 1968	Giants
C—ED IRVIN	May 18, 1912	Tigers
P—BUMPUS JONES	October 15, 1892	Reds

In their first big league games:

McCovey had two triples and two singles. Jacobs singled four times. Travis had five singles in a 12-inning game. Campaneris had two home runs. Nieman went Campaneris one better by becoming the only player in major league history to homer in his first two at bats. Bonds had a grand-slam. Irvin, a sandlot player called upon to play for the Tigers along with a crew of St. Joseph's College students when the Tigers struck to have the suspended Ty Cobb reinstated, had two triples—and never appeared in another major league game.

Most amazing of all was Jones, who entered the Cincinnati clubhouse on the last day of the season, suggested that he was the best pitcher on the premises and, after having had his challenge accepted, went out to the mound and hurled a no-hitter over the Pirates. That day also turned out to be Jones's last moment of glory. Signed to a contract for the 1893 season, he was batted around in both spring training and in early-season games, moved on to the Giants, and disappeared forever. Jones rates as the starter over Bobo Holloman, whose no-hitter for the Browns on May 6, 1953, was his first start but not his first appearance.

RIGHT OFF THE BAT

These players are among the forty-eight in the history of baseball to have homered in their first at bat.

1B—REGGIE SANDERS	Sept. 1, 1974	Tigers
2B—DAVE MACHEMER	June 21, 1978	Angels
3B—GARY GAETTI	Sept. 20, 1981	Twins
SS—JOHNNY LEMASTER	Sept. 21, 1975	Giants
OF—CLYDE VOLLMER	May 21, 1942	Reds
OF—CHUCK TANNER	April 12, 1955	Braves
OF—FRANK ERNAGA	May 24, 1957	Cubs
C—MIKE FITZGERALD	Sept. 13, 1983	Mets
P—PETE RICHERT	April 12, 1962	Dodgers

Richert struck out the first six major league batters he faced.

This team does not include the earlier-mentioned Bob Nieman and Bert Campaneris. Like Campaneris, Vollmer and Tanner are among an even more select number that homered on the first pitch. Ernaga followed his homer (off Warren Spahn) with a triple and actually had five extra base blows in his first eight plate appearances. (His major league career consisted of 11 hits in 43 at bats, with seven of the hits for extra bases.) Fitzgerald is the last catcher to have accomplished the feat.

Honorable mention to Hoyt Wilhelm, who homered his first time up and then played for 21 more years without hitting another.

And to Bill Duggleby, a pitcher with the Phillies in 1898 who was not only the first player to homer his first time up, but who did it with flair—by stroking a grand-slam.

MOST VALUABLE ROOKIES

Since the institution of the Rookie of the Year award in 1947, only 13 players have followed up that honor by also winning recognition as a Most Valuable Player. The first date below refers to the rookie award, the second to the MVP year.

1B—ORLANDO CEPEDA	1958 Giants	1969 Cardinals
2B—PETE ROSE	1963 Reds	1973 Reds
3B—DICK ALLEN	1964 Phillies	1972 White Sox
SS—CAL RIPKEN	1982 Orioles	1983 Orioles
OF—WILLIE MAYS	1951 Giants	1954 and 1965 Giants
OF—FRANK ROBINSON	1956 Reds	1961 Reds, 1966 Orioles
OF—FRED LYNN	1975 Red Sox	1975 Red Sox
C—JOHNNY BENCH	1968 Reds	1970 and 1972 Reds
P—DON NEWCOMBE	1949 Dodgers	1956 Dodgers

Rose, Allen and Ripken had changed positions by the time they won their MVP awards. Rose started at second and moved to the outfield, Allen went from third to first and Ripken was a rookie third baseman and an MVP shortstop.

Newcombe deserves special mention as the only player to win not only Rookie of the Year and MVP honors, but also the Cy Young Award (1956).

So, too, does Lynn, who is the only player to win both awards in the same year.

The other double winners are Jackie Robinson (1947 and 1949 Dodgers), Willie McCovey (1959 and 1969 Giants),

Rod Carew (1967 and 1977 Twins) and Thurman Munson (1970 and 1976 Yankees).

MAJORS ONLY

The list of players who went directly to the majors without minor league experience is a short one, but it includes some impressive names.

1B—FRANK CHANCE
2B—FRANKIE FRISCH
3B—BOB HORNER
SS—ERNIE BANKS
OF—MEL OTT
OF—AL KALINE
OF—DAVE WINFIELD
C—KING KELLY
P—SANDY KOUFAX

Chance and Kelly actually played in the minors, but not until after their major league careers were over. Horner was assigned to the Braves Triple-A affiliate, but refused to go and won an arbitration suit over his demotion. Winfield is worthy of note for having been drafted out of college not only by a baseball team, but also by professional football and basketball franchises.

WHAT DID THEY DO WRONG?

Some players come up to the major leagues, do little, and quickly disappear; others come up to the majors, make the best of limited opportunities, but disappear just as quickly. For instance:

1B—MIKE SCHEMER	.330	1945–46 Giants
	(36-for-109)	
2B—JERRY LIPSCOMB	.326	1937 Browns
	(31-for-96)	
3B—FRANK SKAFF	.320	1935 Dodgers,
	(24-for-75)	1943 Athletics
SS—BOOB FOWLER	.326	1923–25 Reds,
	(57-for-175)	1926 Red Sox
OF—TRIP SIGMAN	.326	1929–30 Phillies
	(42-for-129)	
OF—TOM HUGHES	.373	1930 Tigers
	(22-for-59)	
OF—CHARLIE DORMAN	.367	1923 White Sox,
	(29-for-79)	1928 Indians
C—JACK CUMMINGS	.341	1926–29 Giants,
	(45-for-132)	1929 Braves
P—EDDIE YUHAS	12–2	1952–53
	(2.73 ERA)	Cardinals

Honorable mention to Butch Sanicki for his 17 plate appearances and .294 batting average, on five hits (a single, a double and three home runs) that drove in 8 runs and allowed him to score five; John Paciorek for his 3-for-3 game in which he also walked twice, drove in three runs and scored four; Luis Silverio for a 6-for-11 career that left him with a batting average of .545 and a slugging average of .909; and to John Gaddy, who started two games for the 1938 Dodgers, completed one, won both and finished with an ERA of 0.69.

FLASHES

In their rookie years, or during parts of them, they made everyone sit up and notice; in their second year, or even second time around the league, the only thing to notice was that they had become easy outs.

1B—BOB HALE	1955 Orioles
2B—LOU KLEIN	1943 Cardinals
3B—TED COX	1977 Red Sox
SS—HARRY CHAPPAS	1978 White Sox
OF—BOB HAZLE	1957 Braves
OF—ROY FOSTER	1970 Indians
OF—DINO RESTELLI	1949 Pirates
C—JACK SHEPARD	1954 Pirates
P—VON McDANIEL	1957 Cardinals

Hale's .357 batting average made him the only member of his team with at least 100 at bats to reach .300. Klein batted .287 and scored 62 runs to help win a pennant, went off to war, never won a regular job when he came back, and jumped to Mexico. Cox hit .362 after being called up in September and almost brought Boston a pennant. Chappas was supposed to be another Rizzuto, but the main similarity was their height. Hurricane Hazle hit .403 in 43 games to spearhead Milwaukee's pennant drive and to become the flashiest of all flashes. Foster missed by only a couple of votes of being Rookie of the Year, then quickly faded. Restelli hit eight homers in his first 10 games, and only five in his last 83. Both offensively and defensively, Shepard looked like one of the few major leaguers on the lowly Pirates for a while, but was soon only a hanger-on. McDaniel filled ballparks around the National League with shutout performances and low-hit games, but barely got out of Florida in 1958.

PHENOMS

They couldn't miss. They had incredible minor league or college records, they had major league positions waiting for them, and they had the media constantly telling them how great they were going to be. Unfortunately, they then actually took the field.

PHENOMS

1B—BOB NELSON	1955 Orioles
2B—TED KAZANSKI	1953 Phillies
3B—BILLY HARRELL	1955 Indians
SS—NELSON NORMAN	1978 Rangers
OF—CLINT HARTUNG	1947 Giants
OF—CARLOS BERNIER	1953 Pirates
OF—BOB LENNON	1954 Giants
C—BOB TAYLOR	1957 Braves
P—RUBE MELTON	1941 Phillies

Nelson, ballyhooed as "the Babe Ruth of Texas," never homered in the majors and hit .205. Kazanski, originally a shortstop, hit .217 both in his first season and lifetime. Harrell stopped hitting even in the minors after averaging only .231 for Cleveland. Norman hit .225 and had an elevator career with the Rangers. Hartung, the phenom prototype, warmed a Polo Grounds bench for seven years as a .212 hitter and an even more forgettable pitcher. Bernier lasted a single season (.213) after establishing all kinds of records in the Pacific Coast League. Lennon was called up after belting 64 homers one year in the Southern Association; in the majors he batted .165 and hit one homer in 79 plate appearances. Taylor hung around as a third-string catcher for some years, winding up at .218. Melton's minor league credentials were so seductive that three teams—the Phillies, Cardinals and Dodgers—got into hot water with the commissioner's office over a circus series of tamperings and under-the-table deals orchestrated by Branch Rickey. He ended up with a record of 30 wins and 50 losses.

LEAD STARTS

Some of the best players in the game might have compiled even better career statistics if they had been allowed to subtract their first years in the majors as regulars.

1B—RUSTY STAUB	1963 Astros
2B—NELLIE FOX	1950 White Sox
3B—MIKE SCHMIDT	1973 Phillies
SS—PEEWEE REESE	1941 Dodgers
OF—LOU BROCK	1962 Cubs
OF—ROBERTO CLEMENTE	1955 Pirates
OF—REGGIE SMITH	1967 Red Sox
C—RAY SCHALK	1913 White Sox
P—RED RUFFING	1925 Red Sox

Staub struggled through with six homers and a .224 average. Fox batted .247 and had only four stolen bases. Schmidt managed 18 homers, but also struck out 136 times and batted a mere .196. Reese led the National League with 47 errors and only batted .229. Brock hit .263 and struck out six times as often as he swiped a base (96 to 16). Clemente checked in to Pittsburgh with a .255 mark and five homers. Smith started off at .246 and struck out 95 times. Hall of Famer Schalk could do no better than .244. Ruffing, who was to suffer throughout his career in Boston, debuted with a record of 9-18 and an ERA of 5.01. He also walked 75 batters while striking out only 64.

THE BRIEFEST REGULARS

Playing regularly is the goal of every major leaguer, and having played regularly is the consolation of players consigned to the bench or to a pinch-hitting role after a couple of seasons as daily starters. There have, however, been a few players who have gone directly from a regular job to oblivion—one season appearing in more than a hundred games and the next not considered good enough even to wear a major league uniform.

1B—ART MAHAN	145 games, 1940 Phillies
2B—SPARKY ANDERSON	152 games, 1959 Phillies
3B—BUDDY BLAIR	137 games, 1942 Phillies
SS—GAIR ALLIE	121 games, 1954 Pirates
OF—LARRY MURPHY	107 games, 1891 Washington (AA)
OF—ERNIE SULIK	105 games, 1936 Phillies
OF—GOAT ANDERSON	121 games, 1907 Pirates
C—ARCHIE CLARK	101 games, 1890 Giants
P—BILL SWEENEY	83 games, 1884 Baltimore (UA)

The Phillies obviously had their problems.

Clark is the exception here. He shared the catching duties with three others, appearing in only 36 games behind the plate but also playing both the outfield and three infield positions. He is also the only player in this lineup to have an encore, returning in 1891 for 46 games, almost all of them as a catcher.

Of all the managers who lasted one full season and only one full season we'll take Jack Barry. Once part of Connie Mack's $100,000 Infield, Barry played second base for the Red Sox in 1917, managed the team to a second-place finish (90-62, nine games out of first), was fired and gave up the business forever.

Sweeney finished his only season on the mound with a rather commendable 40-21 record. His twentieth-century counterpart was Harry Schmidt, who was 21-13 with Brooklyn in his rookie year (1903) and then never again appeared in a box score.

YOUNGEST PLAYERS

Otherwise known as the Joe Nuxhall Team.

1B—ED KRANEPOOL	17	1962 Mets
2B—TED SEPKOWSKI	18	1942 Indians
3B—PUTSY CABALLERO	16	1944 Phillies
SS—TOMMY BROWN	16	1944 Dodgers
OF—MEL OTT	17	1926 Giants
OF—AL KALINE	18	1953 Tigers
OF—WILLIE CRAWFORD	17	1964 Dodgers
C—JIMMIE FOXX	17	1925 Athletics
P—JOE NUXHALL	15	1944 Reds

All of these players put in little more than token appearances in their first years. In the case of Nuxhall it was more of a slug appearance, his ⅔ of an inning leading to two hits, five walks, and an ERA of 67.50.

Numerous honorable mentions here, including several outfielders (Lew Malone and Moose Brown, most prominently) who were only a few months older than Kaline. The youngest American League hurler was 16-year-old Carl Scheib of the 1943 Athletics.

The manager is Roger Peckinpaugh, who skippered the 1914 Yankees for 17 games at the age of 23.

THE YOUNGEST REGULARS

As any aging veteran with tired legs will tell you, baseball is a young man's game. These players carried that general rule to the extreme.

1B—PHIL CAVARRETTA	19	1935 Cubs
2B—LARRY DOYLE	20	1907 Giants
3B—SIBBY SISTI	19	1940 Braves
SS—ROBIN YOUNT	18	1974 Brewers
OF—LES MANN	19	1913 Braves
OF—AL KALINE	19	1954 Tigers
OF—TONY CONIGLIARO	19	1964 Red Sox
C—DEL CRANDALL	19	1949 Braves
P—WILLIE McGILL	17	1891 Cincinnati-Milwaukee (AA), St. Louis (AA)

Cavarretta batted .275, Doyle .260, Sisti .251, Yount .250, Mann .253, Kaline .276, Conigliaro .290 with 24 home runs, and Crandall .263. McGill won 20 games in his second season.

Honorable mention to Buddy Lewis (1936 Senators), Mel Ott (1928 Giants) and Ty Cobb (1906 Tigers), all of whom missed this team by being only months older than the players named at their positions here.

A special note on Al Kaline, who won a batting crown in 1955—when he was practically an old man.

The manager is Lou Boudreau, who led the Cleveland Indians to fourth place in 1942—at the age of 25.

FIRST BLACKS

After Moses and Welday Walker were driven out of baseball in 1884, black ballplayers entered the major leagues infrequently and through deception. A catcher named Irwin Sandy passed himself off as a Mexican, a Spaniard and an Italian until 1886; he played under the assumed name, Sandy Nava. George Treadway claimed to be an American Indian and lasted until 1896. Half a century later came Jackie Robinson and . . .

1B—JACKIE ROBINSON	1947	Dodgers
2B—HANK THOMPSON	1947	Browns,
	1949	Giants
3B—OZZIE VIRGIL	1958	Tigers
SS—ERNIE BANKS	1953	Cubs
OF—LARRY DOBY	1947	Indians
OF—CARLOS PAULA	1954	Senators
OF—SAM JETHROE	1950	Braves
C—ELSTON HOWARD	1955	Yankees
P—BOB TRICE	1953	Athletics

For the record, the other first black Americans on teams were: Sam Hairston, 1951 White Sox; Tom Alston, 1954 Cardinals; Nino Escalera, 1954 Reds; Curt Roberts, 1954 Pirates; John Kennedy, 1957 Phillies; and Pumpsie Green,

1959 Red Sox. Obviously some teams were in no hurry to integrate the clubhouse.

Honorable mentions to:

John Wright, Roy Campanella, Don Newcombe and Roy Partlow, signed by the Dodgers after Robinson, but before Doby and Thompson by the Indians and Browns, respectively.

Dan Bankhead, 1947 Dodgers, the first black pitcher in the majors.

Gene Baker, 1953 Cubs, who came up with Banks.

Pat Scantlebury, 1956 Reds, the last player to make the jump from the Negro leagues to the majors.

Frank Robinson, 1975 Indians, the first black manager.

Emmett Ashford, 1966 American League, the first black umpire.

It should also be noted that Virgil, the first black in a Detroit uniform, had played for the Giants in 1956 and 1957.

SOPHOMORE SUCCESSES

One of the more enduring baseball myths is the Sophomore Jinx, which dictates that a fine rookie season can only be followed by a catastrophic second year. These winners of the Baseball Writers Rookie of the Year Award explode that myth.

1B—ORLANDO CEPEDA	1958 and 1959 Giants
2B—TED SIZEMORE	1969 and 1970 Dodgers
3B—BOB HORNER	1978 and 1979 Braves
SS—HARVEY KUENN	1953 and 1954 Tigers
OF—TONY OLIVA	1964 and 1965 Twins
OF—SAM JETHROE	1950 and 1951 Braves
OF—FRANK ROBINSON	1956 and 1957 Reds
C—JOHNNY BENCH	1968 and 1969 Reds
P—HERB SCORE	1955 and 1956 Indians

Cepeda followed his .312, 25 home runs and 96 RBI rookie season with .317, 27 homers and 105 RBIs. Sizemore's average jumped from .271 to .306. Horner's brief rookie year (89 games) ended with a .266 average, 23 homers and 63 RBIs; the following season in 121 games he batted .314, hit 33 home runs and drove in 98. Kuenn's average dropped two points from .308 to .306, but that is hardly proof of a jinx. Oliva also dropped two points, from .323 to .321—but he won the batting championship both years. Jethroe's average went from .273 to .280 and he led the league in stolen bases with 35 each season. Robinson's homers and RBIs declined, from 38 and 83 to 29 and 75, but his batting average jumped from .290 to .322. Bench's numbers were .275, 15 and 82 his first year and .293, 26 and 90 his second season. And Score won rookie honors on the basis of a 16-10 won-lost record with a 2.85 ERA and a league-leading 245 strikeouts; he followed this up with 20-9, 2.53 and a league-leading 263 strikeouts.

JINXED SOPHOMORES

On the other hand there are:

1B—WALT DROPO	1950 and 1951 Red Sox
2B—KEN HUBBS	1962 and 1963 Cubs
3B—GIL McDOUGALD	1951 and 1952 Yankees
SS—ALVIN DARK	1948 and 1949 Braves
OF—ROY SIEVERS	1949 and 1950 Browns
OF—AL BUMBRY	1973 and 1974 Orioles
OF—JOE CHARBONEAU	1980 and 1981 Indians
C—THURMAN MUNSON	1970 and 1971 Yankees
P—HARRY BYRD	1952 and 1953 Athletics

Dropo declined across the board—136 games to 99, .332 average to .239, 34 homers to 11, 144 RBIs (a league-leading total) to 57. Hubbs dropped from a .260 average to .235 and from a league-leading 129 runs scored to 93. McDougald's average dipped from .306 to .263. Dark went from .322 to .276. Sievers declined from .306, 16 home runs and 91 RBIs to .238, 10 and 57.

Bumbry's average fell an astonishing 104 points from .337 to .233. Charboneau—.289, 23 homers and 87 RBIs as a rookie—spent most of the next season in the minor leagues and finished the season with only 48 major league games played, a .210 average, 4 home runs and 18 RBIs. Munson's batting average fell 51 points from .302 to .251. And Byrd—15-15 with a 3.31 ERA as a rookie—closed his second season with an 11-20 record and a 5.51 ERA.

ODDS AND ODDS

Some odd facts regarding rookies:

1B—RON ALLEN	1972	Cardinals
2B—EMMETT MUELLER	1938	Phillies
3B—BUDDY LEWIS	1936	Senators
SS—JIM BAUMER	1949	White Sox
OF—WILLIE MURPHY	Career	
OF—ERNIE KOY	1938	Dodgers
OF—ALLEN LEWIS	1973	Athletics
C—CLINT COURTNEY	1951	Yankees
P—JIM DERRINGTON	1956	White Sox

Allen, brother of Dick Allen, is the only major leaguer whose only hit was a home run (he went 1-for-11). On opening day at Ebbets Field in 1938, Mueller hit his first major league home run in the top of the first inning and Koy hit his maiden homer in the bottom of the same inning. Third baseman Lewis was so daunted by the presence of President Franklin Delano Roosevelt at the Washington opener that he asked to be taken out of the lineup (and was). When manager Jack Onslow told Baumer to grab a bat for the his first major league appearance, the infielder fainted. Murphy's entire career was concentrated into 1884—when he played for three different teams (Cleveland, Washington, Boston) in three different leagues (the National League, the American Association, the Union League, respectively)! Lewis, Charlie Finley's first experiment in specialized pinch-running, appeared in 35 games without once coming to the plate. Courtney was baseball's first bespectacled catcher. At the age of 17, Derrington became the youngest pitcher ever to start a major league game. He lost that game and another the following season, and was washed up as a major leaguer at the age of 18!

THE END AND AFTER

What they did after hanging up their gloves. Or, in some cases, *why* they hung up their gloves when they did.

THEY DIED WITH THEIR SPIKES ON

Although Lou Gehrig was the most noted player forced to the sidelines by a fatal disease, he was actually out of the game two years before finally succumbing. Others met quicker ends.

1B—HARRY AGGANIS	1955	Red Sox
2B—KEN HUBBS	1963	Cubs
3B—TONY BOECKEL	1923	Braves
SS—RAY CHAPMAN	1920	Indians
OF—ED DELAHANTY	1903	Senators
OF—LEN KOENECKE	1935	Dodgers
OF—ROBERTO CLEMENTE	1972	Pirates
C—THURMAN MUNSON	1979	Yankees
P—DON WILSON	1974	Astros

Agganis was felled by a pulmonary embolism. Hubbs, Munson and Clemente died in plane crashes. Chapman, the only on-field fatality, was beaned by Carl Mays. (His last words were, "Tell Mays I'm all right.") Delahanty went on a bender and jumped off the International Bridge into the Niagara River. Wilson died of asphyxiation in his own garage—an apparent suicide. Boeckel was hit by an automobile while looking at the wreckage of a two-vehicle collision he had survived just minutes before.

The Koenecke story is somewhat bizarre. A promising

but streaky outfielder for the Dodgers in the 1930s, he was sent home from a road trip on which he had not hit at all. He took a train from St. Louis to Detroit, then inexplicably chartered a plane. On the flight, his first, Koenecke went absolutely berserk and the co-pilot was forced to hit him on the head with a fire extinguisher to subdue him. A second blow fractured his skull and he died later in a Toronto hospital.

In addition to Delahanty and Wilson, Chick Stahl, Win Mercer and Willard Hershberger also took their own lives.

THE DISABLED

While it is true that Ray Chapman is the only major leaguer ever killed on the field, numerous others have had distinguished or promising careers shortened, when not ended altogether, by serious injuries.

1B—LUKE EASTER	1953 Indians
2B—FELIX MILLAN	1977 Mets
3B—BOBBY VALENTINE	1973 Angels
SS—RAY CORHAN	1911 White Sox
OF—PETE REISER	1946 Dodgers
OF—EARLE COMBS	1934 Yankees
OF—TONY CONIGLIARO	1967 Red Sox
C—MICKEY COCHRANE	1937 Tigers
P—HERB SCORE	1957 Indians

Head injuries from pitched balls or line drives knocked out Corhan, Combs, Conigliaro, Cochrane and Score. Easter and Valentine were victimized by broken legs. Millan had a shoulder bone broken when Pirate catcher Ed Ott picked him up and threw him to the ground after a hard slide at second. Reiser, of course, remains the epitome of the player whose career was devastated by injuries: Among other things, he suffered a fractured skull in 1942, a broken ankle in 1946 and another fractured skull in 1947. Despite the greater physical seriousness of the head injuries, it was the 1946 break that probably contributed most to his abbreviated career, robbing him of his exceptional speed.

THE EXILES

Baseball has had to admit to more dirty wash than just the 1919 Black Sox.

1B—HAL CHASE	1919 Giants
2B—GENE PAULETTE	1920 Phillies
3B—HEINIE ZIMMERMAN	1919 Giants
SS—AL NICHOLS	1877 Louisville
OF—GEORGE HALL	1877 Louisville
OF—BENNY KAUFF	1920 Giants
OF—JIMMY O'CONNELL	1924 Giants
C—BILL CRAVER	1877 Louisville
P—PHIL DOUGLAS	1922 Giants

With the exception of Kauff and Craver, all these players were banned for alleged involvement with gamblers and/or throwing games. Kauff was indicted, but cleared of abetting an auto theft ring. But baseball decided that its sense of morality was more important than a court's sense of legality. Although usually linked with Nichols, Hall and pitcher Jim Devlin as the "Louisville Crooks," catcher-shortstop Craver was actually banned because he refused to sign a non-gambling pledge circulated in the immediate aftermath of the scandal. His conviction that such a pledge constituted an invasion of privacy was a principle recognized neither by club owners of the time nor most subsequent baseball historians.

The manager is Jack O'Connor of the 1910 Browns, who ordered his third baseman, Red Corriden, to play deep against Nap Lajoie in a last-day-of-the-season doubleheader so Lajoie could beat out Ty Cobb for the batting title. Lajoie went 8-for-8, including six bunt singles, but Cobb won anyway.

The umpire is Richard Higham, who was expelled from the National League in 1882 for telling gamblers the probable winners of the games he was scheduled to officiate.

ONE YEAR TOO MANY

There are few sadder sights in baseball than watching an aged star performing from memory. The following is a lineup of players who should have quit while they were ahead:

1B—ERNIE BANKS	1971 Cubs
2B—BILL MAZEROSKI	1972 Pirates
3B—KEN BOYER	1969 Dodgers
SS—BOBBY WALLACE	1913–16 Cardinals, 1917–18 Browns
OF—WILLIE MAYS	1973 Mets
OF—CHUCK KLEIN	1940–44 Phillies
OF—HACK WILSON	1934 Dodgers-Phillies
C—WALKER COOPER	1956–57 Cardinals
P—EARLY WYNN	1961–62 White Sox, 1963 Indians

The most notorious cases are probably those of Mays, who as a member of the 1973 Mets showed the entire country the effects of age during the World Series against the Athletics, and Wynn, who labored long and mightily to notch his 300th win. Special mention must also be made of Cooper, who journeyed from one National League cellar team to another in the last years of his career, and Wallace, who bounced back and forth between the benches of the two St. Louis teams for six years.

TIMING IS ALL

On the other hand, many players have been able to read the writing on the wall even when their general managers and fans have insisted otherwise. Among them have been:

1B—HANK GREENBERG	1947 Pirates
2B—BOBBY DOERR	1951 Red Sox
3B—JOE SEWELL	1933 Yankees
SS—LUIS APARICIO	1973 Red Sox
OF—TED WILLIAMS	1960 Red Sox
OF—TY COBB	1928 Athletics
OF—JOE DiMAGGIO	1951 Yankees
C—WILBERT ROBINSON	1902 Orioles
P—SANDY KOUFAX	1966 Dodgers

Although many of these stars may have lost a step or two before calling it quits, they went out as regulars and with fielding and/or batting averages not appreciably lower than their career marks. The .249 average recorded by Greenborg in 1947 for the cellar-dwelling Pirates included 25 home runs, 74 runs batted in and a league-leading 104 walks, while DiMaggio's .263 (71 runs batted in) was due in good part to a heel injury. Williams, of course, went out at .316 and with a Fenway Park blast that has made John Updike as noted for his nonfiction as his fiction.

ONE LAST SHOT

Some players have second thoughts about retirement and return to give it one more try.

1B—DICK ALLEN	1977 Athletics
2B—JOHNNY EVERS	1922 White Sox,
	1929 Braves
3B—PIE TRAYNOR	1937 Pirates
SS—LEO DUROCHER	1943 and 1945 Dodgers
OF—CURT FLOOD	1971 Senators
OF—BABE HERMAN	1945 Dodgers
OF—SAM DUNGAN	1900 Cubs,
	1901 Senators
C—JIM O'ROURKE	1904 Giants
P—DIZZY TROUT	1957 Orioles

Two years after calling it quits, Allen returned to bat

.240 in 51 games. Evers, who had retired in 1917, was reactivated for single games by both Chicago and Boston. Manager Traynor reactivated himself after a one-year hiatus for five games and a .167 mark. After turning shortstop over to Peewee Reese in 1941, manager Durocher came back for six games in 1943 and two more (as a second baseman) in 1945. In the midst of his protest retirement over the reserve clause, Flood was persuaded by Washington owner Bob Short to come back for 13 games. Eight years after going home, Herman returned to Ebbets Field to bat .265 in 34 at bats. A fair hitter from 1892 to 1894, Dungan failed in a comeback with Chicago, but then hit an astonishing .320 for Washington. O'Rourke had been retired 11 years when, at the age of 52, he caught a pennant-deciding game and went 1-for-4. Five years after his retirement, Trout was so impressive in an Old-Timers game that Baltimore gave him another shot. He appeared in two games, got one batter out, and was belted around to the tune of an 81.00 ERA.

OLDEST PLAYERS

And some players try it at an age when most athletes have long since gone on to other things.

1B—CAP ANSON	46	1897	Cubs
2B—ARLIE LATHAM	50	1909	Giants
3B—JIMMY AUSTIN	49	1929	Dodgers
SS—BOBBY WALLACE	44	1918	Cardinals
OF—SAM THOMPSON	46	1906	Tigers
OF—SAM RICE	44	1934	Indians
OF—CARL YASTRZEMSKI	44	1983	Red Sox
C—JIM O'ROURKE	52	1904	Giants
P—SATCHEL PAIGE	59	1965	Athletics

Anson was the regular first baseman and beats out Dan Brouthers, who was one month younger when he played two games for the Giants in 1904 at the age of 46. Latham played in just two games. And Austin took the field in only one. Wallace played 12 games at short, 17 at second base ind one at third base. Thompson played eight games in the outfield, Rice played 78, and Yastrzemski only one (although he was the regular designated hitter). Over-40 catchers are common for some reason. Gabby Street (1931 Cardinals) and Deacon McGuire (1912 Tigers) each caught a game at the age of 48. But O'Rourke would be the oldest player ever to take up a glove were it not for Paige, who pitched three scoreless innings, giving up one hit and striking out one.

Honorable mention to Charley O'Leary, who singled and scored a run as a pinch-hitter just a few weeks shy of his 53rd birthday (1934 Browns). Also to Minnie Minoso, who as the designated hitter in three games for the 1976 White Sox at the age of 53 went 1-for-8 and became the oldest player to get a hit. Minoso also pinch-hit twice four years later (age 57, 1980 White Sox), but went hitless.

The manager is Connie Mack, who was a few months shy of his 89th birthday when he managed his last game in 1950.

OLDEST REGULARS

Some players don't just hang around, they hang in day after day. The following, for example, played at least 100 games in the seasons cited:

1B—CAP ANSON	46	1897	Cubs
2B—RABBIT MARANVILLE	41	1933	Braves
3B—JIMMY DYKES	39	1936	White Sox
SS—LUKE APPLING	42	1949	White Sox
OF—PETE ROSE	43	1984	Expos—Reds
OF—SAM RICE	41	1931	Senators
OF—STAN MUSIAL	41	1962	Cardinals
C—DEACON McGUIRE	40	1904	Yankees
P—HOYT WILHELM	47	1970	Braves—Cubs

Among the batters the most astonishing members of this lineup are Anson, who batted .302, Appling, who closed at .301, Rice, who hit .310, and Musial, who clouted

.330. Technically, McGuire was behind the plate for only 97 games, but the extra wear and tear of being a catcher entitles him to a place on the team.

Wilhelm's record for the year was 6-5 with 13 saves. Some may object that his 50 game appearances were less than the 57 turned in by Satchell Paige for the 1952 Browns, but the fact is that Paige was officially only 46 that year. In addition, the St. Louis right-hander had a far inferior 3-9 record.

RETURNING SONS

Somebody once said that managing was a temporary job with illusions of permanence. The disillusioning can be particularly painful in the cases of those major leaguers who became identified with one club for most of their playing days, finished out the string with another club, and then were summoned back to take over the team of their best years. Some of these have been:

1B—MICKEY VERNON	1961–63 Senators
2B—RED SCHOENDIENST	1965–76 Cardinals
3B—KEN BOYER	1978–80 Cardinals
SS—JIM FREGOSI	1978–81 Angels
OF—CASEY STENGEL	1934–36 Dodgers
OF—JIM MARSHALL	1974–76 Cubs
OF—TOMMY HOLMES	1951–52 Braves
C—JOE TORRE	1982–84 Braves
P—BURLEIGH GRIMES	1937–38 Dodgers

The moral? You *can* go home again, but don't take too much furniture back with you.

EVERYWHERE BUT HOME

When players become identified with a team during their careers and then go on to managing, the odds are pretty favorable that they will eventually be welcomed back to take over their *alma mater*. The following have *not* been:

```
        1B—FRANK ROBINSON
        2B—GENE MAUCH
        3B—DON ZIMMER
        SS—DONIE BUSH
        OF—TED WILLIAMS
        OF—HARRY CRAFT
        OF—CHUCK TANNER
         C—AL LOPEZ
         P—BOB LEMON
```

Some examples: Mauch played for six teams (Dodgers, Cubs, Pirates, Braves, Cardinals and Red Sox), but has managed four completely different ones (Phillies, Expos, Twins and Angels). Both Robinson and Lopez had only token appearances with the Indians at the end of their careers before taking over as skippers, but have never been invited to take over the teams they starred with (Robinson with the Reds, Orioles and Angels; Lopez with the Dodgers, Braves and Pirates). No players were more identified with single teams during their careers than Williams and Lemon, but they too have had to get their managerial experience elsewhere.

COACHES

Eight men who played gin with the manager and a ninth who had to have doubts about whose hand he was playing.

```
        1B—ELSTON HOWARD    1969 Yankees
        2B—MILT STOCK       1950 Dodgers
        3B—ARLIE LATHAM     1907 Giants
        SS—FRANK CROSETTI    Career
        OF—COZY DOLAN       1916 Giants
        OF—FRED CLARKE      1925 Pirates
        OF—BOB KENNEDY      1963 Cubs
         C—CHARLIE LAU      1983 White Sox
         P—MEL HARDER       1947 Indians
```

Howard was the first black coach. Stock was the man who waved Cal Abrams home to the doom of Brooklyn's pennant hopes in the final game of the 1950 season. Latham was the first contracted coach. Crosetti holds the mark as player, coach and/or manager for being in the most World Series (23). Dolan's only duties as a coach for John McGraw were to serve as the manager's bodyguard and to spy on the players. If Dolan wasn't the most despised coach of his time, then Clarke was—to the point of a player mutiny in 1925 over his allegedly negative influence on the club and on manager Bill McKechnie. (Most of the mutineers were immediately traded away, but Clarke, too, was released at the end of the season.) Kennedy's designation as "head coach" effectively ended the College of Coaches experiment tried out by Phil Wrigley in the early 1960s. When Leo Durocher came along a couple of years later, the "head coach" charade was dropped altogether for the traditional "manager." Only a few months before his death, Lau had become the first coach signed to a multiyear contract. Harder is generally recognized as the first full-time pitching coach.

UMPIRES

With umpires entering the major leagues at younger and younger ages, and only after elaborate training programs, it is unlikely that we will see as many former players wearing blue in the decades to come as we have in the past. Players like:

1B—JAKE BECKLEY
2B—BILL SOMMERS
3B—GEORGE MORIARTY
SS—BABE PINELLI
OF—JOCKO CONLAN
OF—FRANK SECORY
OF—SHERRY MAGEE
 C—CHARLIE BERRY
 P—LON WARNEKE

Among those in the bullpen would be Firpo Marberry, Ed Rommel, George Pipgras, Bill Kunkel and Ken Burkhart.

ANNOUNCERS

Upon retirement some players become coaches, some become managers, and still others become both by going into broadcasting.

1B	—BILL WHITE	Yankees
2B	—JERRY COLEMAN	Padres
3B	—BROOKS ROBINSON	Orioles
SS	—LOU BOUDREAU	Cubs
OF	—JACK GRANEY	Indians
OF	—DUKE SNIDER	Expos
OF	—AL KALINE	Tigers
C	—TIM McCARVER	Mets
P	—WAITE HOYT	Reds

Outfielder Graney merits special mention as the first player to enter a broadcasting booth in pursuit of another career, when he was hired by Cleveland in 1932. (The same Graney has two other footnotes in baseball history: as the first player to bat against a Red Sox southpaw named Ruth and as the first player to wear a number on his uniform.)

Rumor has it that several other former players work the various network games of the week.

HOLLYWOOD ALL-STARS

On the field or on the screen, a player is a player.

HOLLYWOOD ALL-STARS

1B—CHUCK CONNORS
2B—JACKIE ROBINSON
3B—LOU STRINGER
SS—JOHNNY BERARDINO
OF—ERNIE ORSATTI
OF—LEON WAGNER
OF—JOE DiMAGGIO
C—CHARLIE LAU
P—JIM BOUTON

Whether hero or villan, Connors has had much more success as an actor than as a first baseman for the Dodgers and Cubs. There was only one person who could star in *The Jackie Robinson Story* and he did. Stringer has been a Hollywood extra for some years, more or less what he was for the Cubs and Red Sox in the 1940s. *General Hospital* soap fans know all about Berardino's infield play for the Indians, Browns and Pirates. Orsatti was a Hollywood stunt man both during and after his playing days, and later became an agent for actors. Wagner has had small parts in a number of films, including *Bingo Long's Traveling All-Stars*. DiMaggio had a part in something called *Manhattan Merry-Go-Round;* perhaps the acting experience he gained in this movie is what led Mr. Coffee and the Bowery Savings Bank to choose him to be the spokesman in their commercials. Lau had a featured role in Neil Simon's *The Return of Max Dugan;* oddly enough, he played a batting coach named Charlie Lau. Bouton's colorful career as pitcher, sportscaster, author and nemesis of the baseball establishment has also included being the heavy in Robert Altman's *The Long Goodbye* and being the star of a short-lived television sitcom.

Honorable mention to Wes Parker, who did a lot of television acting; Jim Lefebrve, who has appeared on *MASH;* and Babe Ruth, who was in a number of minor films in the 1930s and who played himself very convincingly in *Pride of the Yankees.*

MISCELLANEOUS—ON THE FIELD

Everything you couldn't find out from the other chapters—as long as it happened on the field.

TRIVIA

These are the answers. What are the questions?

> 1B—WALLY PIPP
> 2B—BILLY WAMBSGANSS
> 3B—HARRY STEINFELDT
> SS—RAY CHAPMAN
> OF—GENE STEPHENS
> OF—WILLIE MAYS
> OF—BOBBY BONDS
> C—BILL DICKEY
> P—TRACY STALLARD

Who was the Yankee first baseman before Lou Gehrig?

Who made the only unassisted triple play in a World Series?

Who played third base on the Cubs in the Tinker to Evers to Chance infield?

Who is the only player killed on a major league ballfield?

Who is the only twentieth-century player to get three hits in one inning?

Who was on deck when Bobby Thomson hit the "shot heard round the world"?

Who is the only player to steal 30 bases and hit 30 home runs in a single season five times?

Who broke Carl Hubbell's streak of five consecutive strikeouts in the 1934 All-Star Game?

Who gave up Roger Maris's 61st home run in 1961?

MISCONCEPTIONS

Myths, misconceptions, oversights—baseball history is replete with them. For example:

1B—MARV THRONEBERRY	1962 Mets
2B—EDDIE STANKY	Career
3B—BUCK WEAVER	1919 White Sox
SS—LOU BOUDREAU	Career
OF—BABE RUTH	Career
OF—PETE GRAY	Career
OF—CASEY STENGEL	1917 Dodgers
C—YOGI BERRA	1947 Yankees
P—MONTY STRATTON	Career

Although he became the symbol of Mets' buffoonery in their initial years, Throneberry actually played for the team for only one full season and had the highest fielding average of any regular. Despite Leo Durocher's backhanded compliment that he was able to win without hitting ability, Stanky had averages of .320, .285 and .300 in three consecutive seasons and had no match as a batsman among all his immediate predecessors and successors on the Cubs, Braves and Giants. Weaver was thrown out of baseball as one of the infamous Black Sox, but there has never been a shred of evidence linking him to his seven teammates or gamblers of the era. Boudreau was *not* the youngest manager at 24; that distinction goes to Roger Peckinpaugh, who was 23 when he took over the Yankees for 17 games in 1914. Yankee Stadium is not known as "The House that Ruth Built" because of all the homers the Babe hit in the Bronx; the epithet actually stems from the fact that the ballpark had to be built because Ruth's homers (and the fans who came to see them) made the Yankees *non gratae* in the Polo Grounds, where the landlord New York Giants didn't like being outdrawn by their tenants. The one-armed Gray was not a member of the amazing pennant-winning St. Louis Browns of 1944; his only major league season was the following year, when he hit .218 in 61 games. Stengel did not throw a grapefruit out of a plane to an unwary Wilbert Robinson; the practical joke was actually the work of trainer Frank Kelley. Although he succeeded Bill Dickey in many other respects, Berra did not replace the older Hall of Famer as the Yankee catcher in 1947; that task fell largely to Aaron Robinson. After the 1938 shooting accident that cost him a leg, Stratton did not struggle back to the majors; the furthest he got, and that only for a brief time, was a low minor league team.

RECORDS THAT WILL NEVER BE BROKEN

Play-by-play announcers are always talking about records that will stand forever. These are our picks.

1B—LOU GEHRIG
2B—ROGERS HORNSBY
3B—PIANO LEGS HICKMAN
SS—BILL DAHLEN
OF—CHARLIE JAMIESON
OF—JOE DiMAGGIO
OF—BABE RUTH
  C—DEACON McGUIRE
  P—JACK TAYLOR

Gehrig's 2130 consecutive games, Hornsby's .402 average over five seasons (1921–25), Hickman's 91 errors in 118 games for the Giants in 1900, Dahlen's 972 errors in his 20-year career, Jamieson's starting two triple plays while playing for the Indians in 1928, DiMaggio's 56-game hitting streak, Ruth's .847 slugging average over two seasons (1920–21) and McGuire's 25 years behind the plate should stand the test of time.

But Taylor's streak of 188 consecutive complete games is probably the all-time, never-to-be-broken record. From June 20, 1901, to August 9, 1906, Taylor, hurling for the Cubs and Cardinals, was never taken out for a relief pitcher. In that stretch he not only pitched 188 complete games, but he also finished another 15 as a reliever for a total of 1727 innings pitched without relief.

The manager is Connie Mack, who led the Philadelphia Athletics for the first 50 years of their existence.

Pat Collins is the only player ever to pinch-run and pinch-hit in the same game. On June 8, 1923, while playing for the St. Louis Browns, he appeared as a pinch-runner in the third inning and then came back as a pinch-hitter in the ninth.

THE ECLIPSED

Most of them held their records for decades, all of them had their marks bettered eventually. See if you can remember the record in question.

1B—ROGER CONNOR	Babe Ruth
2B—ROGERS HORNSBY	Dave Johnson
3B—NED WILLIAMSON	Babe Ruth
SS—EVERETT SCOTT	Lou Gehrig
OF—BABE RUTH	Hank Aaron and Roger Maris
OF—TY COBB	Maury Wills
OF—WILLIE KEELER	Joe DiMaggio
C—JOHNNY KLING	John Stearns
P—RUBE WADDELL	Sandy Koufax

Connors's 136 homers were the career high passed by Ruth on his way to compiling 714. Hornsby's 42 homers in 1922 were the most for a second baseman until Johnson hit 43 in 1973. Williamson held the season home run record (27 with the Cubs in 1884) until Ruth hit 29 in 1919. Scott played in 1307 consecutive games—and then came Gehrig with 2130. Aaron's 755 career blasts and Maris's 61 home runs in 1961 have brought attention to them without ex-

actly eclipsing Ruth. Wills's 104 steals in 1962 wiped out
Cobb's 96 thefts in 1915. DiMaggio's 56-game hitting
streak in 1941 topped Keeler's 44 straight games in 1897.
It took 76 years for Kling's 1902 record of most steals by a
catcher in a season (23) to be broken by Stearns. Waddell
whiffed 349 batters for the 1904 Athletics and was not sur-
passed until Koufax struck out 382 in 1965.

OUT OF PROPORTION

It was unlikely that these players would roll up the statistics they did, but that's what they did anyway.

1B—VIC POWER	1958 Indians
2B—DAVE JOHNSON	1973 Braves
3B—MICKEY KLUTTS	Career
SS—LEO CARDENAS	1972 Angels
OF—BILLY HAMILTON	Career
OF—TOMMY LEACH	Career
OF—TOMMY LONG	Career
C—MIKE RYAN	Career
P—VIRGIL TRUCKS	1952 Tigers

In one game Power stole home twice; they were his only
steals for Cleveland all season. In the same year that
Johnson hit his record-breaking 43 homers, he hit only 25
doubles. In his seven-year career between 1976 and 1983,
Klutts was put on the disabled list for various injuries ten
times. Although he played 150 games, Cardenas scored
only 25 runs. On the other hand, Hamilton scored 1690
runs in only 1578 games. Leach hit 62 homers, but 48 of
them were inside-the-park jobs. Long had 49 career triples,
but only 47 doubles. Ryan was the epitome of the player
who couldn't even hit his weight: in 11 major league seasons the 205-pound catcher batted a mere .193. Trucks was
only 5-19 for Detroit in 1952, but two of the victories were
no-hitters.

Honorable mention to pitcher Bob Tiefenauer, who won
a mere nine games in ten years of major league service,
and to outfielder Bill Sharman, the basketball great who

was called up by Brooklyn in 1952, never appeared in a game, but was nevertheless thrown out of one for bench jockeying.

FIELD FOLLIES

Of all the bizarre occurrences to take place on a major league baseball field these were the strangest.

1B—MARV THRONEBERRY	1962 Mets
2B—GERMANY SCHAEFER	1911 Senators
3B—ODELL HALE	1935 Indians
SS—ERNIE BANKS	1959 Cubs
OF—JEFF LEONARD	1979 Astros
OF—JOHNNY DICKSHOT	1937 Pirates
OF—JOE CONNOLLY	1914 Braves
C—MORGAN MURPHY	1898 Phillies
P—JIMMY ST. VRAIN	1902 Cubs

Throneberry tripled on June 17, but was called out on an appeal play for failing to touch second. When Mets manager Casey Stengel came out of the dugout to complain, the umpire told him not to bother since Marvelous Marv had also missed first. Schaefer stole second to draw a throw and allow the runner on third to score. Unsuccessful in this, he "stole first," then repeated the theft of second, this time drawing the desired throw.

Hale received an assist in baseball's oddest triple play (on September 7) when a line drive off the bat of Joe Cronin hit him in the head and landed in the hands of shortstop Billy Knickerbocker, who tossed to second baseman Roy Hughes for the second out; Hughes flipped the ball to Hal Trosky at first.

Banks (on June 30) watched helplessly as two baseballs came at him, one thrown by his third baseman the other by his pitcher; the first originated with the bat boy who had picked it up after what was either a pitch that hit Stan Musial or a wild pitch ball four; the second originated with the home plate umpire who had handed a new ball to the catcher who handed it to the pitcher who threw it to

Banks. (Banks tagged Musial with the first ball as Stan rounded second base and the second ball went into the outfield; initially the umpires sent Musial back to first, then called him out, but the ball should have been declared dead when the bat boy touched it.

Leonard routinely flied out to end a 5-0 game on August 21, but Mets' shortstop Frank Taveras had called time so Leonard got a second chance and singled. However, Mets first baseman Ed Kranepool had left the field so Leonard had to try a third time and flied out again, but an Astros protest was upheld and play had to be resumed the following day with Leonard on first. The next batter, Jose Cruz, grounded out to second.

When the wind blew Dickshot's hat off he allowed two runs to score because he chased the hat instead of the ball. Connolly was knocked out by a line drive that hit him in the head. Murphy, a third-string catcher, was caught stealing opponents' signals when Reds' third base coach Tommy Corcoran kicked the dirt in the coach's box and unearthed a wire that led to Morgan in the clubhouse where he was using a buzzer to relay the stolen signals to his own third base coach. St. Vrain, a weak-hitting, left-handed pitcher who batted from the right side but rarely made contact, took his manager's advice and moved to the other side of the plate; from this unfamiliar vantage point he grounded to Honus Wagner at short and promptly ran as fast as he could—to third base!

BIZARRE AT BATS

And for those of you out there keeping score at home, how would you score these?

1B—STUFFY McINNIS	1911 Athletics
2B—GEORGE CUTSHAW	1916 Dodgers
3B—GEORGE BRETT	1983 Royals
SS—RAY CHAPMAN	1920 Indians
OF—JACK TOBIN	1922 Browns
OF—GEORGE ALTMAN	1960 Cubs
OF—DAVE AUGUSTINE	1973 Pirates
C—TIM McCARVER	1971 Phillies
P—FRANK SULLIVAN	1956 Red Sox

McInnis took advantage of a new (and short-lived) rule prohibiting pitchers to take warm-up pitches between innings (June 27) and walloped one of Ed Karger's warm-ups for an inside-the-park homer—before the outfielders were on the field. Cutshaw broke up a tie game in the eleventh inning with a hard ground ball that struck the right field fence and spun upward and over the fence for a home run. (In those days any ball that went over the fence was a four-bagger.) Brett's home run was disallowed because he had pine tar too far up the bat, then was reallowed by AL President Lee McPhail on the grounds that it had not been Brett's intention to break the rules. Chapman walked away from the plate with an 0-2 count because, with Walter Johnson pitching, a third strike "wouldn't do me any good." Tobin grounded out routinely first-to-pitcher to end a 2-1 game in late May, but after the players had dispersed and the crowd had overrun the field the umpire agreed that the Yankee pitcher Sam Jones had bobbled the ball, allowing the tying run to score. The crowd was sent back to the stands, the players returned to the field and the game continued as the Browns scored five additional runs. (Jones was so shaken he lost his next nine games.) Altman walked on three balls (on April 24) as a balk was incorrectly counted as a ball. In the 13th inning of a crucial game (on September 30) Augustine hit a ball onto the top of the wall in Shea Stadium. The ball bounced straight up in the air and into the hands of Mets' left fielder Cleon Jones whose throw, relayed by the third baseman, helped cut down the potential winning run at the plate. (The Mets went on to win both the game and the pennant.) McCarver hit a ninth-inning, game-winning grand-slam in Philadelphia on Bicentennial Day, July 4, 1976. Obviously excited by the exploding scoreboard, fireworks and other hoopla, he passed the runner in front of him and had to settle for a game-winning single in the record book. Sullivan hit into a double play and drove in a run without being charged with a time at bat (April 17). He flied out to right, the runner on third scored, and the runner on first was out trying to tag up and go to second.

STREAK BREAKERS

The pitchers knew that it had to happen eventually. The batters who made it happen were:

1B—ED KRANEPOOL	1967	Mets
2B—EDDIE STANKY	1947	Dodgers
3B—DEBS GARMS	1938	Braves
SS—MAURY WILLS	1970	Dodgers
OF—BUBBA MORTON	1962	Tigers
OF—HOWIE BEDELL	1968	Phillies
OF—BERNIE CARBO	1972	Cardinals
C—JOHN STEARNS	1982	Mets
P—HAL GRIGGS	1957	Senators

Kranepool's three hits and key runs batted in were the main reason New York ended Larry Jackson's 18-0 record against the team. Stanky singled with one out in the ninth inning to prevent Ewell Blackwell from matching Johnny Vander Meer's consecutive no-hitters feat. Garms was the batter who finally broke through for a single off Vander Meer after 21⅔ no-hit innings. Wills managed to hit the ball against Tom Seaver, ending the Met pitcher's 10 straight strikeouts. Morton drew the first walk off Bill Fischer after the latter's record-setting 84⅓ innings. Bedell's sacrifice fly put an end to Don Drysdale's 58⅔ consecutive shutout innings. Carbo's double off Jim Barr ended the pitcher's mark of retiring 41 straight batters. Stearns touched Greg Minton for the first home run given up by the Giant reliever in 269⅓ innings. It was Griggs who ended Ted Williams's record of reaching first base 16 consecutive times.

The manager is Al Lopez, whose 1954 Indians and 1959 White Sox prevented the Yankees from claiming a hallucinating 16 consecutive pennants!

THE SPOILERS

Some members of this team waited until there were two outs in the ninth inning before they spoiled a no-hitter—and they weren't the cruelest ones.

1B—JOE ADCOCK	1959 Braves
2B—JOE GORDON	1943 Yankees
3B—TED GULLIC	1933 Browns
SS—LARRY KOPF	1917 Reds
OF—SAM MERTES	1901 White Sox,
	1904 Giants
OF—JOHNNY LEWIS	1965 Mets
OF—JOE WALLIS	1975 Cubs
C—GARY ALEXANDER	1978 Indians
PH—ED FITZGERALD	1954 Senators

Adcock sent Harvey Haddix home after 12⅓ hitless innings. Gordon reached Chicago's Orval Grove for a two-out double in the ninth, while Gullic waited for the same moment to single off Chicago's Whitlow Wyatt. Kopf's tenth-inning safety off Hippo Vaughn of the Cubs led to the only run in the "double no-hit" game won by Fred Toney. As an American Leaguer Mertes broke up Cleveland hurler Earl Moore's no-hit bid with a tenth-inning single and did the same thing as a National Leaguer against Bob Wicker of Chicago. Lewis waited until the eleventh inning to homer off Cincinnati's Jim Maloney and give the Mets a win. Wallis waited until two out in the ninth to foil Tom Seaver with a single. Alexander's two-out homer in the ninth not only broke up a shutout as well as a no-hitter, but was followed by two more hits that denied Baltimore's Mike Flanagan even a complete game. Fitzgerald's opposite-field double with two out in the ninth ruined a perfect game for Billy Pierce of Chicago. Other 27th batters who ruined perfect games were Washington's Dave Harris (against Tommy Bridges of Detroit) and Chicago's Jerry Hairston (Milt Wilcox of Detroit).

COLLISIONS

There is no more exciting play than the hard slide. And no more frightening event than the collision of two players in the field. These were the most damaging such occurrences.

1B—STEVE GARVEY	1983 Padres
2B—DAVEY WILLIAMS	1955 Giants
3B—FRANK BAKER	1909 Athletics
SS—WALLY GERBER	1929 Red Sox
OF—DICK HARLEY	1902 Tigers
OF—GEORGE THEODORE	1973 Mets
OF—DAVE PARKER	1978 Pirates
C—CONNIE MACK	1893 Pirates
DH—CLIFF JOHNSON	1977 Yankees

Garvey jammed his thumb in the catcher's mask during a collision at the plate and was injured seriously enough to end his consecutive game streak at 1207 games. Jackie Robinson ran over Williams on a play in which the latter was covering first; Williams's career was effectively ended by the collision. Ty Cobb spiked Baker in a crucial late-season game. The trainer bandaged a deep gash in Baker's arm and the third baseman stayed in the game, but the play brought Cobb much criticism for his ferocity. Gerber and outfielder Ken Williams ran into each other head on; both were unconscious for some time, Gerber never played another game, and Williams barely got through the season before retiring. Harley spiked John McGraw in the knee-cap when the Detroit outfielder was caught off third by a throw from the catcher; the injury virtually ended McGraw's career when he was only 29. Theodore, playing left field, collided with center fielder Don Hahn chasing a fly ball and destroyed a promising career. Mack's leg was broken in a collision at the plate with Herman Long during the 1893 pennant stretch. Johnson blindsided home plate umpire Lou DiMuro while scoring a run and knocked the man in blue unconscious; DiMuro missed the rest of the season.

PLAYER-MANAGERS

Two of the oldest bromides in baseball are that great players make terrible managers and that player-managers make even worse ones. Judge for yourself. The following is a lineup of player-managers enshrined at Cooperstown.

1B—BILL TERRY	1932–36 Giants
2B—ROGERS HORNSBY	1925–26 Cardinals, 1928 Braves, 1930–32 Cubs, 1933–37 Browns
3B—JIMMY COLLINS	1901–06 Red Sox
SS—JOE CRONIN	1933–34 Senators, 1935–45 Red Sox
OF—FRED CLARKE	1897–99 Louisville, 1900–15 Pirates
OF—TRIS SPEAKER	1919–26 Indians
OF—TY COBB	1921–26 Tigers
C—MICKEY COCHRANE	1934–37 Tigers
P—CLARK GRIFFITH	1901–02 White Sox, 1903–07 Yankees, 1909 Reds, 1912–14 Senators

Their success strictly as player-managers? Terry won pennants in 1933 and 1935. Hornsby won in 1926. Collins brought the Sox home first in 1903 and 1904. Cronin took the Senators into the World Series in 1933. Clarke had winners in 1901, 1902, 1903 and 1909. Speaker had one in 1920. And Cochrane had two, in 1934 and 1935. On the other hand, Cobb proved that as a manager he was a good hitter. And worst of all was Griffith, who got nowhere in his 11 years in the dual role (perhaps because he himself made only token mound appearances in six of those years).

RECENT PLAYER-MANAGERS

And while we're at it, some of those who most recently took on a dual playing-managing role:

1B—PETE ROSE	1984 Reds
2B—SOLLY HEMUS	1959 Cardinals
3B—LOU BOUDREAU	1952 Red Sox
SS—DON KESSINGER	1979 White Sox
OF—FRANK ROBINSON	1976 Indians
OF—HANK BAUER	1961 Athletics
OF—TOMMY HOLMES	1951 Braves
C—LUKE SEWELL	1942 Browns
P—FRED HUTCHINSON	1953 Tigers

None of these managers had anything like a pennant-winning team. The last player-manager to sit on a bench during a World Series was Boudreau during a previous tenure, with the 1948 Indians.

FROM BOTH SIDES

Twenty-three players have hit home runs from both sides of the plate in a single game. Most notable are:

1B—EDDIE MURRAY
2B—JOHNNY LUCADELLO
3B—LARRY MILBOURNE
SS—U.L. WASHINGTON
OF—MICKEY MANTLE
OF—REGGIE SMITH
OF—ROY WHITE
C—TED SIMMONS
P—TONY MULLANE

Mantle switch-homered ten times for the all-time record. Other repeaters were Smith, six times; White and Murray, five times each; and Simmons, three times. Tommy Tresh did it three times and Jim Russell, Ellis Burton and Pete Rose, twice each.

Tony Mullane, an ambidextrous pitcher, started a game for Louisville on July 18, 1882, throwing right-handed. In the fourth inning he switched to his left arm and beat Baltimore. This is the only time in history that a pitcher threw with both arms in a game.

COMBINATIONS

There are a number of combinations of offensive categories in which it is rare to achieve a certain level in the same season. Among the more interesting are:

1B—JIM BOTTOMLEY	1928 Cardinals
2B—JOE MORGAN	1973, 1974 and 1976 Reds
3B—EDDIE MATHEWS	1953 and 1959 Braves
SS—ERNIE BANKS	1958 and 1959 Cubs
OF—BABE RUTH	1921 Yankees
OF—BOBBY BONDS	Career
OF—TIM RAINES	1983 Expos
C—ROY CAMPANELLA	1953 Dodgers
P—SANDY KOUFAX	1963 Dodgers

Bottomley is the only player ever to record over 40 doubles, over 30 homers and over 20 triples. Morgan had 50 or more stolen bases and 20 or more homers three times. Mathews is the only third baseman to hit 40 or more homers and bat over .300 twice. (The only other third baseman to do this was Al Rosen with the 1953 Indians.) Banks is the only shortstop to reach 40/.300. Who but Ruth could have scored and driven in over 170 runs in the same season? Bonds stole over 30 bases and hit over 30 homers in five different seasons (1969, 1973, 1975, 1977 and 1978); this combination has been achieved only eleven times. Raines is the most recent player to steal over 70 bases and drive in over 70 runs. Campanella is the only catcher to join the 40/.300 club. Six times pitchers have had 25 or more wins, 300 or more strikeouts and an earned run average below 2.00;

Koufax added to that combination a Won-Lost Percentage over .800. The other five were Rube Waddell (1904 Athletics), Walter Johnson (1910 and 1912 Senators), Koufax (1966 Dodgers) and Steve Carlton (1972 Phillies).

MORE WALKS THAN HITS

Only 19 times in history has a player had more walks than hits—with a minimum of 100 hits—in a single season. The widest margins were:

1B—ROY CULLENBINE	137 BB	104 H	1947 Tigers
2B—MAX BISHOP	128 BB	110 H	1929 Athletics
3B—EDDIE YOST	151 BB	119 H	1956 Senators
SS—EDDIE JOOST	114 BB	111 H	1947 Athletics
OF—JIMMY WYNN	148 BB	133 H	1969 Astros
OF—TED WILLIAMS	136 BB	133 H	1954 Red Sox
OF—MICKEY MANTLE	106 BB	103 H	1968 Yankees
C—GENE TENACE	125 BB	102 H	1977 Padres
P—ROY FACE	18 W	10 Sv	1959 Pirates

Bishop walked more often than he hit safely in four other seasons (1926, 1927, 1930 and 1932). Joost (1949), Wynn (1975), Mantle (1962) and Tenace (1974) did it twice.

The only other players to accomplish this were Eddie Stanky (1945 and 1946) and Hank Greenberg (1947).

Face had eight more wins in relief than he had saves, a considerable margin.

100 STRIKEOUTS, 100 WALKS

Twenty-four players have racked up 100 strikeouts and 100 walks in the same season a total of 46 times. Twenty-six times these players actually struck out more times than they walked. The worst spreads between walks and strikeouts are:

1B—JIMMIE FOXX	105 BB	119 K	1936	Red Sox
2B—DICK McAULIFFE	105 BB	118 K	1967	Tigers
3B—MIKE SCHMIDT	101 BB	180 K	1975	Phillies
SS—EDDIE JOOST	114 BB	110 K	1947	Athletics
OF—HARMON KILLEBREW	106 BB	142 K	1962	Twins
OF—REGGIE JACKSON	114 BB	142 K	1969	Athletics
OF—GREG LUZINSKI	100 BB	135 K	1978	Phillies
C—GENE TENACE	106 BB	127 K	1975	Athletics
P—AMOS RUSIE	218 BB	208 K	1893	Giants

The repeaters in this category are Schmidt (7 times), Mickey Mantle (5), Tenace (4), Dolph Camilli (3), Killebrew (3), Jimmy Wynn (3), Eddie Mathews (2), Dwight Evans (2) and Ken Singleton (2).

Rusie is the only pitcher—since the present distance of 60 feet, 6 inches from mound to home was established—to walk 200 or more batters and strike out more than 200 batters in the same season and to walk more than he struck out.

MODELS AND STYLISTS

A lineup of players who have influenced the playing and dress fashions of the game or have simply been the first word in technique.

1B—VIC POWER
2B—PETE ROSE
3B—BILLY COX
SS—DAVE CONCEPCION
OF—RALPH KINER
OF—JIM LEMON
OF—RUSTY STAUB
C—RANDY HUNDLEY
P—DON LARSEN

Power's snap catches and other one-handed antics helped usher in the Willie Montanez generation. Rose's belly flops into bases showed that the hook slide wasn't the only way to get from first to third ahead of a strong throw. Nobody has ever quite matched Cox's penchant for picking up a grounder, counting the stitches on the ball and then rocketing a throw to first inches ahead of the batter. Concepcion introduced the bounced throw on Astroturf from deep in the hole. Kiner and Phil Rizzuto were the first to wear batting helmets in the majors. Lemon introduced the protective ear flaps on helmets. Staub popularized the wearing of two batting gloves in western show-down fashion. Hundley was the first to use the flip-over mitt that made one-handed catching possible. A few years later Johnny Bench perfected the technique which, in the mitts of less able receivers, has been a contributing factor in the dramatic increase in stolen bases in recent years. Larson and Bob Turley of the Yankees were pioneers in the no-windup delivery.

BATTING STANCES

Coaches tell young players to stand up at the plate in a way that is comfortable even if it is unorthodox. These players are examples of why that is good advice.

1B—STAN MUSIAL
2B—JOE MORGAN
3B—GIL McDOUGALD
SS—BILL RUSSELL
OF—WILLIE KEELER
OF—MEL OTT
OF—AL SIMMONS
 C—JOHN WOCKENFUSS
 P—JUAN MARICHAL

Musial stood with his knees together and the bat perpendicular to the ground; Ted Lyons described Musial in his crouch as similar to "a small boy looking around a corner to see if the cops are coming." Morgan flapped his left elbow in anticipation of each pitch. McDougald's bat was pointed toward the ground. Russell extends both his index fingers away from the bat. Keeler held his hands about six inches apart on the barrel of the bat. Ott lifted his right foot and dropped his hands below his knee when he swung. Simmons stepped in the bucket. Wockenfuss, a right-handed batter, stands with his left foot almost behind his right foot. Marichal had the highest kick of any pitcher.

WHATEVER IT TAKES

Some players have attributed their skills to more than extra batting practice. See if you can remember the talismans, superstitions and unusual aids of:

1B—LOU GEHRIG
2B—ROGERS HORNSBY
3B—WADE BOGGS
SS—DAVE CONCEPCION
OF—LOU SKIZAS
OF—DARRELL EVANS
OF—JOE DiMAGGIO
C—BRIAN DOWNING
P—MIKE MARSHALL

Gehrig always credited his mother's pickled eels with assisting his batting prowess. Hornsby claimed he was a good hitter because he never went to the movies. The obsessive Boggs eats chicken on 14-day cycles. Concepcion is one of the numerous Catholics who blesses himself before every at bat. Skizas used to rub an Orthodox medal in his back pocket between pitches. Evans says it was the sighting of a UFO from his back porch that spurred his career into a second life in 1982. DiMaggio would never run from the outfield to the dugout without touching second base. Downing was the first to employ a Nautilus training program for upper body strength. Marshall credited his studies in kinesiology with giving him the long career he had.

Honorable mentions to Steve Carlton for punching his sack of rice and, unconsciously, to Dock Ellis for throwing the only no-hitter of his career while under the influence of LSD.

GREATEST FIGHTS
OF THE CENTURY

Fans love a good fight. And these, in our opinion, were the best.

1B—JOE ADCOCK	Ruben Gomez
2B—BILLY MARTIN	Jim Brewer
3B—JOHN McGRAW	Tommy Tucker
SS—PHIL RIZZUTO	Clint Courtney
OF—TY COBB	Mr. Lueker
OF—CARL FURILLO	The Giants
OF—AL COWENS	Ed Farmer
C—JOHN ROSEBORO	Juan Marichal
P—BILL GULLICKSON	Mike Jorgensen

Adcock became infuriated when Gomez threw at him (in July, 1956); brandishing a bat he chased Gomez all the way to the center field clubhouse in the Polo Grounds. When Brewer threw at Martin (August 4, 1960), the latter tossed his bat down the first base line; when Martin went to retrieve the bat, Brewer followed and Martin broke his jaw with a punch. Tucker slid hard into McGraw, who kicked Tucker in the face (May 16, 1894). The ensuing fight so distracted everyone that a fire in the right field bleachers went ignored—even though it eventually burned down Boston's South End Grounds. Courtney slid hard into Rizzuto (April 28, 1953) and the fight that resulted involved both benches, flying bottles, a dislocated collarbone for umpire John Stevens, and the summoning of a police escort to keep angry fans away from the Yankees as they returned to their hotel. Cobb went into the stands behind third base and attacked a heckling fan (Lueker) in New York (May 15, 1912). His actions earned him a ten-day suspension and led to a strike by the rest of the Tigers. When Furillo, who had been taunted by Leo Durocher throughout 1953, was hit by a pitch, he yelled at the Giants manager from first base; Durocher challenged Furillo, who plunged into the

Giants dugout, punched Monte Irvin, and had his hand stepped on and broken by Jim Hearn. Nevertheless, Furillo was the NL batting champion that year. In 1979 Farmer broke Cowens's jaw with a pitch. The next time they faced each other (in 1980) Cowens grounded out, ran directly at Farmer, attacked him, and was sued by Bill Veeck, the White Sox owner. On August 22, 1965, Marichal made a comment to Roseboro about a pitch that came too close to the pitcher, Marichal tapped Roseboro on the head with his bat, Roseboro took a swing, Marichal raised his bat in earnest, and both benches emptied. Jorgensen, who had been hospitalized and near death after being beaned in the American League in 1979, went after Gullickson with a bat when the NL pitcher threw at him (1980); both teams entered the fray.

The managers are Harry Walker of the Cardinals and Birdie Tebbets of the Reds, who tangled and rolled around in the dirt throwing punches at each other (July 5, 1955) after Tebbetts protested Walker's delaying tactics; each manager was fined $100.

PINCH-HITTING ODDS AND ODDS

Some facts involving pinch-hitters and the players they batted for.

1B—DAVE PHILLEY	1958–59 Phillies
2B—JACK DOYLE	1892 Cleveland
3B—JIMMY DYKES	1928 Athletics
SS—PEEWEE WANNINGER	1925 Yankees
OF—JOHNNY FREDERICK	1932 Dodgers
OF—CHARLIE MAXWELL	1951 Red Sox
OF—CARROLL HARDY	Career
C—CLIFF JOHNSON	Career
P—MIKE O'NEILL	1902 Cardinals

Philley hit safely in his last eight 1958 at bats and in his first 1959 appearance to set the record for most consecutive pinch-hits. Doyle is credited with the very first pinch-hit, a single. Dykes was lifted for pinch-hitter Ty

Cobb in the latter's last major league appearance; Cobb popped out. Lou Gehrig's consecutive game streak of 2130 began when he batted for Wanninger on June 1, 1925. Frederick's six pinch-homers are the major league record for a season. Maxwell's first three big league homers were pinch-hit jobs against future Hall of Famers Bob Feller, Bob Lemon and Satchel Paige. A lifetime .225 hitter, Hardy batted for Ted Williams, Roger Maris and Carl Yastrzemski at various points in his career. Johnson holds the record for most career pinch-homers with 19. O'Neill hit the first pinch-grand-slam.

BASE-RUNNING ODDS AND ODDS

Some players have made running the bases a historic moment, others have made it a historic misadventure.

1B—TIM MURNANE	1876 Braves
2B—RAY MORGAN	1917 Senators
3B—JIMMY SEXTON	1982 Athletics
SS—LUIS APARICIO	1972 Red Sox
OF—BILL O'HARA	1909 Giants
OF—JIM DELSING	1951 Browns
OF—DON BAYLOR	1974 Orioles
C—GUS TRIANDOS	Career
P—TIPPY MARTINEZ	1983 Orioles

Murnane stole major league baseball's first base in the inaugural NL game with Philadelphia. Morgan was the player walked by Babe Ruth and then thrown out trying to steal on reliever Ernie Shore's first pitch; Shore went on to retire the next 26 batters. Sexton's 16-for-16 is the highest perfect stolen base mark for a season in baseball history. In a pennant-deciding series with Detroit on the last weekend of the season, aged speedster Aparicio fell down twice as he rounded third base with crucial runs. On both September 1 and September 2 in 1909, O'Hara was sent in as a pinch-runner and proceeded to steal second and third; he is the only one to have accomplished this. Delsing was the runner for midget Eddie Gaedel after the latter had walked as a pinch-hitter for Frank Saucier. Baylor is the only player to be thrown out twice in an inning on attempted steals. The positive side of Triandos's legendary lethargy on the bases (one stolen base in his career) is that he also holds the record for the most consecutive games (1206) without being thrown out trying to steal. In a game against Toronto, reliever Martinez got out of an inning by picking off three Blue Jays.

MISCELLANEOUS— OFF THE FIELD

Everything you wanted to know that isn't somewhere else in this book.

SPECIAL ROSTER SPOTS

They were one of twenty-five, but not for the usual reasons.

1B—STEVE BILKO	1958 Dodgers, 1961 Angels
2B—JOE AMALFITANO	1954 Giants
3B STEVE MACKO	1981 Cubs
SS—GEORGE DAVIS	1903 Giants
OF—ROBERTO ORTIZ	1950 Senators
OF—SHERRY ROBERTSON	Career
OF—DAN McGARVEY	1912 Tigers
C—GUS BRITTAIN	1937 Reds
P BARNEY SCHULTZ	1967–68 Cardinals

Because of Bilko's popularity as a minor league slugger in Los Angeles, both California clubs made sure he was part of their inaugural major league seasons. Amalfitano was one of several bonus babies teams were required to carry for two years in the 1950s. The fatally ill Macko was carried by Chicago for the entire season. Although filling a roster spot, Davis was kept out of the lineup for all but four games as part of the agreement between the National and American leagues concerning players who had jumped to the new circuit the year before. Ortiz was kept around as an interpreter for pitcher Connie Marrero. Mainly because he was in the Griffith family, Robertson hung on with Washington for nine seasons in the 1940s despite a leaden glove and an anemic bat. McGarvey was one of the semi-pros hastily signed to a Detroit contract after Tiger players went on strike in solidarity with the suspended Ty Cobb. Brittain was brought to Cincinnati to act as an enforcer during field brawls deliberately provoked by manager Charlie Dressen in the interests of making the team "more aggressive." Schultz was put on the St. Louis roster in both years in order to give him pension eligibility.

LOUD FOULS

You couldn't blame this team for complaining; in one way or another, each of its members was done dirty.

1B—DAVE ORR	Career
2B—MANNY TRILLO	1982 Phillies
3B—TONY CUCCINELLO	1945 White Sox
SS—PHIL RIZZUTO	1956 Yankees
OF—SHERRY MAGEE	1906 and 1914 Phillies
OF—TAFFY WRIGHT	1938 Senators
OF—TITO FRANCONA	1959 Indians
C—JOE TORRE	Career
P—SAMMY STEWART	1981 Orioles

Despite the fact that he compiled a lifetime .353 average as a regular, Orr has been denied entry into the Hall of Fame because he did not play the requisite ten years (he played eight). Although he holds the record for the most consecutive errorless games (89) by a second baseman in a season, Trillo was denied the absolute big league mark (91) when manager Pat Corrales, unaware of the streak, sat him down toward the end of the season. With less than two weeks left in the season and while leading the AL in batting, Cuccinello was told that he would be released by Chicago at the end of the year; the dispirited infielder ended up losing the title by less than a point. Rizzuto was cut loose by the Yankees after 13 years of service on Old-Timers Day. Magee lost two homers to a special rules committee verdict that game-winning blasts be credited only to the base necessary for driving in the run; the hits were changed to a double and a triple. Wright was specifically denied a batting title because, although he appeared in the 100 games necessary for the title in the period in question, he got into 39 box scores as a one-time pinch-hitter. On the other hand, Francona suffered because of the letter of the rule when his 399 at bats were one short of eligibility for winning the title. Torre joined the Braves after the team had been involved in postseason play for the third consecutive year, played with them for a seven-year period when they won nothing, left them just as they once again got into postseason competition, and joined the Cardinals just as St. Louis failed to qualify for championship games for the first time in three years. Steward lost the ERA crown to Steve McCatty when his lower mark was rounded off (as the rules dictated) to the nearest complete inning.

TROUBLE IN THE CLUBHOUSE I

When players don't get along with their managers and/or general managers, somebody usually moves on.

1B—HAL TROSKY	1940 Indians
2B—GERRY PRIDDY	1947 Senators
3B—BILL MADLOCK	1979 Giants
SS DONIE BUSH	1912 Tigers
OF—DICK COOLEY	1897 Phillies
OF—MAX CAREY	1925 Pirates
OF—REGGIE JACKSON	1978 Yankees
C—GLENN MYATT	1935 Indians
P—SCHOOLBOY ROWE	1943 Phillies

Trosky was a leader of the "crybaby Indians" who eventually succeeded in getting manager Oscar Vitt replaced. Priddy became an unwanted presence when he declined to sign a letter drawn up by manager Ossie Bluege asserting that the team admired its skipper. Madlock's ongoing battles with manager Joe Altobelli ultimately won him a trade to Pittsburgh and a World Series ring. Bush was a leader of the solidarity strike over the suspended Ty Cobb that ultimately forced Detroit to field a semi-pro team in a game against Philadelphia. Cooley was the team spokesman in a successful bid to get rid of manager George Stallings. Carey was packed off to the Dodgers after he and several other players sought to pressure the removal of coach Fred Clarke as a negative influence on the club. Jackson's ongoing battles with manager Billy Martin were a significant factor in the latter's first of several departures from the Bronx. Myatt was sold to the Giants when manager Walter Johnson decided he was "anti-Johnson." Rowe organized the team in an unsuccessful effort to force the reinstatement of manager Bucky Harris.

TROUBLE IN THE CLUBHOUSE II

Or, wearing the same uniform doesn't necessarily mean they're teammates.

1B —HAL CHASE	Career
2B—ROB ANDREWS	1979 Giants
3B—DICK ALLEN	1965 Phillies
SS—DICK BARTELL	1941 Tigers
OF—TY COBB	Career
OF—ALEX JOHNSON	1970–71 Angels
OF—REGGIE JACKSON	1977 Yankees
C—MOSES WALKER	1884 Toledo (AA)
P—FRED KLOBEDANZ	1902 Braves

Chase was so disliked by teammates wherever he played that his own infielders threw balls in the dirt to make his life on the diamond more difficult. Andrews was a member of the so-called "God Squad" of born-again Christians that created a great deal of divisiveness on the Giants and ultimately led to the dismissal of two managers. Allen and Frank Thomas got into such a violent fight during batting practice on July 3, 1965, that the latter was released that very evening despite a game-saving home run. When the

Tigers won the pennant in 1940, Bartell's constant hectoring was considered a plus; a year later the same taunts were regarded as divisive and he was traded away. Cobb's legendary troubles with teammates included feuds with Germany Schmidt and Sam Crawford. Among the many who went after the unpopular Johnson were Ken Berry with his fists and Chico Ruiz with a gun. Jackson, "the straw that stirred the drink," was especially successful in stirring up Thurman Munson and Graig Nettles. In order to show up the black catcher Walker, Toledo pitchers made a habit of throwing warmup tosses into the dirt. Klobendanz was hounded off Boston by teammates for having scabbed during a theatrical union strike in the off-season.

LABOR RELATIONS

Curt Flood and Andy Messersmith aren't the only players meriting mention in a labor history of baseball. Some others are:

1B—TONY LUPIEN
2B—NAP LAJOIE
3B—JERRY TERRELL
SS—JOHN MONTGOMERY WARD
OF—DAVE FULTZ
OF—HERSCHEL BENNETT
OF—DANNY GARDELLA
C—TED SIMMONS
P—ALLIE REYNOLDS

Lupien challenged his postwar release by the Phillies on the grounds that it violated federal laws covering the reintegration of World War II veterans into their jobs; economic necessity forced him to settle out of court after a protracted legal battle. Lajoie's jump from the same Phillies to the Athletics in 1901 spurred lengthy courtroom maneuvers that ended with Ban Johnson's move of the second baseman to Cleveland. On the grounds of religious principles, Terrell was the only major leaguer to vote against the 1981 players' strike. Ward and Fultz were the

game's first union organizers—Ward with the Brotherhood
that led to the Players League in 1890 and Fultz with the
Players Fraternity that established minimum guidelines
for the farming out of players in the years around World
War I. Bennett successfully appealed to Commissioner
Kenesaw Landis in the early 1930s about being "buried"
in the minors, but his personal victory also led to an
indirect confirmation of the legality of the farm system.
Gardella, one of the players who jumped to Mexico briefly
in the mid-'40s, undertook a direct challenge to the reserve
clause, but, like Lupien, was forced by economic need to
settle out of court. Simmons played for most of the 1972
season without a contract in order to challenge the "option
year" basis of the reserve clause, but then inked a new
pact with the Cardinals. Reynolds and Ralph Kiner were
the chief spokesmen for the pension rights won by players
in the early '50s and were also the immediate prelude to
the Marvin Miller era.

HOLDOUTS

Many baseball fans seem attached to the notion that it is
only the players of recent years who have concerned themselves with trivialities like pay raises and better contracts.
The following is a lineup of players who, long before Curt
Flood and the Major League Players Association forged
free agency, backed up their contract demands by sitting
out entire seasons or significant parts of them.

1B—DICK SIEBERT	1946 Browns
2B—NAP LAJOIE	1902 Athletics
3B—FRANK BAKER	1915 Athletics
SS—CHARLIE HOLLOCHER	1924 Cubs
OF—JOE JACKSON	1918 White Sox
OF—MIKE DONLIN	1907 Giants
OF—EDD ROUSH	1930 Giants
C—JOHNNY KLING	1909 Cubs
P—JOE WOOD	1916 Red Sox

Siebert never played another major league game after

his protest. Lajoie, Roush and Wood were traded away in retaliation for their holdouts. Baker refused his sale to the Yankees for a year, but then went to the New Yorkers. Hollocher settled his dispute in time to play 74 games for Chicago, but they were the last 74 he played in the majors. Jackson went to work in a military plant, came back the following year, then went out for good with the eruption of the Black Sox scandal. Donlin came back and had a great 1908 season for the Giants. Kling returned the following season, hung around for about a year and a half, then went off to Boston.

THE ROBINSONS

It is, of course, possible to create teams out of the Johnsons, Jacksons, Smiths and Browns who have appeared on major league diamonds. But none of these teams can compare with:

1B—EDDIE ROBINSON
2B—JACKIE ROBINSON
3B—BROOKS ROBINSON
SS—CRAIG ROBINSON
OF—FRANK ROBINSON
OF—FLOYD ROBINSON
OF—BILL ROBINSON
C—WILBERT ROBINSON
P—DON ROBINSON

Admittedly a little weak at shortstop, but with four Hall of Famers to take up the slack, who'll notice?

The backup battery? Humberto and Aaron.

FATHERS AND SONS

The trick here is to use both generations in both teams.

1B—GEORGE SISLER	DICK SISLER
2B—EDDIE COLLINS	BUMP WILLS
3B—RAY BOONE	BUDDY BELL
SS—MAURY WILLS	DALE BERRA
OF—CLYDE BARNHART	VIC BARNHART
OF—GUS BELL	EDDIE COLLINS, JR.
OF—YOGI BERRA	DEL UNSER
C—AL UNSER	BOB BOONE
P—MEL QUEEN	MEL QUEEN, JR.

Left out are the Camillis (Dolf and Doug), the Smalleys (Roy and Roy, Jr.), the Averills (Earl and Earl, Jr.), the Hegans (Mike and Jim), the Franconas (Tito and Terry), the Laws (Vern and Vance) and the Laniers (Max and Hal)—not to mention George Sisler's other son, Dave.

The only father-son managerial combination are our first basemen above. George managed the Browns in 1924, 1925 and 1926; Dick piloted the Reds for part of 1964 and all of 1965.

In any event our money would be on the Dads in any best-of-seven series.

MOST COLORFUL CHARACTERS

It is often said that today's players lack the color of their predecessors, that the modern athlete is nothing but a businessman. Perhaps that is so, but much of what passed for color was actually the effect of excessive drinking.

> 1B—BABE HERMAN
> 2B—BILLY MARTIN
> 3B—JOHN McGRAW
> SS—RABBIT MARANVILLE
> OF—PETE BROWNING
> OF—BABE RUTH
> OF—PEPPER MARTIN
> C—OSSEE SCHRECKENGOST
> P—BUGS RAYMOND

Herman may not ever have been hit on the head by a fly

ball, but by his own admission "the shoulder doesn't count"; he may never have tripled into a triple play, but he did double into a double play. Martin fought with everyone in sight both as a player and as a manager; his most famous escapade was the Copacabana brawl in 1957 that got him exiled to Kansas City. McGraw scrapped, clawed and sometimes even cheated: He would hold baserunners by the belt to slow them down, he would cut across the field directly from first to third when the umpire wasn't looking, and he would plant baseballs in the high outfield grass so his teammates wouldn't have to bother chasing long hits. As a manager he became a Broadway dandy and, recalling his own carousing days, often assigned detectives to follow his players on their nocturnal adventures. Maranville quit drinking in the late 1920s, but before that he was a hell raiser of all-star proportions; with the Pirates in the early 1920s he and Chief Moses Yellowhorse partied with the best of them. Browning was a combination of Dizzy Dean and Ted Williams: He talked a blue streak (mostly about hitting), referred to himself invariably in the third person (by one of his many nicknames such as Ole Pete, Pietro, the Gladiator, Gladdy, or Glad), shouted (because he was hard of hearing), and drank himself to death (in an insane asylum) at the age of 44. Ruth's appetites for food, women and booze were legendary; so was his informality with everyone from women of the night to presidents. Martin was the ringleader of the Gas House Gang. He organized a mudcat band, rode fire engines and engaged in midget car racing—all to the detriment of manager Frankie Frisch's peace of mind. Schreckengost and pitcher Rube Waddell drove their manager, the gentlemanly Connie Mack, to distraction with their regular benders and equally regular jokes and pranks. Raymond was perhaps the wildest of many wild pitchers. He was thrown out of the sanitarium to which McGraw sent him because he was making the other patients crazier and McGraw eventually had to get rid of him for drinking during a game.

NICKNAMES

As much as anything else baseball is a game of colorful nicknames. In our opinion these were the best.

        1B—THE IRON HORSE
        2B—THE FORDHAM FLASH
        3B—THE WILD HORSE OF THE OSAGE
        SS—THE SCOOTER
        OF—THE SULTAN OF SWAT
        OF—THE GEORGIA PEACH
        OF—THE SPLENDID SPLINTER
         C—THE DUKE OF TRALEE
         P—THE BIG TRAIN

The players attached to these titles were Lou Gehrig, Frankie Frisch, Pepper Martin, Phil Rizzuto, Babe Ruth, Ty Cobb, Ted Williams, Roger Bresnahan and Walter Johnson.

FOOTBALL PROS

Since the days of Jim Thorpe, more than one athlete has gotten it into his head that he could excel in more than one professional sport. Among those who have combined major league baseball with the National Football League are:

1B—TOM BROWN	Majors, 1963	NFL, 1964–69
2B—CHUCK CORGAN	Majors, 1925, 1927	NFL, 1924–27
3B—CHARLIE DRESSEN	Majors, 1925–31, 1933	NFL, 1920, 1922–23
SS—JIM LEVEY	Majors, 1930–33	NFL, 1934–36
OF—EVAR SWANSON	Majors, 1929–30, 32–34	NFL, 1924–27
OF—WALT FRENCH	Majors, 1923–29	NFL, 1922, 1925
OF—PID PURDY	Majors, 1926–29	NFL, 1926–27
C—CHARLIE BERRY	Majors, 1925–38	NFL, 1925–26
P—GARLAND BUCKEYE	Majors, 1918, 1925–28	NFL, 1920–24

This is a very mixed bunch. On the one hand, there are Brown and Corgan, who hit .147 and .221, respectively. On the other hand, there are Swanson and French, who both ended their careers at .303.

Buckeye makes the team despite a lifetime mark of 30 wins and 39 losses. In fact, the only footballer-pitcher who won more than he lost was Sandy Vance, who played in the NFL in 1931 and who won three and lost two in three fragmented seasons in the American League (1935, 1937–38).

Cal Hubbard deserves honorable mention since he is in the Hall of Fame of both sports—as a baseball umpire and a football player.

So does George Halas, who played in the NFL from 1920 to 1929 and coached the Chicago Bears four times (1920–29, 1933–42, 1946–55 and 1958–68), and who also played 12 games for the Yankees in 1919, compiling a batting average of .091 on 2 hits in 22 times at bat.

Honorable mention to Red Badgro, Paddy Driscoll, Greasy Neale, Ernie Nevers, Ace Parker and Jim Thorpe, who, with Halas, are in the Football Hall of Fame. Only Neale was more than a journeyman baseball player, however.

BASKETBALL PROS

On balance, the athletes who have mixed major league baseball with professional basketball have fared much better on the diamond than their football counterparts. Among them:

1B—GEORGE CROWE	Majors: 1952–53, 1955–61
	NBL: 1948–49
2B—RALPH MILLER	Majors: 1920–21, 1924
	ABL: 1925–31
3B—DANNY AINGE	Majors: 1979–81
	NBA: 1981-present
SS—DICK GROAT	Majors: 1952, 1955–67
	NBA: 1952–53
OF—IRV NOREN	Majors: 1950–60
	NBL: 1946–47
OF—FRANKIE BAUMHOLTZ	Majors: 1947–49, 1951–57
	NBL: 1945–46, BAA: 1946–47
OF—RUSTY SAUNDERS	Majors: 1927
	ABL: 1925–31, NBL: 1940–41, 1945–46
C—DEL RICE	Majors: 1945–61
	NBL: 1945–46
P—GENE CONLEY	Majors: 1952, 1954–63
	NBL: 1952–53, 1958–64

Backup pitchers include Hall of Famer Bob Gibson, who spent the 1957–58 season with the Harlem Globetrotters, and the still-active Ron Reed, who played in the NBA from 1965 to 1967. For a pinch-hitter there is Howie Schultz, who was in the majors from 1943 to 1948, in the NBL between 1946 and 1949, and in the NBA from 1949 to 1953. The manager-coach is Red Rolfe, who piloted the Tigers between 1949 and 1952 and coached in the Basketball Association of America (BAA) in 1946–47.

OTHER SPORTS

Tennis, anyone? No, but on the other hand. . . .

1B—JIM THORPE	Track and field
2B—BUDDY BLATTNER	Table tennis
3B—DON HOAK	Boxing
SS—ANDRE RODGERS	Cricket
OF—SAMMY BYRD	Golf
OF—BILL MAHARG	Boxing
OF—WES SCHULMERICH	Wrestling
C—ERNIE LOMBARDI	Bocci
P—LOU KRETLOW	Golf

Technically, very technically, Thorpe and Lombardi did not have the professional status of the other members of this lineup. Thorpe, of course, suffered for the distinction, while Lombardi became so renowned in the Bay Area for his skills in the Italian game that he was known as "Bocci" to fellow National Leaguers. At one point Blattner was the national table tennis champion. Hoak fought professionally in Pennsylvania. Maharg was one of the teenagers pressed into service in 1912 by the Tigers to replace the players striking in solidarity with the suspended Ty Cobb; he put in another one-game appearance for the Phillies many years later. Rodgers has been the only Caribbean cricket player to reach the majors. Kretlow has laid claim to sinking the longest hole-in-one (427 feet!) in the history of the game.

Honorable mentions to, among others, golfer Ken Harrelson, Illinois horseshoe pitching champion Don Erickson and New York State Boxing Commissioner Frank Dwyer.

MOVIE STARS

Hollywood has found several players' lives worthy of film or television treatment—with a seeming emphasis on pitchers. Among the players portrayed on the big or small screen have been:

1B—LOU GEHRIG	*The Pride of the Yankees*	Gary Cooper
2B—ROGERS HORNSBY	*The Winning Team*	Frank Lovejoy
3B—JACKIE ROBINSON	*The Jackie Robinson Story*	Jackie Robinson
SS—CASEY	*Casey at the Bat*	Wallace Beery
OF—JIMMY PIERSALL	*Fear Strikes Out*	Tony Perkins
OF—RON LeFLORE	*One in a Million: The Ron LeFlore Story*	LeVar Burton
OF—BABE RUTH	*The Babe Ruth Story*	William Bendix
C—ROY CAMPANELLA	*It's Great to Be Alive*	Paul Winfield
P—GROVER CLEVELAND ALEXANDER	*The Winning Team*	Ronald Reagan

A question about shortstop? Well, neither the original Ernest Thayer ditty, "Casey at the Bat" (in which the hero struck out), nor Grantland Rice's subsequent "Casey's Revenge" (in which he homered) mention any position for Casey. So why not shortstop and the 1927 silent film?

Lefty Gomez made a brief appearance in *The Babe Ruth Story*. He was supposed to throw a pitch to Bendix, who would swing a Ruthian swing, whereupon there would be a cut to actual footage of a Ruth home run. Bendix must have been truly into the part, however, because he knocked the pitch over the right-field wall.

The Babe himself starred in some minor films of his own in the 1930s and also appeared as himself in *The Pride of the Yankees*.

Among the other players given life on the big screen were Dizzy Dean (Dan Dailey), Monty Stratton (Jimmy Stewart) and Jim Thorpe (Burt Lancaster).

MEMORABLE QUOTES

These players either said it or had it said about them.

1B—LOU GEHRIG
2B—RON HUNT
3B—DICK ALLEN
SS—JOHNNY LOGAN
OF—WILLIE KEELER
OF—COOL PAPA BELL
OF—CARMELO MARTINEZ
C—YOGI BERRA
P—SATCHEL PAIGE

Gehrig's famous farewell included the line, "But today I can say I consider myself the luckiest man on the face of the earth."

Hunt described his hit by pitch records thusly: "Some people give their bodies to science, I give mine to baseball."

Allen dismissed Astroturf with the line, "If a horse can't eat it, I don't want to play on it."

Logan, told that what had appeared in the *Milwaukee Journal* was a typographical error, replied, "The hell it was; it was a clean base hit."

Keeler's "I hit 'em where they ain't" is still the best formula for success at bat.

Josh Gibson said of Bell, "Cool Papa was so fast he could get out of bed, turn out the light across the room, and be back in bed under the covers before the lights went out."

Martinez declared that, "The only problem I have in playing the outfield is catching the fly balls."

Take your pick of Berraisms. Our favorites are his philosophical "It ain't over till it's over," and his recapitulation of the 1960 World Series, "We made too many wrong mistakes."

Paige's philosophy of life included, "Don't look back. Something may be gaining on you."

The manager is Leo Durocher for "Nice guys finish last." Or perhaps Earl Weaver for his outburst at a player who wanted to hold a clubhouse chapel because "You have to walk with the Lord": "I'd rather walk with the bases loaded." Or Bill Lee's description of Don Zimmer as a "designated gerbil."

The coach is Mike Gonzalez of the Dodgers, who coined the phrase "Good field; no hit" to describe rookie catcher Moe Berg.

The announcer is Gerry Coleman: "Rich Folkers is throwing up in the bullpen."

And the sportswriter is Red Smith for his response to critics of baseball: "Baseball is a dull game only for those with dull minds."

EAT YOUR WORDS

Sometimes things get said that just don't turn out the way the speaker intended.

1B—BILLY TERRY
2B—BILLY MARTIN
3B—GRAIG NETTLES
SS—LUKE APPLING
OF—BABE RUTH
OF—REGGIE JACKSON
OF—CARL FURILLO
C—MUDDY RUEL
P—WARREN SPAHN

In 1934 Terry asked, "Is Brooklyn still in the league?" That was before the season started; in September the hapless sixth-place Dodgers beat the Giants twice to knock them out of the pennant race. In 1953 Martin said: "The Dodgers are the Dodgers. If they had eight Babe Ruths, they couldn't beat us"; two years later the Dodgers beat the Yankees in the World Series. In 1977 Nettles declared, "I guess it's in my nature to be quiet"; subsequent statements belied this. (His comments equating the 1978 Yankees with a circus and describing Sparky Lyle's passage from "Cy Young to Sayonara" are two cases in point.)

The line, "You hit singles, you drive a Ford; hit home

runs, you drive a Cadillac," or a variation on it has been attributed to several players, Appling among them. Whoever said it, Pete Rose would disagree. Ed Barrow, the Red Sox manager in 1918, said, describing his ace pitcher, "I'd be the laughing-stock of baseball if I changed the best left-hander in baseball into an outfielder." Jackson in 1972: "I hate [Billy] Martin. But if I played for him, I'd probably love him"; not quite. Furillo told Robin Roberts that the wild southpaw throwing batting practice was "Some Jew kid who'll never learn to pitch as long as he has a hole in his ass"; that was Sandy Koufax he was talking about.

Ruel was the first to describe the catcher's equipment as "the tools of ignorance," even though most good catchers are rather astute. "Spahn, Sain and two days of rain" was hardly an adequate way of describing a pitching staff that included Vern Bickford (11-5) and Bill Voiselle (13-13).

The manager is Tommy Holmes, who headed the Braves Triple-A team in 1952 and said of one young player, "That kid can't play baseball. He can't pull the ball." Hank Aaron proved him wrong. The owner—and there are many candidates—is Clark Griffith of the old Washington Senators in 1935: "There is no chance of night baseball ever becoming popular in the bigger cities because high-class baseball cannot be played under artificial lights."

STENGELESE

As Casey Stengel once put it, "I never coulda done it without my players." These are some of the players he never coulda done it without.

    1B—MARV THRONEBERRY
    2B—BILLY MARTIN
    3B—BOBBY BROWN
    SS—JERRY LUMPE
    OF—MICKEY MANTLE
    OF—GREG GOOSEN
    OF—CASEY STENGEL
     C—HOBIE LANDRITH
     P—JOHNNY SAIN

And this is what he had to say to and about them:

Throneberry: "We was going to get you a birthday cake, but we figured you'd drop it."

"Now you take Ernie Lombardi who's a big man and has a big nose and you take Martin who's a little man and has a bigger nose. How do you figger it?"

"Bobby Brown reminds me of a feller who's been hitting for twelve years and fielding one."

Lumpe: "He looks like the greatest hitter in the world till you play him."

"Son, it ain't the water cooler that's strikin' you out," he told his famous slugger after Mantle demolished the dugout water cooler.

"I got a kid, Greg Goosen, he's nineteen years old and in ten years he's got a chance to be twenty-nine."

Himself: "I broke in with four hits and the writers promptly decided they had seen the new Ty Cobb. It took me only a few days to correct that impression."

"You gotta have a catcher. If you don't have a catcher, you'll have all passed balls." (This was Casey's response to a question about why Landrith was the first draft pick of the Mets).

"Sain don't say much, but that don't matter much, because when you're out there on the mound, you got nobody to talk to."

FIELDING

Fielding statistics are much neglected by numbers buffs, but here are the best and some of the worst in defensive categories. And, remember, pitchers are fielders, too.

HIGHEST FIELDING AVERAGE—CAREER

With 1000 or more games played these players have posted the highest fielding averages.

1B—WES PARKER	.996
2B—DAVE CASH	.984
3B—BROOKS ROBINSON	.971
SS—LARRY BOWA	.981
OF—PETE ROSE	.992
OF—JOE RUDI	.991
OF—MICKEY STANLEY	.991
C—BILL FREEHAN	.993
P—DON MOSSI	.990

The best fielding average for a pitcher is based not on 1000 games, but on 1500 innings pitched.

HIGHEST FIELDING AVERAGE—SEASON

This team is a pitcher's delight, the players with the highest fielding averages in a season with a minimum of 150 games.

1B—STUFFY McINNIS	.999	1921 Red Sox
2B—BOBBY GRICH	.995	1973 Orioles
3B—DON MONEY	.989	1974 Brewers
SS—EDDIE BRINKMAN	.990	1972 Tigers
OF—CURT FLOOD	1.000	1966 Cardinals
OF—TERRY PUHL	1.000	1979 Astros
OF—BRIAN DOWNING	1.000	1982 Angels
C—RANDY HUNDLEY	.996	1967 Cubs
P—RANDY JONES	1.000	1976 Padres

While many outfielders and pitchers have had perfect fielding marks in a season, the four players on this team had the most chances accepted in 150 games. Flood had 396; Puhl, 359; Downing, 330; and Jones, 112.

MOST ERRORS—SEASON

Nowadays an error is a minor calamity, a relatively infrequent event. There was, however, a time when that wasn't true at all.

1B—JOE QUINN	62	100 games, 1884 St. Louis (UA)
2B—POP SMITH	88	80 games, 1880 Cincinnati
3B—PIANO LEGS HICKMAN	91	118 games, 1900 Giants
SS—BILL SHINDLE	115	132 games, 1890 Philadelphia (PL)
OF—ED BEECHER	52	125 games, 1890 Buffalo (PL)
OF—GEORGE VAN HALTREN	47	143 games, 1892 Baltimore-Pirates
OF—CY SEYMOUR	36	135 games, 1903 Reds
C—NAT HICKS	94	45 games, 1876 New York
P—TIM KEEFE	63	68 games, 1883 New York (AA)

A few extenuating circumstances are involved. Quinn made his blunders as a rookie and later was moved to second base. Hickman's errors came in the only year in which

314

he played third; primarily a first baseman, he also played second and the outfield, and was a pretty good hitter. And Keefe won 41 and lost 26 in 1883, so his errors couldn't have hurt him that much.

Dishonorable mention to Bob Ferguson (1883 Phillies), who tied Smith's total, but took 85 games to do it.

Dishonorable mention also to Pop Snyder (1881 Braves) and Mike Hines (1883 Braves) for their 99 passed balls each—in 58 and 56 games, respectively; Phil Knell (1891 Columbus, AA) for his 54 hit batsmen in 58 games; and Steve Carlton for his 11 balks (1979 Phillies).

MOST ERRORS—GAME

Modern gloves make a duplication of these dubious achievements unlikely.

1B—JOE QUINN	5	July 4, 1884	St. Louis (UA)
2B—ANDY LEONARD	9	June 14, 1876	Braves
3B—BILLY ALVORD	6	May 22, 1890	Toledo (AA)
SS—GERMANY SMITH	7	June 17, 1885	Brooklyn (AA)
OF—MIKE TIERNAN	5	May 16, 1887	Giants
OF—MARTY SULIVAN	5	May 18, 1887	Cubs
OF—KIP SELBACH	5	August 19, 1902	Orioles
C—BILL TAYLOR	7	May 29, 1886	Baltimore
P—ED DOHENY	5	August 15, 1889	Giants

Quinn, Alvord and the three outfielders are merely the most recent to make so many miscues. The others stand alone.

And honorable mention to Frank Gardner (Washington, NL), who had 12 passed balls on May 10, 1884; Ed Knouff, who hit 6 batters while pitching for Baltimore (AA) on

April 25, 1887; John Ryan, who threw 10 wild pitches for Louisville (NL) on July 22, 1876; and Bob Shaw, who balked 5 times on May 4, 1963, while trying to throw the ball for the Braves.

CONSECUTIVE ERRORLESS GAMES

This lineup includes those players who played the most games in a row without making an error. Included are the number of games, the number of chances accepted during the streak and the seasons in which the streak took place.

1B—STEVE GARVEY	188	1572	1983–present
2B—JOE MORGAN	91	418	1977–78
3B—JIM DAVENPORT	97	209	1966–68
SS—ED BRINKMAN	72	331	1972
OF—DON DEMETER	266	449	1962–65
OF—BRIAN DOWNING	244	471	1982–83
OF—AL KALINE	242	375	1970–72
C—YOGI BERRA	148	950	1957–59
P—PAUL LINDBLAD	385	126	1966–74

Davenport is the only one who played other positions during his streak.

CONSECUTIVE CHANCES WITHOUT AN ERROR

Looking at the same phenomenon, consistent fielding excellence, from another angle, we come up with quite a few different names. Included are the number of chances accepted during the streak, the number of games played during the streak and the seasons covered.

1B—STUFFY McINNIS	1700	163	1921–22
2B—MANNY TRILLO	479	89	1982
3B—DON MONEY	261	88	1973–74
SS—BUDDY KERR	383	70	1946–47
OF—CURT FLOOD	568	227	1965–67
OF—KEN BERRY	510	211	1971–73
OF—BRIAN DOWNING	471	244	1982–83
C—YOGI BERRA	950	148	1957–59
P—CLAUDE PASSEAU	273	145	1941–46

Downing and Berra are the only repeaters from the previous team.

MOST PUTOUTS—CAREER

Casey Stengel once said that "You got to get twenty-seven outs to win." By that standard, this team would have accounted for over 2500 victories.

1B—JAKE BECKLEY	23,709
2B—EDDIE COLLINS	6526
3B—BROOKS ROBINSON	2697
SS—RABBIT MARANVILLE	5139
OF—WILLIE MAYS	7095
OF—TRIS SPEAKER	6791
OF—MAX CAREY	6363
C—BILL FREEHAN	9941
P—FERGUSON JENKINS	363

Beckley's number here is the highest statistic in this book.

MOST PUTOUTS—SEASON

This team would account for almost 180 wins.

1B—JIGGS DONOHUE	1846	1907	White Sox
2B—BID McPHEE	529	1886	Cincinnati (AA)
3B—DENNY LYONS	255	1887	Philadelphia (AA)
SS—HUGH JENNINGS	425	1895	Baltimore
OF—TAYLOR DOUTHIT	547	1928	Cardinals
OF—RICHIE ASHBURN	538	1951	Phillies
OF—CHET LEMON	512	1977	White Sox
C—JOHNNY EDWARDS	1135	1969	Astros
P—DAVE FOUTZ	57	1886	St. Louis (AA)

Donie Bush (1914 Tigers) tied Jennings's record, but it took him 157 games to do it; Jennings played only 131.

Ashburn had 514 putouts in 1949, giving him two of the four highest season totals. Indeed, Ashburn had four of the eight 500-plus seasons by an outfielder and six of the ten highest season totals ever.

Edwards is the only catcher ever to have 1000 or more putouts in a season—and he did it twice. The other season was 1963 when he was credited with retiring 1008 opposing batters with the Reds.

MOST PUTOUTS—GAME

These players had the stated number of putouts in a regulation nine-inning game.

1B—ERNIE BANKS	22	May 9, 1963	Cubs
2B—BOBBY KNOOP	12	August 30, 1966	Angels
3B—WILLIE KUEHNE	10	May 24, 1889	Pirates
SS—HOD FORD	11	Sept. 18, 1929	Reds
OF—EARL CLARK	12	May 10, 1929	Braves
OF—LYMAN BOSTOCK	12	May 25, 1977	Twins
OF—TONY ARMAS	11	June 12, 1982	Athletics
C—JERRY GROTE	20	April 22, 1970	Mets
P—BERT BLYLEVEN	6	June 25, 1984	Indians

Banks is the most recent of three first basemen to make 22 putouts in a game. Knoop is one of two—and the only one in the twentieth century—to make a dozen putouts at second. Kuehne holds his record alone. Ford is the most recent of several shortstops with 11 putouts. Clark and Bostock were playing center field when they caught 12 fly balls; a number of outfielders have caught 11 in one game, but Armas is the only one to do so in right field. Grote had a lot of help from Tom Seaver in piling up his total. And Blyleven is the only pitcher with 6 putouts in a game.

MOST ASSISTS—CAREER

The next time you see an infielder scoop up a ground ball or an outfielder throw out a runner trying to take an extra base, think of the players on this team, who did just that most often.

1B—GEORGE SISLER	1528
2B—EDDIE COLLINS	7630
3B—BROOKS ROBINSON	6205
SS—LUIS APARICIO	8016
OF—TRIS SPEAKER	448
OF—TY COBB	392
OF—JIMMY RYAN	375
C—DEACON McGUIRE	1859
P—CY YOUNG	2013

Young must have had a knack for making batters hit back to the box.

MOST ASSISTS—SEASON

And these are the players who threw out an opponent the most times in a single season.

1B—BILL BUCKNER	159	1982 Cubs
2B—FRANKIE FIRSCH	641	1927 Cardinals
3B—GRAIG NETTLES	412	1971 Indians
SS—OZZIE SMITH	621	1980 Padres
OF—TOM DOLAN	62	1883 St. Louis (AA)
OF—ORATOR SHAFFER	50	1879 Cubs
OF—HUGH NICOL	48	1884 St. Louis (AA)
C—BILL RARIDEN	238	1915 Newark (FL)
P—ED WALSH	227	1907 White Sox

Relatively recent infield records and ancient outfield records would indicate that infield play has improved, probably because of advanced equipment, while outfield defensive play was better back when, probably because the dead ball allowed outfielders to play much shallower than they do now.

MOST ASSISTS—GAME

And the most assists in one (nine-inning) game:

1B—BOB ROBERTSON	8	June 21, 1971	Pirates
2B—DON MONEY	12	June 24, 1977	Brewers
3B—MIKE FERRARO	11	Sept. 14, 1968	Yankees
SS—TOMMY CORCORAN	14	August 7, 1903	Reds
OF—WALLY BERGER	4	April 27, 1931	Braves
OF—ELTON LANGFORD	4	May 1, 1928	Indians
OF—BOB MEUSEL	4	Sept. 5, 1921	Yankees
C—MIKE HINES	9	May 1, 1883	Braves
P—RIP SEWELL	11	June 6, 1941	Pirates

Money, Ferraro, Sewell and the outfielders are the most recent to throw out that many opponents. The others hold the record exclusively.

MOST DOUBLE PLAYS—CAREER

These players turned over the most pitcher's best friends in their careers.

1B—MICKEY VERNON	2044
2B—BILL MAZEROSKI	1706
3B—BROOKS ROBINSON	618
SS—LUIS APARICIO	1553
OF—TRIS SPEAKER	135
OF—TY COBB	107
OF—MAX CAREY	86
C—RAY SCHALK	217
P—WARREN SPAHN	82

Obviously, longevity is an essential part of making this team, but in addition to longevity you have to have range, a good arm and better-than-average teammates.

MOST DOUBLE PLAYS—SEASON

And these did it most often in a single season.

1B—FERRIS FAIN	149	1949 Athletics
2B—BILL MAZEROSKI	161	1966 Pirates
3B—GRAIG NETTLES	54	1971 Indians
SS—RICK BURLESON	147	1980 Red Sox
OF—HAP FELSCH	15	1919 White Sox
OF—JACK TOBIN	15	1919 Browns
OF—JIMMY SHECKARD	14	1899 Baltimore
C—BLIMP HAYES	29	1945 Indians
P—BOB LEMON	15	1953 Indians

Relatively recent infielders and relatively older outfielders tell us something about the history of fielding prowess at various positions.

MOST DOUBLE PLAYS—GAME

And the most in a nine-inning game . . .

1B—CURT BLEFARY	7	May 4, 1969	Astros
2B—BOBBY KNOOP	6	May 1, 1966	Angels
3B—KEN McMULLEN	4	August 13, 1965	Senators
SS—NELSON NORMAN	5	April 23, 1979	Rangers
OF—JOHN NELSON	3	June 9, 1887	New York (AA)
OF—JOHN McCARTHY	3	April 26, 1905	Cubs
OF—IRA FLAGSTEAD	3	April 19, 1926	Red Sox
C—RICK DEMPSEY	3	June 1, 1977	Orioles
P—HAL NEWHOUSER	4	May 19, 1948	Tigers

McMullen is the most recent of five third basemen with four DPs in a game. Norman is the most recent of 47 shortstops. Dempsey is the most recent of eight catchers. And Newhouser is the most recent of two pitchers. All the others stand alone in the record book. The outfield contingent consists of the only three outfielders to start three double plays in a regulation-length game.

UNASSISTED

Some players who did it without help.

1B —GEORGE BURNS	Second inning, Sept. 14, 1923, Giants
2B—MIKE EDWARDS	August 10, 1978, Athletics
3B—JOE DUGAN	1924 Yankees
SS—RON HANSEN	First inning July 30, 1968, Orioles
OF—TRIS SPEAKER	Career
OF—ELMER SMITH	Career
OF—JOSE CARDENAL	1968 Indians
C—FRANK CROSSIN	1914 Browns
P—BILL WHITE	1879 Cincinnati

Burns was the first of two first baseman to make an unassisted triple play. (The other is Johnny Neun.) Edwards is the only second baseman to make two unassisted double plays in one game in this century. Dugan is the only third baseman to make four unassisted double plays in a season. Hansen is the most recent shortstop to make an unassisted triple play. (The others are Neal Ball, Ernie Padgett, Glenn Wright and Jim Cooney.) Speaker and Smith are the only outfielders to make four unassisted double plays in their careers. Cardenal is the most recent of four outfielders to make two unassisted double plays in a season. Crossin is the only catcher to make two unassisted double plays in a season. White has the most complete games in a season, 74—out of the 75 in which he pitched.

Honorable mention to Jim Carleton and Claude Passeau, the only pitchers to make two unassisted double plays in their careers.

NOT MUCH TO DO

Little Leaguers are taught to increase their self-confidence by repeating over and over to themselves, "Hit it to me. Hit it to me." Sometimes, however, neither that nor anything else works. This team consists of players who went through the longest game without a putout or an assist.

1B—GENE TENACE	9 inn.	Sept. 1, 1974	Athletics
2B—STEVE YERKES	15 inn.	June 11, 1919	Red Sox
3B—TONY BOECKEL	15 inn.	June 6, 1921	Braves
		Sept. 12, 1921	Braves
SS—JOHN GOCHNAUER	12 inn.	July 14, 1903	Indians
LF—PAT MULLIN	16 inn.	May 9, 1952	Tigers
CF—BILLY BRUTON	22 inn.	June 24, 1962	Tigers
RF—CAP PETERSON	22 inn.	June 12, 1967	Senators
C—GENE DESAUTELS	14 inn.	August 11, 1942	Indians
P—MILT WATSON	20 inn.	July 17, 1918	Phillies

Tenace is the most recent of four first basemen to play a regulation contest without accepting a chance. Boeckel actually played *two* 15-inning games in 1921 without a chance. Gochnauer shares his accomplishment—or lack of it—with one other shortstop, from the nineteenth century. And Mullin is the most recent of four left fielders to be inactive for so many innings.

BUSY, BUSY, BUSY

On the other hand, some days you just can't stop the ball from coming your way. These players had the most chances accepted in a nine-inning game.

1B—ERNIE BANKS	22	May 9, 1963	Cubs
2B—TERRY HARMON	18	June 12, 1971	Phillies
3B—ROY HUGHES	13	August 29, 1944	Cubs
SS—EDDIE JOOST	19	May 7, 1941	Reds
LF—WILLIE HORTON	11	July 18, 1969	Tigers
CF—EARL CLARK	13	May 10, 1929	Braves
RF—TONY ARMAS	12	June 12, 1982	Athletics
C—GEORGE BIGNALL	23	October 3, 1884	Milwaukee (UA)
P—NICK ALTROCK	13	August 6, 1904	White Sox

Banks is the most recent first baseman to accept 22 chances. One other second baseman—in the nineteenth century—had 18 chances. Hughes is the most recent of eight third basemen to be in on 13 plays. Joost's total was matched by a shortstop in the last century. Horton is the most recent of five left fielders with 11 chances. Eighteen of Bignall's 23 chances were strikeouts.

Ed Walsh (1907 White Sox) tied Altrock's record.

ODDS AND ODDS

A collection of fielding peculiarities.

1B—GEORGE SISLER	1922 Browns
2B—BID McPHEE	1882–89 Cincinnati (AA)
	1890–96 Reds
3B—NED WILLIAMSON	1885 Cubs
SS—LEE TANNEHILL	1911 White Sox
OF—BABYDOLL JACOBSON	1926 Red Sox
OF—CHARLIE JAMIESON	1928 Indians
OF—WILLIE MAYS	1951 Giants
C—JOE GARAGIOLA	1949 Cardinals
P—BILL HUBBELL	1921 Phillies

Sisler, the slickest fielding first baseman of all time, started a routine first-to-pitcher putout, realized the pitcher was not covering the base, caught up with his own toss and stepped on the bag. McPhee played in about 1700 games before he thought it necessary to use a glove. Williamson's fielding average was .891—and that was the *highest* for all third basemen in the National League that year. Tannehill is the only shortstop to make two unassisted double plays in a single game.

Jacobson played right field in seven consecutive games without either a putout or an assist. Jamieson started two triple plays in the same season. Mays's exploits in the field were spectacular, but never more so than in his rookie year. On one play he ran out from under his hat and caught the ball in his left hand and the hat in his right. On another, he caught a line drive in right center, spun in the

325

air, threw the ball like a shortstop and nailed Billy Cox at the plate. But his greatest catch, according to both Leo Durocher and Branch Rickey, came in Pittsburgh's Forbes Field, when he outran a long, hooking line drive by Rocky Nelson, realized the ball was sinking and bending to his right, and, with his back to the plate, reached out with his bare right hand and caught the ball.

Garagiola had five chances accepted in one inning—a neat trick. And Hubbell had perhaps the most painful assist in the history of the game when Rogers Hornsby bounced a line drive off his head and directly into the hand of Russ Wrightstone.

Honorable mention to Steve Gromek, who pitched a complete game for the Indians in 1945 without any of his infielders getting credit for an assist. There were 15 fly balls to the outfield, four infield popups, two popups to the catcher, four strikeouts and two unassisted putouts by the first baseman.

POST-SEASON PLAY AND THE ALL-STAR GAMES

Bests, worsts, and a lot more in between for the World Series, the inter-divisional League Championship Series, the sudden death playoffs and the All-Star Games.

BEST WORLD SERIES—CAREER

Although he has certainly earned rights to one-ninth of the title, Reggie Jackson is not the only Mister October. Among the most productive players in the World Series have been:

1B—LOU GEHRIG	Yankees	
2B—BILLY MARTIN	Yankees	
3B—PEPPER MARTIN	Cardinals	
SS—PEEWEE REESE	Dodgers	
OF—BABE RUTH	Yankees	
OF—REGGIE JACKSON	Yankees and Athletics	
OF—MICKEY MANTLE	Yankees	
C—YOGI BERRA	Yankees	
P—BOB GIBSON	Cardinals	

In seven World Series Gehrig swatted 10 home runs. In the four series in which he actually batted, Martin went 33-99 (.333), walloped five homers and drove in 19 runs. Martin the Cardinal went 23 for 55 (.418) for the two series in which he came to the plate. In seven series Reese got 46 hits for a .272 average and made about one error per series. Ruth hit at least .300 six out of ten times and slugged 15 home runs. In five series Jackson has hit 10 homers and accumulated a slugging average of .755. Mantle hit 18 homers in 12 series. Berra's .274 mark over 14 series includes 12 homers. Gibson has a mark of seven wins and two losses for three series.

Honorable mention to Lou Brock for the highest World Series batting average (over three series) of .391 and to Duke Snider for 11 homers in six series.

BEST WORLD SERIES

The best World Series, of course, is the one your team has won. But for individual performances in post-season play between the leagues, we'll take:

1B—LOU GEHRIG	1928 Yankees
2B—BOBBY RICHARDSON	1960 Yankees
3B—BROOKS ROBINSON	1970 Orioles
SS—MARK KOENIG	1927 Yankees
OF—BABE RUTH	1928 Yankees
OF—REGGIE JACKSON	1977 Yankees
OF—LOU BROCK	1968 Cardinals
C—GENE TENACE	1972 Athletics
P—CHRISTY MATHEWSON	1905 Giants

Odd about all those Yankees. Anyway, in the cited years: Gehrig hit four homers and had a slugging average of 1.727. Richardson went 11-for-30 and batted in 12 runs. Robinson not only turned singles into outs and doubles into double plays, but ended up with 17 total bases in five games. Koenig rapped out nine hits in 18 at bats to help the Yankees sweep. In another four-game sweep, Ruth banged out three doubles, three homers and four singles in 16 at bats for a .625 average. Jackson's five homers helped him to a slugging average of 1.250. Brock stole seven bases, hit two homers, drove in five runs, and ended up with a .464 average (13-for-28) for the seven-game series against the Tigers. Tenace was the difference in the seven-game Series against the Reds, going 8-for-23 (.348) with four homers and nine runs batted in. Mathewson merely threw three shutouts in a five-game series against the Athletics.

BEST WORLD SERIES GAME

Anyone who disagrees with us about the pitcher in this lineup is reading the wrong book.

1B—VIC WERTZ	1954 Indians
2B—BOBBY RICHARDSON	1960 Yankees
3B—PAUL MOLITOR	1982 Brewers
SS HONUS WAGNER	1909 Pirates
OF—REGGIE JACKSON	1977 Yankees
OF—BABE RUTH	1926 and 1928 Yankees
OF—LOU BROCK	1967 and 1968 Cardinals
C—JOHNNY BENCH	1976 Reds
P—DON LARSEN	1956 Yankees

Everybody knows about Willie Mays's great catch against Wertz in the opening game of the 1954 World Series; what many may not remember is that the drive was Wertz's bid for a *fifth* hit in the game! The other single-game accomplishments were: Richardson, six runs batted in; Molitor, five hits; Wagner, three hits and three stolen bases; Jackson and Ruth, three home runs; Brock, three stolen bases; Bench, two homers and five runs batted in. As for Larsen, he struck out pinch-hitter Dale Mitchell in a key situation.

DRAMATIC FINAL PLAYS

Most World Series have ended with relatively routine plays—a fly ball to left, an easy grounder to short. But some have not been so routine. Aside from those Series that ended with a hit, these were the most exciting.

1B—WILLIE McCOVEY	1962 Giants
2B—JOHNNY RAWLINGS	1921 Giants
3B—LARRY GARDNER	1912 Red Sox
SS—MAURY WILLS	1963 Dodgers
OF—CURT WELCH	1886 St. Louis (AA)
OF—BABE RUTH	1926 Yankees
OF—EARLE COMBS	1927 Yankees
C—BOSS SCHMIDT	1907 and 1908 Tigers
P—DOLF LUQUE	1933 Giants

McCovey's wicked line drive to Bobby Richardson with two on ended the seventh game with a score of 1-0. Rawlings made a sensational stop on the outfield grass and threw out Frank Baker to start a double play as first baseman George Kelly caught Aaron Ward off third; final score: 1-0. Gardner ended one of the most dramatic sequences in World Series history with a sacrifice fly to right in the bottom of the tenth to win the eighth game by a 3-2 score. Gardner's game winner came after the Snodgrass muffed fly ball and Tris Speaker's single that followed a dropped foul pop. With the score 2-1 in the top of the ninth in the fourth game Elston Howard grounded to Wills only to have Dick Tracewski drop the potential force out at second; the next batter, Hector Lopez, unintentionally dribbled the ball to short again and Wills threw him out at first. Welch, a journeyman outfielder, stole home in the tenth inning of the sixth game to break a 3-3 tie; he had taken a long lead and opposing catcher King Kelly called for a pitchout, but Welch streaked home on an unsuccessful 2-5-2 pickoff. Ruth inexplicably tried to steal second with the score 3-2 in the seventh game and Bob Meusel at the plate; Cards catcher Bob O'Farrell threw him out easily with Tommy Thevenow making the tag. With the score tied 3-3 in the fourth game Combs walked, moved to second on Mark Koenig's bunt single, went to third on a wild pitch, waited as Babe Ruth was intentionally passed, made a fake start toward home on each pitch to Tony Lazzeri, and so rattled Pirates pitcher John Miljus that he let go with his second wild pitch of the inning to score the Series-ending run. Schmidt made the last out in two successive World Series—on a pinch-hit popout to Joe Tinker and on a ball tapped in front of the plate that Johnny Kling tossed to Frank Chance. The score of both games was 2-0. Luque's strikeout of Joe Kuhel was the most dramatic of the ten Series-ending whiffs; Mel Ott had hit a home run in the top of the tenth to put the Giants ahead 1-0, but Luque allowed a single to Joe Cronin and a walk to Fred Schulte before reaching back for whatever it took to get Kuhel to fan.

FIELDING GEMS

Every fan has seen the replay of Willie Mays's astonishing catch off Vic Wertz. But there have been any number of other great plays. These are our picks of the very best.

1B—PETE ROSE	Game 6	1980 Phillies
2B—BILLY WAMBSGANSS	Game 5	1920 Indians
3B—GRAIG NETTLES	Game 3	1978 Yankees
SS—PEEWEE REESE	Game 7	1955 Dodgers
OF—SANDY AMOROS	Game 7	1955 Dodgers
OF—WILLIE MAYS	Game 1	1954 Giants
OF—TOMMIE AGEE	Game 3	1969 Mets
C—JIM HEGAN	Game 6	1948 Indians
P—BOB GIBSON	Game 5	1964 Cardinals

With one out and the bases loaded in the ninth inning catcher Bob Boone waved Rose off a foul popup that jumped out of Boone's glove; Rose, in the play all the way, snatched it before it hit the ground. In the fifth inning Wambsganss snatched a line drive by Clarence Mitchell, stepped on second to retire Pete Kilduff and tagged Otto Miller to complete the only World Series triple play. With all due respect to Brooks Robinson, the finest performance by a third baseman was Nettles's diving stops with the bases loaded in the fifth and sixth innings that turned sure runs into force outs. Amoros's running, one-handed catch of a ball sliced into the left field corner by Yogi Berra killed a Yankee rally in the sixth inning. Reese took the relay from Amoros and doubled Gil McDougald off first. Mays raced, hat flying and back to the plate, and grabbed

Wertz's blast deep into the far reaches of center field in the Polo Grounds. Game 3 in 1969 belonged to Tommie Agee: In the third he made a backhanded, fingertip catch against the wall to rob Elrod Hendricks of a two-run triple and in the seventh he made a diving catch in right-center to take a bases-loaded extra base hit away from Paul Blair. With a man on first and none out in the ninth, pinch-hitter Sibby Sisti bunted the ball in the air; Hegan grabbed it and doubled the runner off first, and one out later the Indians sealed the 4-3 victory and the Series. In the ninth inning Gibson took a line drive off the bat of Joe Pepitone on his hip, chased it over toward third base, picked it up, turned 180 degrees in the air, and nipped Pepitone at first with a falling-away, one-handed jump shot.

Honorable mention to Billy Martin (1952), Harry Hooper (1912), Ron Swoboda (1969), Dwight Evans (1975), and to Andy Pafko, Duke Snider and Carl Furillo for their catches in the same game in 1952.

PERFECT SERIES

With the exception of the pitcher, the following is a lineup of very forgettable players. Nevertheless, each and every one of these players can also say that he retired with a World Series batting average of 1.000.

1B—CHICO SALMON	1969–1970 Orioles
2B—JERRY BUCHEK	1964 Cardinals
3B—RIP RUSSELL	1946 Red Sox
SS—JIM MASON	1976 Yankees
OF—ED KING	1922 Giants
OF—BOB MAIER	1945 Tigers
OF—AL FERRARA	1966 Dodgers
C—CLAY DALRYMPLE	1969 Orioles
P—LEFTY GOMEZ	1932, 1936–38 Yankees

Russell and Dalrymple were 2-for-2, the others got a hit in one official at bat. Mason is the only player to have homered. Other October Perfectos are catchers Bobby Bragan, Virgil Davis and Buddy Rosar.

Gomez won six games without losing. Jack Coombs and Herb Pennock each won five.

WORST SERIES

Sometimes established players can't do anything right in the fall . . .

1B—GIL HODGES	1952 Dodgers
2B—DAVEY LOPES	1981 Dodgers
3B—BUCK WEAVER	1919 White Sox
SS—ROGER PECKINPAUGH	1925 Senators
OF—JACK MURRAY	1911 Giants
OF—WILLIE DAVIS	1966 Dodgers
OF—WILLIE WILSON	1980 Royals
C—JOHNNY BENCH	1972 Reds
P—DON NEWCOMBE	1956 Dodgers

Hodges was hitless in 21 at bats. Lopes made six errors and could have been charged with more. Weaver went to the plate 34 times without driving in a run, which did much to offset indications that he did not cooperate in the Black Sox fix. Peckinpaugh, usually the most sure-handed of shortstops and the AL MVP that year, committed eight errors in 40 chances. Murray, the Giants cleanup hitter, went 0-for-21. Davis went 1-for-16 and made three errors. After a regular season of .326 and 79 stolen bases, Wilson batted only .154 (4-26) and stole only two bases; he also struck out 11 times. Bench was not only limited to one RBI, but he also managed to strike out on an intentional pass. (The pitcher was Rollie Fingers of Oakland.) Newcombe could never do anything right in World Series competition. His career record is 0-4 with an 8.49 ERA, but he hit bottom in 1956 when he yielded 11 runs and 11 hits in less than five innings for an ERA of 21.21.

STARS THAT DIDN'T SHINE

And sometimes even superstars couldn't get up for the Fall Classic.

1B—JIM BOTTOMLEY	1930 Cardinals
2B—FRANKIE FRISCH	1930 Cardinals
3B—EDDIE MATHEWS	1957 Braves
SS—HONUS WAGNER	1903 Pirates
OF—TY COBB	1907 Tigers
OF—BABE RUTH	1922 Yankees
OF—TED WILLIAMS	1946 Red Sox
C—GABBY HARTNETT	1938 Cubs
P—BOB LEMON	1954 Indians

Bottomley batted .045, getting only one hit in 22 at bats. Frisch did a little better, compiling a .208 average. Mathews batted .160. Wagner, in the very first Series, disappointed everyone by hitting .222. Cobb was even lower in his post-season debut—.200. Ruth went 2-for-17 (.118) with only one RBI. Williams also had only one RBI and a .200 average. Hartnett was 1-for-11 (.091). Lemon lost two games, won none and had a 6.75 ERA.

SURPRISE STARTERS

Managers love to pull surprises in the World Series. Fans and players alike were shocked when they heard the announcement "Now playing . . ."

1B—TONY PEREZ	1983 Phillies
2B—HAL JANVRIN	1916 Red Sox
3B—JACK SHEEHAN	1920 Dodgers
SS—MICKEY STANLEY	1968 Tigers
OF—AMOS STRUNK	1910 Athletics
OF—TILLIE SHAFER	1913 Giants
OF—CLYDE BARNHART	1927 Pirates
C—JIMMY WILSON	1940 Reds
P—HOWARD EHMKE	1929 Athletics

Perez replaced Pete Rose in the third game, much to Rose's irritation. Jack Barry had appeared in five World Series in six years, but when he was injured for the 1916 Series there was some question about who would replace him; Janvrin got the nod over Mike McNally. Sheehan was only on the Brooklyn roster as part of the deal that allowed Joe Sewell to replace Ray Chapman, who had been killed by a pitch, on the Indians. When Jimmy Johnstone, the regular Dodger third baseman, was injured, Sheehan, who had played only three games during the regular season, started the last three Series games. Stanley, the regular Tiger center fielder, was moved to short to get the bats of the other three outfielders (Willie Horton, Jim Northrup and Al Kaline) into the lineup and to get the bat of shortstop Ray Oyler (.135 average) out. With Rube Oldring injured, everyone expected Topsy Hartsell to replace him; Connie Mack, however, used rookie Strunk in the first four games. John McGraw had two reserve outfielders—Jim Thorpe and Claude Cooper—on his bench when Fred Snodgrass got hurt. Instead, McGraw used third baseman Tilly Shafer in the first game. Kiki Cuyler's various disputes with manager Donie Bush kept him on the bench most of the second half of the season, and Barnhart played every game of the Series. With Ernie Lombardi felled with an injured leg and Willard Hershberger a suicide, the Reds were left with two inadequate catchers, Bill Baker and Richard West. The Reds activated Wilson, a 40-year-old coach, who batted .353 and had the only stolen base of the Series. Connie Mack had a starting rotation in 1929 that included Lefty Grove, George Earnshaw, Rube Walberg and Ed Rommel, but Mack, a lover of surprises, gave the opening game assignment to Ehmke, who had pitched only 55 innings all year. All Ehmke did was pitch a neat 8-hitter, strike out 13, and win 3-1.

GETTING OFF ON THE RIGHT FOOT

A select few players have been able to ignore all the hoopla surrounding a World Series, walk up to the plate and belt a home run in their first October classic appearance. These include:

1B—DON MINCHER	1965 Twins
2B—BUCKY HARRIS	1925 Senators
3B—BROOKS ROBINSON	1966 Orioles
SS—JIM MASON	1976 Yankees
OF—GEORGE WATKINS	1930 Cardinals
OF—MEL OTT	1933 Giants
OF—GEORGE SELKIRK	1936 Yankees
C—ELSTON HOWARD	1955 Yankees
P—JOSE SANTIAGO	1967 Red Sox

Others who have performed the feat are infielders Bob Watson (1981 Yankees) and Doug DeCinces (1979 Orioles); outfielders Dusty Rhodes (1954 Giants), Roger Maris (1960 Yankees), Don Buford (1969 Orioles), Amos Otis (1980 Royals) and Jim Dwyer (1983 Orioles); catcher Gene Tenace (1972 Athletics); and pitcher Mickey Lolich (1968 Tigers).

CLASSIC TWO-TIMERS

Babe Ruth and Reggie Jackson are the only players ever to hit three homers in a World Series game—Ruth in the fourth game of the 1926 Series and again in the fourth game of the 1928 classic, and Jackson in the sixth game of 1977. Ruth is also one of 26 players ever to hit two four-baggers in one October game. He would be part of a team of:

1B—LOU GEHRIG	1928 and 1932 Yankees
2B—TONY LAZZERI	1932 Yankees
3B—BOB ELLIOTT	1948 Braves
SS—TONY KUBEK	1957 Yankees
OF—BABE RUTH	1923 and 1932 Yankees
OF—DUKE SNIDER	1952 and 1955 Dodgers
OF—MICKEY MANTLE	1958 and 1960 Yankees
C—YOGI BERRA	1956 Yankees
PH—WILLIE AIKENS	1980 Royals (twice)

Aikens makes the team as the chief reserve because he, Gehrig, Ruth, Snider and Mantle are the only players to have more than one multiple-homer game in World Series history.

For the record, the first player to hit more than one circuit blast in a Series game was Patsy Dougherty, an outfielder for the 1903 Red Sox.

THE UNKINDEST CUT OF ALL

While these players played a substantial part in getting their teams into the World Series, they themselves were forced to the sidelines for the championship games by injuries.

1B—HANK GREENBERG	1935 Tigers
2B—WILLIE RANDOLPH	1978 Yankees
3B—RED SMITH	1914 Braves
SS—GEORGE DAVIS	1906 White Sox
OF—DON MUELLER	1951 Giants
OF—REGGIE JACKSON	1972 Athletics
OF—JIM RICE	1975 Red Sox
C—CHIEF MEYERS	1913 Giants
P—RUBE WADDELL	1905 Athletics

Greenberg broke a wrist in the second game of the Series. Randolph's injury in the Championship Series created the opportunity for Brian Doyle to become a Series hero. Smith broke a leg and missed the Miracle Braves sweep of the Athletics. Davis's pre-Series injury forced third baseman Lee Tannehill to move to short and allowed utility man George Rohe to come off the bench and play third; Rohe batted .333 for the Series and it was Tannehill who had to make way when Davis unexpectedly returned for the final three games. Mueller was sidelined with a broken ankle suffered on the next-to-last play in the playoffs with the Dodgers. Jackson pulled a hamstring in the Championship Series. Rice missed both the Championship Series and the classic 1975 Series. Meyers broke a finger in the first game of the Series, but Larry McLean filled in admirably, batting .500 in a losing cause. Waddell's sore arm saved him from facing Christy Mathewson, a development which disappointed many fans, but which probably saved Waddell from defeat since Matty pitched three shutouts.

WORLD SERIES SPECTATORS

They were good players, they hung around for a long time, but they never managed to find a team able enough to get them into the fall classic.

> 1B—GEORGE SISLER
> 2B—NAP LAJOIE
> 3B—GEORGE KELL
> SS—BOBBY WALLACE
> OF—ELMER FLICK
> OF—KEN WILLIAMS
> OF—RALPH KINER
> C—JOE TORRE
> P—TED LYONS

Wallace had the longest career (25 years) without playing in a World Series, so he beats out fellow-spectators Luke Appling and Ernie Banks.

The manager is Gene Mauch, who has managed four different teams for a total of 23 seasons without winning a pennant.

DOUBLE AGENTS

Some players go through their entire careers without playing a World Series game, while others seem to have the October classic follow them even when they go from one league to the other.

1B—STUFFY McINNIS	1910–11, 1913 Athletics, 1918 Red Sox, 1925 Pirates
2B—DAL MAXVILL	1964 Cardinals, 1974 Athletics
3B—EDDIE MATHEWS	1957–58 Braves, 1968 Tigers
SS—MARK KOENIG	1926–28 Yankees, 1932 Cubs
OF—ENOS SLAUGHTER	1942, 1946 Cardinals, 1956–57 Yankees
OF—ROGER MARIS	1960–64 Yankees, 1967–68 Cardinals
OF—FRANK ROBINSON	1961 Reds, 1966, 1969–71 Orioles
C—DARRELL PORTER	1980 Royals, 1982 Cardinals
P—DON GULLETT	1970, 1972, 1975–76 Reds, 1977 Yankees

Maxvill also played shortstop for the Cardinals in 1967 and 1968; Koenig played second base for the Giants in 1936; and Slaughter pinch-hit for the Yankees in 1958.

The only managers who have won pennants in both leagues are Joe McCarthy (1929 Cubs and 1932, 1936–39 and 1941–43 Yankees), Alvin Dark (1962 Giants and 1974 Athletics), Yogi Berra (1964 Yankees and 1973 Mets), Dick Williams (1967 Red Sox, 1972–73 Athletics, 1984 Padres), and Sparky Anderson (1970, 1972, 1975–76 Reds, 1984 Tigers). Anderson is the only one to win world championships in both leagues.

THREE-TIME WINNERS

Then there are the players who, without neccessarily switching leagues, have appeared in the World Series in three different uniforms.

1B—FRED MERKLE	1911–13 Giants, 1916 Dodgers, 1918 Cubs
2B—EDDIE STANKY	1947 Dodgers, 1948 Braves, 1951 Giants
3B—HEINIE GROH	1912, 1922–24 Giants, 1919 Reds, 1927 Pirates
SS—MARK KOENIG	1926–28 Yankees, 1932 Cubs, 1936 Giants
OF—ANDY PAFKO	1945 Cubs, 1952 Dodgers, 1957–58 Braves
OF—MIKE McCORMICK	1940 Reds, 1948 Braves, 1949 Dodgers
OF—VIC DAVALILLO	1971 Pirates, 1973 Athletics, 1977–78 Dodgers
C—WALLY SCHANG	1913–14, 1930 Athletics, 1918 Red Sox, 1921–23 Yankees
P—BURLEIGH GRIMES	1920 Dodgers, 1930–31 Cardinals, 1932 Cubs

Schang aside, this clearly has been a trick easier to accomplish in the National League than in the American.

For the record, the other three-timers are first baseman Stuffy McInnis, catcher Earl Smith, and pitchers Joe Bush, Paul Derringer, Dutch Reuther and Grant Jackson.

Bill McKechnie (1925 Pirates, 1928 Cardinals and 1939 and 1940 Reds) and Dick Williams are the only managers to lead three different teams into the World Series.

PINCH-HITTING ODDS AND ODDS

These players are worth remembering for either coming off the bench or being called back to it during World Series play:

PINCH-HITTING ODDS AND ODDS

1B—CLYDE ENGLE	1912 Red Sox
2B—EDDIE STANKY	1947 Dodgers
3B—CLETE BOYER	1960 Yankees
SS—FRED STANLEY	1976 Yankees
OF—DEL HOWARD	1907 Cubs
OF—YOGI BERRA	1947 Yankees
OF—CHUCK ESSEGIAN	1959 Dodgers
C—IRA THOMAS	1908 Tigers
P—BABE RUTH	1915 Red Sox

Pinch-hitter Engle hit the fly ball muffed by Fred Snodgrass that led to Boston's Series victory over the Giants. Stanky was the batter called back in favor of Cookie Lavagetto against Bill Bevens. Boyer was lifted by manager Casey Stengel for pinch-hitter Dale Long in the second inning of the first game against Pittsburgh; Stengel excused the embarrassing move by saying he wanted to go for "a big inning." Sixteen years later, the even weaker-hitting Stanley was removed so quickly and so often for another batter that he managed only six plate appearances in four infield starting assignments. A catcher's error allowed Howard to reach first after striking out and led to the tying run scoring; suspicions that the miscue was deliberate prompted the ruling that World Series teams can share in the proceeds only from the first four games. Berra hit the first World Series pinch-homer. Essegian was the first to hit two pinch-homers in one Series. Thomas singled for the first World Series pinch-hit. Although he was the American League's top pitcher with an 18-6 record, Ruth's only appearance in the 1915 Series was an 0 for 1 pinch-hitter.

BASE-RUNNING ODDS AND ODDS

Some were involved in key plays, others in comical plays, and still others played their way into the record book.

1B—ROCKY NELSON	1960 Pirates
2B—EDDIE COLLINS	Career
3B—EDDIE MIKSIS	1947 Dodgers
SS—HONUS WAGNER	1909 Pirates
OF—JOHN ANDERSON	1904 Yankees
OF—FRANK SCHULTE	Career
OF—LEON CULBERSON	1946 Red Sox
C—JIMMY WILSON	1940 Reds
P—RED FABER	1917 White Sox

Nelson almost cost the Pirates the championship when he froze with the ball late in the seventh game and watched both Gil McDougald slide home and Mickey Mantle slide back to first in rundowns that didn't happen. Collins and Lou Brock share the stolen base mark for total World Series at 14. Miksis was the pinch-runner who scored from first on Cookie Lavagetto's double off Bill Bevens. Wagner was the first to steal three bases in a World Series game. (The feat was later emulated by Willie Davis and Lou Brock.)

Both Anderson and pitcher Faber "stole" bases already occupied by teammates, thereby ending rallies. Schulte holds the mark for being thrown out stealing most often— nine times in 21 games; he was successful only three times. It was Culberson who went in to run for Dom DiMaggio after the latter injured himself doubling in the tying runs in the eighth inning of the final game; it was the same Culberson who pursued (some say too lethargically) the Harry Walker double that scored Enos Slaughter from first with the championship run. The 40-year-old Wilson, reactivated for the Series after an injury to Ernie Lombardi, stole the only base in the seven games between Cincinnati and Detroit.

DRAMATIC FINAL HITS

There is nothing more exciting than a game-ending hit, especially in post-season play.

1B—CHRIS CHAMBLISS	1976 Yankees	Championship Series
2B—BILL MAZEROSKI	1960 Pirates	World Series
3B—BOBBY THOMSON	1951 Giants	Playoff
SS—BERT CAMPANERIS	1973 Athletics	Championship Series
OF—EARL McNEELY	1924 Senators	World Series
OF—BING MILLER	1929 Athletics	World Series
OF—GOOSE GOSLIN	1935 Tigers	World Series
C—CARLTON FISK	1975 Red Sox	World Series
PH—COOKIE LAVAGETTO	1947 Dodgers	World Series

The singles by McNeely (the famous "bad hop" base hit) and Goslin, the double by Miller and the home run by Mazeroski ended entire Series. Chambliss's homer off Mark Littell and Thomson's blast off Ralph Branca decided pennants. Campaneris's homer was a turning point in the division playoffs against Baltimore, while Fisk's decided what many believe was the greatest single game in World Series history. Lavagetto's double, of course, ended Bill Bevens's no hitter with two out in the ninth.

Honorable mention to Steve Garvey, who won the fourth game of the 1984 NL Championship Series with a two-run homer in the bottom of the ninth.

MOMENTS IN THE SUN

The World Series brings out the best in some players—and not only the best players. These are our candidates for average performers who stood in the sunshine in October.

1B—FRED LUDERUS	1915 Phillies	World Series
2B—AL WEIS	1969 Mets	World Series
3B—BUCK HERZOG	1912 Giants	World Series
SS—BUCKY DENT	1978 Yankees	Playoff
OF—AL GIONFRIDDO	1947 Dodgers	World Series
OF—DAVE ROBERTSON	1917 Giants	World Series
OF—DUSTY RHODES	1954 Giants	World Series
C—HANK GOWDY	1914 Braves	World Series
P—DON LARSEN	1956 Yankees	World Series

Luderus, a .277 lifetime hitter, batted .438 with a home run and 12 RBIs in his only World Series. Weis, .219 lifetime, hit .455 and clouted a game-tying homer in the final game of the Series for the Miracle Mets. Herzog, a .259 lifetime hitter, went 12-for-30 in a losing cause. Dent hit the homer that mattered in the one-game playoff against the Red Sox.

Gionfriddo made the catch that set DiMaggio to kicking dirt around second base. Robertson, who had had a few good years at bat, but was coming off a regular season batting average of .259, collected 11 hits in 22 at bats in the Series. Rhodes is remembered for his first game pinch-hit homer in 1954, but he also hit another while playing right field in Game 2 and batted .667 for the Series. Gowdy, a .243 hitter during the season, led the Miracle Braves to a four-game sweep over the mighty Athletics by batting .545 with five extra base hits. And if you don't think Larsen was average, account some other way for his lifetime record of 81 wins and 91 losses.

OVERLOOKED FEATS

Some players should be remembered for more than one thing in post-season play.

1B—GIL HODGES	1955 Dodgers	World Series
2B—AL WEIS	1969 Mets	World Series
3B—BOBBY THOMSON	1951 Giants	Playoff
SS—PHIL RIZZUTO	1951 Yankees	World Series
OF—JOE JACKSON	1919 White Sox	World Series
OF—AL GIONFRIDDO	1947 Dodgers	World Series
OF—HANK BAUER	1951 Yankees	World Series
C—GENE TENACE	1972 Athletics	Championship Series
P—DON LARSEN	1962 Giants	Playoff

Most famous for his 0-for-21 effort in the 1952 Series, Hodges also drove in both runs in the Johnny Podres game that gave the Dodgers their first world championship. Weis not only hit a clutch homer in the last game of the Series, but also singled in the winning run in the first Met victory. Two days before his "shot heard around the world," Thomson iced the first playoff game with another homer off Ralph Branca; two innings before his three-run shot, he drove in the first run against Don Newcombe to tie the game at that point. One day after he had cost the Yankees a World Series game by being dropkicked by Eddie Stanky, Rizzuto eluded a pickoff attempt by the same Stanky, was hit on the head by the ball during a rundown, and scored the winning run on the play.

Jackson was outlawed as a Black Soxer despite a series in which he had 12 hits, batted .375, scored five runs, drove home six runs, and committed no errors in the field. In addition to his sensational catch against Joe DiMaggio, Gionfriddo was the pinch-runner for Carl Furillo, who stole second base against Bill Bevens and set up Cookie Lavagetto's memorable pinch-double. Bauer ended the World Series with a dramatic catch of a Sal Yvars line drive; two innings earlier he had slammed a bases-loaded triple to give the Yankees the lead in the game. Best known for his slugging in the 1972 World Series, Tenace wouldn't have gotten that far if he hadn't chosen his last at bat in the division playoffs to break an 0-for-16 drought and single in the pennant-deciding run. The perfect Larsen was also good enough in relief to be the winning pitcher in the final playoff game against the Dodgers.

OVERSHADOWED FEATS

Each of these players played a supporting role that made possible the star's dramatic hit.

1B—WHITEY LOCKMAN	1951 Giants	Playoff
2B—BUCKY HARRIS	1924 Senators	World Series
3B—GEORGE BRETT	1976 Royals	Championship Series
SS—GLENN WRIGHT	1925 Pirates	World Series
OF—CARL FURILLO	1953 Dodgers	World Series
OF—NORM LARKER	1959 Dodgers	Playoff
OF—BERNIE CARBO	1975 Red Sox	World Series
C—HAL SMITH	1960 Pirates	World Series
P—SAL MAGLIE	1956 Dodgers	World Series

Lockman doubled to set the table for Bobby Thomson in the third game of the playoffs with the Dodgers. Harris had a bad hop single over the head of Giants third baseman Fred Lindstrom to tie the score in the eighth inning of the seventh game of the World Series; in the twelfth, another bad hop hit over Lindstrom's head won the game and the Series. Brett hit a homer in the fifth game of the Championship Series that made Chris Chambliss's ninth-inning homer necessary. Wright, who batted only .185 for the Series and hit only 93 homers in eleven years, tied game two with a round-tripper and paved the way for Kiki Cuyler's game-winning blast.

Furillo homered in the ninth inning of the last game of the World Series to tie it up; the Yankees scored in the bottom half, however, and negated his efforts. Larker singled in two runs in the ninth inning of the last game of the 1959 playoffs and made it possible for Furillo to receive credit for a sacrifice fly that tied the game and an infield hit that led to the pennant-winning run. Carbo hit a two-out, three-run homer in the eighth inning to tie the sixth game of the World Series; the score remained tied until Carlton Fisk homered to win it for the Red Sox in the twelfth inning. Smith put the Pirates ahead 9-7 in the eighth inning of the last game of the Series with a dramatic homer; it was up to

Bill Mazeroski to put them ahead for good after the Yankees tied it in the top of the ninth. Maglie pitched a neat five-hitter, retiring the first eleven batters—on the same day that Don Larsen pitched his perfect game.

CONTROVERSIAL CALLS

Were the umpires right or wrong?

1B—GIL HODGES	10th inn., 5th game	1952 Dodgers	World Series
2B—LARRY DOYLE	10th inn., 5th game	1911 Giants	World Series
3B—JACKIE ROBINSON	8th inn., 1st game	1955 Dodgers	World Series
SS—LOU BOUDREAU	8th inn., 1st game	1948 Indians	World Series
OF—CLEON JONES	6th inn., 5th game	1969 Mets	World Series
OF—BERNIE CARBO	6th inn., 1st game	1970 Red Sox	World Series
OF—REGGIE JACKSON	6th inn., 4th game	1978 Yankees	World Series
C—CARLTON FISK	10th inn., 3rd game	1975 Red Sox	World Series
P—VERN RUHLE	4th inn., 4th game	1980 Astros	Championship Series

Hodges got the call on a grounder from umpire Art Passarella despite photos that showed batter Johnny Sain clearly on first before the ball arrived. Doyle scored the winning run on a sacrifice fly, and umpire Bill Klem admitted later that Doyle never touched home. Years later, Yogi Berra had the last word on Robinson's controversial steal of home; according to Berra, Robinson never touched the plate and he never tagged Robinson. (Ed Summers had called Robinson safe.) When Boudreau called for a pickoff on Phil Masi at second, Bill Stewart said no dice; Masi later scored the game's only run.

Lou DiMuro awarded Jones first after manager Gil

Hodges came out of the Mets dugout with a ball streaked with shoe polish, supposedly proving a hit batsman; Donn Clendenon followed with a homer and the Mets were championship bound. The Reds lost by one run when Ken Burkhart, who had his back to the play the entire time, called Carbo out at home on a sweeping tag by catcher Elrod Hendricks; Hendricks made his sweep with his glove, but the ball was in his bare hand. Three umpires— Marty Springstead, Joe Brinkman and Ed Vargo—saw no interference in Jackson's hip movement that broke up a crucial double play; the Yankees went on to score two runs and win the game, 4-3. Larry Barnett was likewise unconvinced of interference when Ed Armbrister ran into Fisk while the latter was fielding a bunt and made a wild throw that sent the eventual winning run to third base. In the NL championship game, Ruhle fielded a soft liner and threw to first for a double play, but the Phillies protested that he had trapped the ball. While an argument ensued, Art Howe realized that nobody had called time, so he took the ball and stepped on second to catch a Phillie elsewhere on the field, claiming a triple play. Doug Harvey, after consulting with NL president Chub Feeney, finally ruled a double play and sent the runner back to second.

Honorable mention to J.C. Martin, who pinch-hit in the bottom of the tenth inning in the fourth game of the 1969 World Series for the Mets with runners on first and second. Pete Richert fielded Martin's bunt, but his throw to first struck Martin on the wrist. The Orioles claimed Martin was out of the baseline, but umpire Lou DiMuro's ruling of "safe" stood and the winning run scored.

OOPS!

World Series and playoff games can magnify the most common offensive and defensive goofs to a legendary degree. For example:

1B—EDDIE MURRAY	1979 Orioles	World Series
2B—MIKE ANDREWS	1973 Athletics	World Series
3B—HEINIE ZIMMERMAN	1917 Giants	World Series
SS—JOHNNY PESKY	1946 Red Sox	World Series
OF—FRED SNODGRASS	1912 Giants	World Series
OF—HACK WILSON	1929 Cubs	World Series
OF—GARRY MADDOX	1978 Phillies	Championship Series
C—HANK GOWDY	1924 Giants	World Series
P—RALPH BRANCA	1951 Dodgers	Playoff

Murray cut off an outfield throw in the ninth inning of the third game and allowed the winning run to score. Andrews made two errors in the twelveth inning of the second game and allowed three runs to cross. In the fourth inning of the sixth game Zimmerman made a two-base error and then chased Eddie Collins across the plate during a rundown. Pesky held the ball on a relay, allowing Enos Slaughter to score from first with the winning run in the final game.

Snodgrass dropped a fly in the tenth inning of the fifth game, setting up a two-run inning that gave Boston the championship. Wilson misjudged a fly into a three-run inside-the-park homer during the seventh inning of the fourth game; the Athletics ended up scoring ten runs to overcome an 8-0 Chicago lead. Maddox dropped a two-out line drive in the tenth inning of the fourth game of the divisional playoffs, thereby allowing Los Angeles to score the pennant-winning run. Gowdy dropped a "$50,000 foul ball" when he tripped over his mask in the ninth inning of the last game. Given a second life, Washington catcher Muddy Ruel doubled and scored the winning run of the Series. And if you don't think Branca should have wasted one against Bobby Thomson, ask the nearest Brooklyn Dodger fan.

The manager is Bucky Harris for insisting on an intentional walk to a hobbled Pete Reiser in the 1947 game in which Bill Bevens was working on a no-hitter. The walk put the winning run on base and allowed Cookie Lavagetto to come to the plate.

POST-SEASON COLLISIONS, CLASHES AND CONTRETEMPS

A variety of collisions, fights, arguments and donnybrooks after the end of the regular season.

1B—CHARLES COMISKEY	1885 St. Louis (AA)	"World Series"
2B—LARRY DOYLE	1911 Giants	World Series
3B—GEORGE BRETT	1977 Royals	Championship Series
SS—BERT CAMPANERIS	1972 Royals	Championship Series
OF—BABE RUTH	1927 Yankees	World Series
OF—JOE MEDWICK	1934 Cardinals	World Series
OF—PETE ROSE	1973 Reds	Championship Series
C—ERNIE LOMBARDI	1939 Reds	World Series
P—DIZZY DEAN	1934 Cardinals	World Series

In the second game of the post-season championship series between the NL Cubs and the AA Brown Stockings, Comiskey, the St. Louis player-manager, objected so strenuously to base umpire Dan Sullivan's calls that he took his team off the field and forfeited the game. Doyle scored the winning run in the tenth inning of the fifth game, but never touched home plate. Athletics manager Connie Mack saw it, but said nothing for fear of starting a riot by Giants fans, who still remembered the Merkle boner three years earlier. The stir in the newspapers was considerable since both plate umpire Bill Klem and Giants manager John McGraw both admitted what had happened. In the first inning of the fifth game of the AL Championship Series Brett tripled and slid hard into Graig Nettles; Brett came up from his slide swinging, the two third basemen wrestled on the ground, and both benches emptied. Campaneris threw his bat at Detroit pitcher Lerrin LaGrow during the 1972 AL Championship Series after LaGrow hit Campaneris on the ankle with a pitch. Tiger manager Billy Martin had to be restrained by three umpires and Campaneris was suspended for the rest of the playoffs and the first three games of the 1973 season.

Ruth and the Giants clashed repeatedly in game three of the 1922 World Series. Ruth was hit by a pitch and later crashed into Heinie Groh at third base. After the game Ruth and Bob Meusel went into the Giants clubhouse looking for Johnny Rawlings, the Giants chief bench jockey, but manager John McGraw and coach Hughie Jennings threw them out. Medwick spiked Tigers third baseman Marv Owen in the sixth inning of the last Series game. When Medwick went back to left field the Tiger fans pelted him with scorecards, food and anything else they could find until Commissioner Landis ordered him removed from the game. Rose tried to break up a 3-6-3 double play in game three of the 1973 NL Championship Series and he and Mets shortstop Bud Harrelson wrestled and fought. The partisan Mets crowd was so irate that a police escort was needed to usher the Reds' wives out of the park.

Lombardi was knocked cold by Charlie Keller in the tenth inning of the last Series game and lay a yard from the ball as Joe DiMaggio also scored. Dean, pinch-running in the ninth inning of the sixth Series game, broke up a double play when the relay by Tigers shortstop Billy Rogell hit him in the head and knocked him out. Dean was rushed to the hospital, but came back to win the seventh game.

BEST ALL-STAR GAMES

The best of the best players who had the best days.

1B—PHIL CAVARRETTA	1944 NL
2B—RED SCHOENDIENST	1950 NL
3B—AL ROSEN	1954 AL
SS—ARKY VAUGHAN	1941 NL
OF—TED WILLIAMS	1941 and 1946 AL
OF—STAN MUSIAL	1955 NL
OF—JOHNNY CALLISON	1964 NL
C—GARY CARTER	1981 NL
P—CARL HUBBELL	1934 NL

Cavarretta reached base five times. Schoendienst hit a 14th-inning homer to down the AL. Rosen had two homers. Vaughan blasted two out in a losing cause. Williams offset Vaughan's homers in 1941 with one of his own and hit two more to lead an AL rout in 1946. Musial's 12th-inning homer in 1955 and Callison's 9th-inning shot in 1964 brought NL victories. Carter walloped two homers in another NL win. Hubbell made NL fans forget their team's loss by striking out Babe Ruth, Lou Gehrig, Jimmie Foxx, Al Simmons and Joe Cronin in succession with his infamous screwball.

ALL-STAR FIXTURES

Some players have appeared in so many All-Star games that it has become their natural right. Since the midseason exhibition became a fixture, however, the players who have absolutely dominated their positions (with their number of appearances) are:

1B—STAN MUSIAL	24
2B—NELLIE FOX	13
3B—BROOKS ROBINSON	18
SS—LUIS APARICIO	10
OF—HANK AARON	24
OF—WILLIE MAYS	24
OF—TED WILLIAMS	18
C—YOGI BERRA	15
P—TOM SEAVER	8

Purists will point out that, since the first All-Star Game wasn't played until 1933, the Ruths, Cobbs and Speakers didn't get the opportunity to match or better these numbers. Okay, purists: Point it out.

It should also be noted that from 1959 to 1963 there were two All-Star contests a year, a fact which gives some of these players a few extra appearances.

Fox and the still-active Seaver are the only members of this team not in the Hall of Fame.

Seaver is the most recent pitcher to appear in eight All-Star Games. The others are Jim Bunning, Don Drysdale and Juan Marichal.

ALL-LEAGUE ALL-STARS

One of the side effects of inter-league trading in recent years has been to increase the number of players who have appeared in All-Star games for both the National and American leagues. In fact, only the first baseman in this lineup predates the winter periods of inter-league swapping.

1B—JOHNNY MIZE	Cardinals, Giants, Yankees
2B—PHIL GARNER	Athletics, Pirates
3B—DICK ALLEN	Phillies, Cardinals, White Sox
SS—CRAIG REYNOLDS	Mariners, Astros
OF—HANK AARON	Braves, Brewers
OF—FRANK ROBINSON	Reds, Orioles, Angels
OF—REGGIE SMITH	Red Sox, Cardinals, Dodgers
C—TED SIMMONS	Cardinals, Brewers
P—JIM BUNNING	Tigers, Phillies

No player has ever appeared for one league, then appeared for the other, then made a third appearance with his original league.

The manager has to be Alvin Dark, who is the only man ever to lead the All-Star squads of both leagues. Dick Williams and Sparky Anderson will join him in 1985.

THESE TOO WERE STARS: A.L.

All-Star games aren't only for future Hall of Famers. Almost every year, in fact, otherwise ordinary players enjoy half-seasons that make it impossible for managers to ignore them when compiling league rosters. Here are some dim names from past American League All-Star teams:

1B—HARRY SIMPSON	1956 Athletics
2B—BILLY MORAN	1962 Angels
3B—DAVE CHALK	1974 Angels
SS—BILLY HUNTER	1953 Browns
OF—LOU FINNEY	1940 Red Sox
OF—THURMAN TUCKER	1944 White Sox
OF—ORIS HOCKETT	1944 Indians
C—DUANE JOSEPHSON	1968 White Sox
P—BOB KEEGAN	1954 White Sox

Simpson's lifetime average was .266, Moran's .263, Chalk's .252, Hunter's .219, Finney's .287, Tucker's .255, Hockett's .276 and Josephson's .258. Keegan ended up with a record of 16-9 in the year he was selected, only once more won as many as ten games, and finished with a career mark of 40 wins and 36 losses.

THESE TOO WERE STARS: N.L.

It may be further testimony of the National League's often-argued superiority that even its most undistinguished All-Star game selections were anything but shabby players.

THESE TOO WERE STARS: N.L.

1B—JOE CUNNINGHAM	1959	Cardinals
2B—PETE COSCARART	1940	Dodgers
3B—PINKY MAY	1940	Phillies
SS—WOODY ENGLISH	1933	Cubs
OF—HERSHEL MARTIN	1938	Phillies
OF—MORRIE ARNOVICH	1939	Phillies
OF—MAX WEST	1940	Braves
C—RAY LAMANNO	1946	Reds
P—LOU FETTE	1939	Braves

Cunningham's lifetime average was .291, Coscarart's .243, May's .275, English's .286, Martin's .285, Arnovich's .287, West's .254 and Lamanno's .252. Fette finished up with a lifetime mark of 41 and 40.

SUMMARY

By way of summation . . .

THE ALL-TIME ALL-STAR
EVERYTHINGS

These are the players whose names appear most often in the lineups in this book.

1B—LOU GEHRIG	33
2B—ROGERS HORNSBY	30
3B—BROOKS ROBINSON	19
SS—HONUS WAGNER	27
OF—BABE RUTH	51
OF—TY COBB	37
OF—TED WILLIAMS	29
C—YOGI BERRA	22
P—SANDY KOUFAX	10

Wagner is on 26 teams as the shortstop and one as an outfielder. Ruth is on 47 as an outfielder and four in the pitcher's spot. And Berra appears 20 times as the catcher and twice as an outfielder.

The runners-up are less clear in some cases. At first you can choose from among Rod Carew (nine teams at first base and three at second), Jimmie Foxx (11 at first and one as the catcher) and George Sisler (11 at first). At second base there is Eddie Collins (20, plus one at shortstop). Eddie Mathews is the third baseman (16 teams). Ernie Banks is at short (22 teams plus three at first base). Choose three outfielders from among Pete Rose (10 in the outfield, seven at third base, four at second base, and three at first base), Willie Mays (23), Stan Musial (14 in the outfield and eight at first base), and Hank Aaron (21, plus one as the DH). The catcher is Mickey Cochrane (16). And on the mound is Walter Johnson (9, plus one team as an outfielder).

LEFT OUT

When all is said and done, after 427 teams and about 2000 players, these are the best at each position who failed to make any other team in this book.

1B—GEORGE KELLY
2B—BOOTS GRANTHAM
3B—FRANK MALZONE
SS—RED KRESS
OF—TOMMY HENRICH
OF—BUG HOLLIDAY
OF—HARRY HOOPER
C—BOB O'FARRELL
P—MICKEY WELCH

Kelly, a .297 lifetime hitter between 1915 and 1932, had his best years with the Giants, for whom he batted over .300 six times; he also hit 148 home runs while playing much of his career before the lively ball. Grantham hit .302 with four National League teams between 1922 and 1934. Malzone, with a .274 lifetime average and 133 homers, was a standout third baseman for the Red Sox in the late 1950s and early 1960s. Kress batted .286 playing for four AL teams (1927–40) and the Giants (1946). Henrich batted .282 with 183 home runs—and was one of the greatest clutch hitters in history—during his eleven years (1937–42, 1946–50) with the Yankees. Holliday's .320 average, compiled with Cincinnati, both in the AA and the NL (1889–98), is the highest by any player on no previous team. Hooper, a .281 lifetime hitter and an outstanding defensive outfielder, played with the Red Sox (1909–20) and the White Sox (1921–25). O'Farrell batted

.273 and caught 1492 games with four National League teams between 1915 and 1935. Welch won 307 games and lost only 209 with the Troy Haymakers and the Giants between 1880 and 1892; he is the only pitcher with 300 or more wins whose name is not otherwise found in this book.

Kelly, Hooper and Welch are in the Hall of Fame. Other Hall of Famers to be shut out in this volume are shortstop Joe Tinker, outfielder Tommy McCarthy and pitchers Herb Pennock and Jesse Haines.

Honorable mention to Lee May, whose 354 home runs is the most by anyone who appears on no team here.

THE AVON A★L★L-S★T★A★R★S